Social Democratic Parties in the European Union

History, Organization, Policies

Edited by

Robert Ladrech
Lecturer in Politics
University of Keele
Staffordshire

and

Philippe Marlière
Lecturer in Politics
University College
London

First published in Great Britain 1999 by
MACMILLAN PRESS LTD
Houndmills, Basingstoke, Hampshire RG21 6XS and London
Companies and representatives throughout the world

A catalogue record for this book is available from the British Library.

ISBN 0–333–68940–2

 First published in the United States of America 1999 by
ST. MARTIN'S PRESS, INC.,
Scholarly and Reference Division,
175 Fifth Avenue, New York, N.Y. 10010

ISBN 0–312–22007–3

Library of Congress Cataloging-in-Publication Data
Social democratic parties in the European Union : history,
organization, politics / edited by Robert Ladrech and Philippe
Marlière.
p. cm.
Includes bibliographical references and index.
ISBN 0–312–22007–3
1. Socialist parties—European Union countries.   I. Ladrech,
Robert.   II. Marlière, Philippe, 1966–   .
JN50.S62   1998
324.2'172'094—dc21   98–30660
                                                                  CIP

This book is printed on paper suitable for recycling and made from fully managed and
sustained forest sources.

10   9   8   7   6   5   4   3   2   1
08   07   06   05   04   03   02   01   00   99

Printed and bound in Great Britain by
Antony Rowe Ltd, Chippenham, Wiltshire

Contents

List of Tables		v
Preface		ix
Notes on the Contributors		xi
List of Abbreviations and Party/Union Acronyms		xiv
Acknowledgements		xix

Introduction: European Social Democracy *in Situ*   1
Philippe Marlière

1	The Social Democratic Party of Austria	16
	Kurt Richard Luther	
2	The Belgian Socialist Party	30
	Pascal Delwit	
3	The Danish Social Democratic Party	43
	Lars Bille	
4	The Finnish Social Democratic Party	56
	Jan Sundberg	
5	The French Socialist Party	64
	Robert Ladrech and Philippe Marlière	
6	The German Social Democratic Party	79
	Johan Jeroen De Deken	
7	The British Labour Party	95
	Paul Webb	
8	The Panhellenic Socialist Movement	110
	Gerassimos Moschonas	
9	The Irish Labour Party	123
	Michael Holmes	
10	The Italian Democrats of the Left	133
	Stefano Guzzini	
11	The Luxembourg Socialist Workers' Party	148
	John Fitzmaurice	

12 The Dutch Labour Party   155
    Kees van Kersbergen

13 The Portuguese Socialist Party   166
    José Magone

14 The Spanish Socialist Workers' Party   176
    Paul Kennedy

15 The Swedish Social Democratic Party   189
    Nicholas Aylott

16 The Party of European Socialists   204
    Simon Hix

Postscript: Social Democratic Parties and the European Union   218
Robert Ladrech

Index   223

List of Tables

1.1 SPÖ absolute membership and membership density in election
    years, 1913–97   23
1.2 SPÖ vote share at all general elections, 1919–95   25
1.3 Social structure of SPÖ electorate, 1986 and 1995   25
2.1 Number of members of the PS and the SP, 1978–95   34
2.2 Electoral performance of the Belgian Socialists, 1945–95   38
3.1 SD Party membership, 1945–95   47
3.2 Sociology of SD membership, 1971 and 1990   48
3.3 Sociology of the Danish electorate; votes for the Social
    Democratic Party, 1964–94   49
3.4 Distribution of Danish left-wing votes and seats at general
    elections, 1945–94   50
3.5 Party composition of national governments in Denmark,
    1945–96   52
4.1 Party members in SDP, 1945–95   59
4.2 Party membership in SDP according to age groups, 1977–96   60
4.3 Socialist seats won in the Finnish Parliament, 1945–95   61
4.4 SDP party leaders, 1899–1993   62
5.1 Evolution of the occupational structure of French PS
    members, 1951–90   70
5.2 French PS membership, 1905–95   71
5.3 PS share of the votes at French general elections, 1919–97   72
6.1 SPD membership, 1946–96   85
6.2 Development of the occupational structure of SPD members,
    1952–96   86
6.3 Electoral performance of the SPD in federal elections, 1949–94   87
6.4 Electoral support for the SPD according to occupation,
    1976–90   87
7.1 Major British parties, 1945–97: seats and share of the total vote   100
7.2 Class basis of electoral support in Britain, 1950–97   104
7.3 Labour Party's individual membership since 1960, UK   104
8.1 PASOK membership, 1974–96   114
8.2 Social penetration of PASOK, 1993–6   118
8.3 PASOK Electoral performance, 1974–96   119
9.1 Labour Party leaders in Ireland, 1922–97   124
9.2 Labour Party electoral performance in Ireland, 1948–97   125
9.3 Number of Labour Party branches and individual members
    in Ireland, 1961–95   127

9.4	Parliamentary representation of other left-wing parties in the Republic of Ireland, 1927–97	128
9.5	Labour party participation in government in Ireland, 1948–97	129
10.1	PCI and FGCI membership, 1947–90	137
10.2	Regional distribution of PCI membership and vote, 1976 and 1990	138
10.3	Change in the socio-economic composition of PCI electorate, 1968–87	140
11.1	LSAP/POSL election results, 1959–94	152
12.1	PvdA membership, 1946–95	159
12.2	Class composition of the PvdA vote, 1971–94	159
12.3	PvdA share of the votes at parliamentary elections, 1946–94	162
13.1	Membership of the PS, Portugal 1974–92	170
13.2	Left vote over time in Portuguese legislative elections, 1975–95	172
13.3	PS in constitutional government in Portugal, 1976–95	174
14.1	PSOE membership, 1888–1997	182
14.2	Sociological characteristics of PSOE members, 1980–93	183
14.3	Share of the vote and seats won by PSOE at general elections, 1977–96	184
14.4	Sociological characteristics of PSOE voters, 1977–93	185
15.1	Swedish governments, 1945–98	189
15.2	SAP members' age, educational and socio–economic profiles, 1960–94	195
15.3	SAP voters' age, educational and socio–economic profiles, 1960–94	196
15.4	Recent Swedish national elections	200
16.1	Member parties of the PES, 1957–95	208
16.2	Leaders of the PES Party Federation and EP Group, 1974–94	209
16.3	PES leadership, 1997	210
16.4	The Socialist Group/Group of the PES in the EP, 1979–94	212

Preface

Clear, concise and accessible coverage of one of the main party families in Western Europe is currently unavailable in English. This is surprising in light of the historic changes to social democracy since the end of the Cold War. Certainly the transformations brought about by the European integration process, notably the drive toward monetary union and all of its attendent economic dynamics, make the need all the greater for a comprehensive guide covering all of these key political players. As a reference work, we hope to provide a focused description of the organizational and main political issues that have faced social democratic parties since 1945 and thereby contributed to their present profile.

A new book on European social democratic parties is justified for two main reasons. Political party analysis, a traditional focus in study of politics, has recently begun to emphasize the organizational aspects of parties to a greater degree. This is most notably represented in the Katz and Mair (1994) project on party organization as well as in the launch of the scholarly journal *Party Politics*. In addition to this focus on party organization, the European Union as a political–economic factor affecting social democratic party fortunes has begun to attract attention, leading scholars to combine party analysis with EU studies.

A renewed interest in political party organizational features, and increasing attention to the impact of European integration on social democratic parties, thus requires a work which can provide necessary background information on all of these parties for students and researchers alike. One of the key features of the book in consequence is its comprehensive coverage. Contributions include all of the relevant social democratic parties in the member states of the European Union, plus the transnational party federation, the Party of European Socialists. In order to facilitate its accessibility, the chapters maintain the same structural format, presenting a history of the party, which in many cases includes references to competing parties on the left, the organizational structure of each party, with reference to relations with trade unions and any significant changes which may have recently occurred, and a brief presentation of selected policy concerns. The structural format also incorporates a feature we hope will provide much needed help for those using the book for research, and this is our inclusion of contact information for each party. This information includes e-mail and postal addresses of the parties and any affiliated research institutes, as well as, where available, the party's web site.

The contributors have produced chapters rich in information, and the limitations placed upon them in terms of length have led them to produce a true feat, concise and yet comprehensive introductions to sixteen party organizations, some of which have been in existence for over 100 years. We are grateful to them for coping with these restraints and also for producing accounts accessible to a wide audience. Finally, the editors wish to thank Professor John Gaffney for helpful suggestion at the beginning of the project, and Iain Ogilvie and Patrick ffrench for their technical assistance and interest during the final completion of the manuscript.

ROBERT LADRECH
PHILIPPE MARLIÈRE

Notes on the Contributors

Nicholas Aylott is Lecturer in Politics at Keele University, UK. His research interests centre on Nordic and comparative European politics, political parties and European integration. His doctoral thesis was on the Swedish Social Democratic Party's handling of the European issue, and he has had several articles published on this topic.

Lars Bille is Senior Lecturer at the Department of Political Science, University of Copenhagen. His main research interests are political parties and party systems. He has published in *Party Organizations: A Data Handbook* (1992) and *How Parties Organize* (1994) both edited by Katz and Mair. His most recent book is *Partier I forandring* (1997).

Johan Jeroen De Deken is Lecturer in Political Sociology and Social Policy at the Humboldt University in Berlin. Earlier he taught at the Central European University and at Comenius University. He was educated at the Free University Brussels, Brown University and at the European University Institute in Florence.

Pascal Delwit is Lecturer in Political Science at the University of Brussels (ULB). His doctoral thesis was on socialist parties in Belgium, France and the UK regarding the question of European integration from 1945 to 1994. He has most recently published *Les partis socialistes et l'intégration européenne (France, Belgique, Grande Bretagne)* (1995); *Les partis politiques en Belgique* (1996); and *Ecolo: Les verts en politique* (1996).

John Fitzmaurice has been an administrator in the Secretariat of the European Commission since 1973 and currently is in charge of relations with the European Parliament. Educated at the Universities of Bristol, Oxford and Brussels, he has published extensively, including studies of the politics of Denmark, Quebec and Belgium, and teaches at the University of Brussels (ULB).

Stefano Guzzini is Assistant Professor in International Relations at the Central European University, Budapest College and completed his PhD at the European University Institute in Florence. His publications include: 'Structural Power: The Limits of Neorealist Power Analysis' (*International Organization,* Summer 1993), 'The "Long Night of the First Republic": Years of Clientelistic Implosion in Italy' (*Review of International Political Economy,*

xi

Winter 1995) and *Realism in International Relations and International Political Economy: The Continuing Story of a Death Foretold* (1998).

Simon Hix is Lecturer in EU Politics and Policy in the Department of Government at the London School of Economics and Political Science. He has published on several issues relating to the European Union and (with C. Lord) *Political Parties in the European Union* (1997). His current research is on EU executive–legislative relations.

Michael Holmes is Lecturer in European Studies in University College Cork and a Visiting Lecturer at the Centre for Peace Studies in Dublin. He has recently completed a doctoral thesis on Irish left-wing parties and European integration, and has published a number of works on Irish politics, Irish foreign policy and the European Union.

Paul Kennedy is Lecturer in Iberian Studies at the Department of European Studies, Loughborough University, UK. He has published in the *International Journal of Iberian Studies* and contributed a chapter on the PSOE to *Looking Left: European Socialism After the Cold War*, Donald Sassoon (ed.) (1997).

Kees van Kersbergen is Professor of National Political Systems and Dutch Politics at the University of Nijmegen in the Netherlands. His main areas of interests are comparative politics, welfare state development and Dutch politics. He is the author of *Social Capitalism* (1995) which was awarded the 7th Stein Rokkan Prize (1996) in Comparative Social Research.

Robert Ladrech is Lecturer in Politics at Keele University, UK, and researches mainly into social democratic parties, French politics and European integration. He has co-authored *Europe since 1945: A Concise History* (4th edn, 1996), and has published widely in journals and books. He is currently preparing a manuscript on the relationship between social democratic parties and the European Union.

Kurt Richard Luther lectures in Politics at Keele University and researches into political parties, consociational democracy and federalism. His main empirical focus has of late been Austrian politics. He has co-edited *Politics in Austria: Still a Case of Consociationalism?* (1992), *Austria 1945–95: Fifty Years of the Second Republic* (1998), *Austria and the European Union Presidency: Background and Perspectives* (1998) and *Party Elites in Divided Societies: Political Parties in Consoaciational Democracy* (1998). He is currently preparing a monograph on the Freedom Party of Austria.

José Magone is Lecturer in European Politics at the University of Hull, UK, and has published extensively on Southern European politics. Among his publications are *The Changing Architecture of Iberian Politics* (1996) and *European Portugal: The Difficult Road to Sustainable Democracy* (1997). He is currently working on a project devoted to European integration and trade union strategies in Spain and Portugal.

Philippe Marlière is Lecturer in Politics at University College London. He was a Research Fellow at the French *Centre National de la Recherche Scientifique* (CNRS) and at the European University Institute (Florence). He has published articles on French Socialism, carried out fieldwork on the collective memory of French Socialists activists and is writing a book on François Mitterrand and the French Left.

Gerassimos Moschonas is Assistant Professor of Comparative Politics in the Department of Political Science and History at Pantheion University (Athens). He is the author of articles on political cleavages in the Greek party system and on European socialist parties. He has published *La social-démocratie de 1945 à nos jours* (1994). A revised version of the book in English will soon be published by Verso.

Jan Sundberg holds the Swedish Chair in Political Science at the University of Helsinki, where he is President of the Nordic Political Science Association. He has published books and articles in Swedish and English on ethnic politics, local politics and more extensively on party organizations.

Paul Webb is Senior Lecturer in Government at Brunel University and a former Visiting Fellow in Social Sciences at Curtin University in Western Australia. He is author of *Trade Unions and the British Electorate* (1992), Reviews Editor for the journal *Party Politics*, and is currently writing a book on British political parties.

List of Abbreviations and Party/Union Acronyms

ADAV	General Workers' Association (Germany)
Agalev	Green Party (Belgium)
Alös	Austrian Socialists' Foreign Bureau
APU	United People's Alliance (Portugal)
ARCI	Italian Association for Recreational Culture
CAP	Common Agricultural Policy
CC.OO	Worker's Commissions (Spain)
CES	Economic and Social Committee (Portugal)
CD	Centre Democrats (Denmark)
CEDA	Confederation of Autonomous Right-Wing Groups (Spain)
CDU	Christian Democratic Union (Germany)
CDU	Communist Coalition (Portugal)
CDU	Democratic Unity Coalition (Portugal)
CDS	Democratic (and) Social Centre (Portugal)
CERES	Centre for Socialist Studies, Research and Education (France)
CFDT	French Democratic Confederation of Labour
CFSP	Common Foreign and Security Policy (EU)
CGIL	Italian General Confederation of Labour
CGT	General Confederation of Labour (France)
CGTB	Belgian General Confederation of Labour (later FGTB)
CGTP	General Confederation of Portuguese Workers
CGTP-In	General Confederation of Portuguese Workers
CGTU	Unified General Confederation of Labour (France)
CIR	Convention of Republican Institutions (France)
CiU	Convergeance and Union (Spain)
CLP	Constituency Labour Party (Great Britain)
CnaP	Clann na Poblachta (Ireland)
CNP	Dutch Communist Party
CPCS	Permanent Council of Social Concertation (Portugal)
CPN	Dutch Communist Party (1918)
CSU	Christian Socialist Union (Germany)
DA	Democratic Alternative (Finland)
DC	Christian Democrats (Italy)
DGB	German Federation of Trade Unions
DKP	Danish Communist Party
DL	Democratic Left (Ireland)

DR	Justice Party (Denmark)
DS	Democrats of the Left (Italy)
EC	European Community
ECB	European Central Bank
ECSC	European Coal and Steel Community
EEC	European Economic Community
EFTA	European Free Trade Association
EL	Unity List (Denmark)
ELDR	Federation of European Liberal Democratic and Reform Parties
EMS	European Monetary System
EMU	Economic and Monetary Union
EP	European Parliament
EPP	European People's Party–Christian Democrats
ESP	European Socialist Party
ETUC	European Trade Union Confederation
EU	European Union
FDP	Free Democratic Party (Germany)
FDF	Democratic Front for French-speakers (Belgium)
FEN	National Federation of Education (France)
FEPU	Front of the United Political Left (Portugal)
FF	Fianna Fáil (Ireland)
FG	Fine Gael (Ireland)
FGCI	Federation of Young Communists (Italy)
FGTB	Belgian General Federation of Labour
FNTT	Land-Workers' Association (Spain)
FNV	Federation of Dutch Trade Unions
FO	Workers' Strength (France)
FPÖ	Austrian Freedom Party
FSG	Caucus of Social Democratic Trades Unionists
FSP	People's Socialist Front (Portugal)
GAPS	Autonomous Political Socialist Group (Portugal)
Højre	Conservative People's Party (Denmark)
HRG	University Directive (1976) (Germany)
IGC	Inter-Governmental Conference (EU)
ILP	Independent Labour Party (Great Britain)
IMF	International Monetary Fund
IRI	Institute for Industrial Reconstruction (Italy)
KF	Conservative people's Party (Denmark)
KPD	Communist Party of Germany
KPÖ	Austrian Communist Party
KRF	Christian People's Party (Denmark)
LO	Swedish Trade Union Confederation
LP	Labour Party (Great Britain)

LRC	Labour Representation Committee (Great Britain)
LSAP/POSL	Luxembourg Socialist Workers' Party
MEP	Member of the European Parliament
MDC	Citizen's Movement (France)
MFA	Movement of Armed Forces (Portugal)
MRP	Popular Republican Movement (France)
MRRP	Movement for the Reorganization of the Party of the Proletariat (Portugal)
MSDP	Majority SPD (Germany)
MSP	Socialist People's Party (Portugal)
NATO	North Atlantic Treaty Organization
NEC	National Executive Committee (Great Britain)
NGO	Non-Governmental Organization
NLP	National Labour Party (Ireland)
NVB	Dutch People's Movement
OECD	Organization for Economic Co-operation and Development
ÖGB	Austrian Labour Federation
OGBL	Luxembourg Trade Union Federation
ÖTV	Public Service, Transport and Communication Workers Union (Germany)
ÖVP	Austrian People's Party
PAK	Panhellenic Liberation Movement
PASKE	Panhellenic Militant Trade Union Movement
PASOK	Panhellenic Socialist Movement
PCB	Communist Party of Belgium
PCF	French Communist Party
PCE	Spanish Communist Party
PCI	Italian Communist Party
PCL	Communist Party of Luxembourg (1921)
PCL	Luxembourg Communist Party
PCP	Portuguese Communist Party
PCS/CSV	Christian Democratic Party (Luxembourg)
PD/DP	Liberal Party (Luxembourg)
PDS	Party of Democratic Socialism (Germany)
PDS	Democratic Party of the Left (Italy)
PEP	Progressive European Party
PES	Party of European Socialists
PLI	Italian Liberal Party
PLP	Parliamentary Labour Party (Great Britain)
POB	Belgian Workers' Party
PP	Popular Party (Spain)
PPD	People's Democratic Party (Portugal)
PPI	Italian Popular Party

PRC	Party of the Communist Refoundation (Italy)
PRD	Democratic Renewal Party (Portugal)
PRI	Italian Republican Party
PRP	Portuguese Republican Party
PS	Portuguese Socialist Party
PS	Socialist Party (France)
PS	Socialist Party (French-speaking Belgium)
PSC/CVP	Social Christians (Belgium)
PSD	Social Democratic Party (Luxembourg) (1971)
PSD	Social-Democratic Party (Portugal)
PSDI	Italian Social Democratic Party
PSE–PSOE	(Basque) Spanish Socialist Workers' Party
PSI	Italian Socialist Party
PSLI	Socialist Party of the Italian Workers
PSOE	Spanish Socialist Workers' Party
PSOP	Portuguese Socialist Party
PSP	Portuguese Socialist Party
PSR	Trotskyist Revolutionary Socialist Party (Portugal)
PSU	Unified Socialist Party (France)
PvdA	Labour Party (The Netherlands)
QMV	Qualified Majority Voting
RMI	Minimum Income for Reintegration (France)
RPR	Rally for the Republic (France)
RS	Revolutionary Socialists
RV	Social Liberal Party (Denmark)
RW	Walloon Rally (Belgium)
SAK	Finnish Workers' Central Union
SAP	Social Democratic Workers' Party (Germany)
SAP	Swedish Social Democratic Party
SD	Danish Social Democratic Party
SDAP	Austrian Social Democratic Workers' Party
SDAP	Dutch Social Democratic Workers' Party
SDB	Social Democratic Union (The Netherlands)
SDLP	Social Democratic and Labour Party (Ireland)
SDP	Finnish Social Democratic Party
SDP	Social Democratic Party of the GDR
SED	Socialist Unity Party of Germany
SF	Danish Socialist Peoples' Party
SFIO	French Section of the Workers' International
SG	Youth Organization of PDS
Sl	Socialist International
SKDL	Finnish People's Democratic Union
SMIC	Minimum Wage (France)

SP	Socialist Party (Flemish-speaking Belgium)
SPD	Social Democratic Party of Germany
SPÖ	Socialist Party of Austria (Social Democratic Party of Austria since 1991)
TD	Member of the Irish Parliament
TPSL	Social Democratic League of Workers and Smallholders (Finland)
TUC	Trades Union Confederation (United Kingdom)
UCD	Democratic Centre Union (Spain)
UDF	Union for French Democracy
UDP	Democratic People's Union (Portugal)
UDP	Maoist People's Democratic Union (Portugal)
UEDS	Left Union of Socialist Democracy (Portugal)
UGT	General Union of Workers (Portugal)
UGT	General Workers's Union (Spain)
USC	Communal Socialist Union (PS, Belgium)
USDP	Independent Socialist Party (Germany)
V	Liberal Party (Denmark)
VAS	Left-Wing Alliance (Finland)
VS	Left Socialists (Denmark)

Acknowledgements

The editors and publishers wish to thank the following for permission to reproduce copyright material: H.-D. Klingemann and M. Kaase (eds), for data in Table 6.4, from *Wahlen and Wähler: Analysen aus Anlaß der Bundestagwahl 1990* (Westdeutscher Verlag, 1994); J. Coakley and M. Gallagher (eds), for data in Tables 9.1, 9.2 and 9.5, from *Politics in the Republic of Ireland* (PSAI and Folens, 1993); R. Sinnott for data in Table 9.4, from *Irish Voters Decide: Voting Behaviour in Elections and Referendums Since 1918* (Manchester University Press, 1995); Pinter Publishers for data in Table 9.3, from P. Mair, *The Changing Irish Party System: Organization, Ideology and Electoral Competition* (1987); G. Voerman for data in Table 12.1, from *Jaarboek Documentatiecentrum Nederlandse Politieke Partijen 1995* (DNPP/ RU-Groningen, 1996); J. F. Tezanos for data in Tables 14.1, 14.2 and 14.4, from *Historia ilustrada del socialismo español* (Editorial Sistema, 1993); A. Widfeldt for data in Tables 15.2 and 15.3m from *Linking Parties with People? Party Membership in Sweden 1960–1994* (Göteborg University Press, 1997).

Introduction: European Social Democracy *in Situ*

Philippe Marlière

EUROPEAN SOCIAL DEMOCRACY: A DEFINITION

The Many Faces of Social Democracy

Social democracy has greatly influenced capitalism in Europe and in turn, capitalism has also shaped the face of social democracy. Despite the natural antagonism between the two political forces, their fate has been to work alongside and influence one another. The historic aim of social democracy was to fight back the most oppressive aspects of capitalism and even to overthrow the liberal–capitalist order prevailing in all European societies at the end of the nineteenth century. As we head towards the twenty-first century, however, the situation appears to be the reverse: capitalism has been more successful at transforming social democracy than vice versa. From its origins as a revolutionary political movement which aimed to free the working class from the exploitation of the capitalist system, social democracy has gradually become a force integrated within the capitalist order. This integration has been so effective that social democracy has now become one of the central pillars of liberal–capitalist societies.

However, social democracy should not be seen as a mere political force. The term 'social democracy', the substantive 'social democrat', or the adjective 'social democratic' can be used to refer to a number of different realities. In the wake of the Second World War, when the influence of social democracy was at its most prominent – notably due to the implementation of the Welfare State right across Europe – the terminology was used to refer to a régime or a political system. The popularized expression 'social democratic compromise' or 'consensus' served to highlight the fact that the achievements of social democratic governments in office in most European countries at the time, or at least influential in opposition, were recognized and accepted by their political opponents on the other side of the left–right political axis. Viewed from this perspective, social democracy embodies a generally accepted way of tackling mainstream social and economic issues and policies which are taken for granted by the political class as a whole.

While social democracy can be studied both as a coherent political force and as a specific way of dealing with socio-economic issues, a closer look at the social democratic parties in the European Union shows that in terms of historical background, organization and policies, it is in fact remarkably diverse. A consecutive reading of the sixteen chapters which form the core of this book will reveal the extent of this political diversity: each chapter highlights the way in which it has been shaped both by external factors and by party features arising from a specific national political climate. The purpose of this introductory chapter is to emphasize the common elements of all European social democratic parties with a view to proposing an accessible political paradigm. In other words, it aims to assess the extent to which it is possible to speak of a typical social democratic mode of organization as well as a set of public policies. Furthermore, it addresses the most recent trends within social democratic parties in the European Union in order to establish their new political agenda.

The Origins of Social Democracy

Historians date the founding of the first 'social democratic' party to France in 1849, in the aftermath of the 1848 Revolution, when left-wing republicans and socialists merged to found the Social Democratic Party which united working-class activists with representatives of the French bourgeoisie. In Germany in 1869, Karl Liebknecht and August Bebel organized the Workers' social democratic Party which rapidly became known as the Social Democratic Party. The birth of these social democratic parties in Europe also coincided with the founding of the First International (1864–76) which gave the proletariat a voice and facilitated the expression of a more unified working-class movement. This political structure was composed of the three following main streams: (1) Socialist and reformist, holding rather moderate positions and composed of petty-bourgeois elements; (2) Collectivist and Anarchist, under the leadership of Bakunin; (3) Communist and Marxist, influenced by Karl Marx' writings. Within the First International, the new social democratic parties contributed to crucial debates such as the issue of the conquest of political power by the working class. From 1875 onwards within the German social democratic party (SPD) and from the 1880s onwards in Europe, Marxism was to exercise increasing intellectual and political domination. From then on, the term 'social democrat' became synonymous with 'class struggles' and 'the political action of the working class with a view to achieving the conquest of power'. When the Second International was launched in 1889, the Marxist element predominated, emphasizing a clear-cut opposition to the liberal–capitalist order and calling for the development of world-wide class solidarity. Before the First World War, the Second International hosted leaders with rather contrasted political stances and personalities: Rosa Luxemburg, Karl Kautsky, Lenin and Jean Jaurès.

Ironically, it was the failure of the Second International to preserve a united front against the 'Capitalist war' foreseen by social democratic leaders which gave social democratic parties the definitive shape they still have today to some extent. In other words, the fact that the working-class alliance had been battered by the war made social democratic parties re-position along more national or even 'nationalistic' lines from 1914 onwards. The unity of the movement was to be further shaken by the other great event in Russia in 1917, the Bolshevik Revolution. When the Third International (soon to be called the 'Communist International') was founded by Lenin and Zinoviev in 1919, social democratic parties were asked to join and transform into 'communist parties', the reason being that for the Bolsheviks in 1914 the Second International had been too 'nationalistic' and 'reformist' in tone and action and had failed to reinforce working-class solidarity. As a consequence, they wanted it to be superseded by a new International that was clearly 'revolutionary'. This sparked off passionate debate within national social democratic parties between 1917 and 1921. In numerous cases, social democratic parties were divided, with some members leaving to join the Third International and form communist parties alongside social democratic ones. In 1923, the 'reformist Right' of social democracy set about trying to heal the rift and decided on the re-launch of the Second International, that is the Socialist International. But after this particularly painful moment in its history, the European left remained divided into two rival camps: a communist one, such as that already in power in the USSR, which argued for revolutionary socio–political changes in liberal–capitalist societies; and a social democrat one, associated by contrast with reformism as a result of its more progressive approach to change and its willingness in practice to abide by the rules of liberal–capitalist régimes in order to conquer political power.

The moderate stance taken by social democratic parties became even more striking after the Second World War. When the so-called 'Cold-War' period started in 1947 between the two main world powers, the United States and the USSR, social democratic parties in the West clearly backed the Western liberal–capitalist camp against Communism. The 'radical trend' of the First International was thus exhausted and with it the ambition to supersede capitalism with a radically different socio–political system. The use of violence and illegal devices to access power were emphatically condemned by all social democratic parties. The collectivization of the means of production, although still advocated in most party manifestos, became *de facto* a kind of unreachable 'Garden of Eden', whereas the grim reality of the here and now was capitalism. In most European countries the social democratic accommodation with capitalism was the idea of a 'mixed economy' combining public and private sectors. Representative of this new trend, the German

SPD denounced its own set of ideological Marxist values at its Bad Godesberg congress in 1959 in order to match practice to theory and present itself to the electorate as an unequivocal 'reformist party'. On the international level, the Second International gave unwavering support during the 'Cold-War' period to the western capitalist camp and its institutions such as NATO, as did fiercely anti-communist social democratic leaders and activists.

A General Typology of European Social Democracy

From 1945 until the early 1970s, all European social democratic parties combined some or all of the following features:

1 They were parties with a *strong working-class anchoring* as far as membership and electorate were concerned.
2 They were *mass parties* – that is, parties with a large membership providing substantial financial resources.
3 They had developed close relationships and in some cases solid organic links with *representative and centralized trade-union organizations*.
4 Although their political basis was clearly of a working-class or 'popular' nature, *they were not 'class parties'* (unlike communist parties) – that is, parties which present themselves to the electorate as solely 'defending the interests of the working class'.
5 Their electoral and sociological basis had an *interclassist profile* which combined strong support among working-class segments of the population with the ability to attract significant proportions of the middle and even upper segments of salaried employees.
6 They were in a position to cover most or all of the left-wing segment of the left–right political axis. In other words, they were the *dominant force on the left* when they were in competition with other left-wing parties.
7 They accepted the mode of electoral and political competition implemented in western capitalist systems based upon the rules of political majority in parliament and, as a corollary, they also accepted the *alternation of political power* between left-wing and conservative parties.
8 Their ideological and programmatic stances were moderate enough to be viewed by a large majority of the electorate as 'acceptable', a fact which entitled them to legitimately compete for power with conservative parties. Another underlying factor, one which differentiated them from communist parties, was public acceptance of social democrats as a legitimate and eligible force at governmental level, whereas

communist parties aroused a marked hostility from the majority of voters and as a consequence lacked the same *'governmental vocation'*.

9   Although they advocated 'Internationalism' and political solidarity with other sister parties of the Second International, their political actions and references were in fact firmly rooted in their respective nations and they presented themselves to their electorates as a 'National Party'. Their marked anti-communism also led them to oppose Eastern block communist régimes from the beginning of the Cold War onwards and most of them were clearly in favour of supporting the *American–Atlanticist camp* against the USSR.

10 In some countries, most notably in Sweden and Austria, they encouraged the implementation of a mode of social relationship between workers and employers which involved a series of concerted trade-offs organized by the state, the trade unions and the employers. They were able to propose a system in which the implementation of public and social policies was agreed through *compromise and collaboration*, thus avoiding serious conflict or opposition between the different protagonists.

11 Although most party manifestos and constitutions called for the 'collectivization of all means of production', no social democratic force in office actually undertook the complete nationalization of the economy. Therefore, from 1945 onwards, the market economy only ever existed alongside nationalized industries and utilities, to form what was called a *'mixed economy'*.

This typology of post-war Social Democracy, like any ideal-typical construction, should evidently be seen as a kind of heuristic device to help identify the key features within it systematically. This in turn does not mean that such a strict paradigm could be applied *mutatis mutandis* to all social democratic forces in the European Union. With the notable exception of the Swedish SAP, which did seem to embrace all eleven variables in a quasi-paradigmatic manner, all other parties combined only a certain number of them. It is possible, however, to locate and separate two characteristic sub-groups among the social democratic parties: one, established in the northern countries of Europe (Sweden, Finland, Denmark, Austria, Germany, Great Britain, Belgium and Luxembourg) and the other located roughly in southern Europe (France, Spain, Italy, Greece, Portugal). The Republic of Ireland and the Netherlands are more problematic cases: although they are both geographically speaking northern European parties, the weakness of their organization makes it difficult to include them in the first group. However, their more conciliatory and pragmatic style in terms of policy could equally justify the opposing view. The dual division therefore remains somewhat unsatisfactory, since some parties do not fit easily into either sub-group. The distinction should therefore be applied with great caution since it appears that even within each sub-group, important socio-logical and political disparities prevail (see below). It is worth noting that in the Belgian, Dutch, Danish, Irish and Finnish cases, the socialist or social democratic forces have always had to form coalition governments with con-servative and liberal forces in order to exercise power. It is clear that the ideological and structural compromises which have to be made in such a situation have undoubtedly limited the room for manoeuvre of all these social democratic parties once in office.

It is in the first group that the 'social democratic model' was most fully developed. In the second group, in contrast, the pattern was much less readily applied and even, in some extreme cases, non-existent (France, Greece). The weakness of social democracy – or even its absence – can be explained by a series of factors: strong competition on the left from com-munist parties, deep divisions within the trade unions, no real party–trade union link, weak party membership particularly among the working-class segment, while the middle classes were somewhat over-represented. This shows that despite a generally shared set of values and beliefs (parliamentary democracy, social justice, hostility to the 'communist pattern'), social democratic parties proved to be very heterogeneous forces in terms of organization and policy.

THE SOCIAL DEMOCRATIC PATTERN AS IMPLEMENTED IN EUROPE AFTER 1945

A Specific Type of Party Organization

From their formation at the end of the nineteenth century until the 1970s, social democratic parties, at least of the 'northern' variety, relied heavily on a significant membership of working-class extraction. Since its aims were to mobilize and politicize the proletariat with a view to conquering political power, social democracy insisted on the full participation of the greatest number of workers in party affairs. As a corollary, the link with the trade unions was from the beginning not only favoured, but also necessary in order to attract the greatest possible number of working class activists. The organic party–trade union link implied a particular type of relationship to the party. Most members joined it indirectly, that is they became *ipso facto* members of the social democratic party because the union to which they belonged was collectively affiliated to it. This explains the impressive number of activists in some northern parties and also their wealth – union members of the party paid a 'political levy' for each of their members. The foundation of a mass party on this indirect structure had a distinct disadvantage, however: most indirect party members were scarcely aware of their party membership and were in fact politically apathetic and showed minimal, if any, commitment to the party. The British Labour Party (LP) and the Swedish Social Democratic Party (SAP), although both have allowed direct adhesion to the party, are the two European Union parties which best typify this very specific mode of party organization. This organizational system still prevails in these parties, although the current trend, especially in Britain, is to encourage direct membership.

Although the politicization of party activists always remained confined to importing a set of general political principles, the party also acted as a 'political community' operating beyond strictly political matters and offering its members a series of cultural or social services through friendly associations or unions. This caused the party itself to formulate a para-political mode of socialization and in some cases a kind of 'micro-society' emerged within the national community which was endowed with specific cultural features largely shaped by the working-class nature of its membership. This trait was noticeably less effective from the 1920s onward when the social democratic parties began to make overtures to the middle classes. Nonetheless, it remained part of the social democratic culture until the 1970s.

Another significant element of the social democratic party which has continued to predominate is the fact that it is a highly structured and hierarchical organization which employs a significant number of party workers at different levels of party bureaucracy. Parties which are still organized according to this kind of pyramidal bureaucratic structure include the SPD, the SAP, the Austrian Social Democratic Party (SPÖ) and to a lesser extent the LP which, in many respects, owes much to the bureaucratic trade union organization surrounding the Trades Union Congress (TUC). Here, once again the north–south divide prevails: parties from the first group as indicated above tend to have high levels of organization and bureaucratization, whereas parties from the second group have weak party organization and rely on a small number of activists who, for the most part, do not contribute effectively to party affairs. In two 'extreme cases', France and Greece, party organization and membership play only a marginal role: like bourgeois parties, these parties appear to function according to the cadre party structure, that is structures which rely primarily on an élite of party workers and especially professional politicians who, as in the Weberian distinction, do not live *for* politics (unlike activists), but *from* politics.

From the 1950s onward, the sociological profile of social democratic parties began to change. Traditionally they had had a mainly working-class membership and hence a working-class agenda, but they began to look towards the middle classes in an attempt to renew and widen their traditional basis. Although 'working-class atavism' (see below) remained alive, the sociology of most parties betrayed an increasingly marked interest in the middle classes. Hence the ambiguity of post-war European social democracy: on the one hand, it was primarily a political force aimed at political integration of the working class into the liberal–capitalist system, but on the other it progressively became a 'catch-all-party' which, notably for electoral purposes, hoped to attract a substantial part of the middle-class vote.

Elements of Electoral Sociology

From Working Class Party to 'Catch-all Party'
From the 1960s onward, the transformation of social democratic parties into 'catch-all-parties' meant a retreat from one of their original objectives: the political and cultural training of the proletariat. On a purely electoral level, this new trend was clearly reflected in all parties by the decreasing importance of working-class suffrage within the total share of the vote. However, despite the consistent weakening of the working-class vote in the overall voting pattern, most parties have retained relatively solid popular support among the electorate in general – at least enough to argue that the working-class vote still constitutes an important part of most social democratic parties. In fact, many social democratic forces have experienced steady electoral decline because the loss of popular votes has not been satisfactorily compensated for by enough new middle-class suffrage. This is especially clear in the case of the SAP which had to concede power to conservative parties in the 1970s after more than 40 years of uninterrupted social democratic rule. In the same way, the LP experienced a severe electoral setback in the early 1970s because of the defection of a significant part of its traditional working-class support.

Until the 1970s, the high level of working-class votes in most social democratic party results constituted a constant feature of their political identity, most notably in parties which combined several of the 'social democratic features' stated in the above typology, that is, the SAP, the LP, the SPÖ and the Danish Social Democratic Party (SD).

Supremacy on the Left Wing of the Political Spectrum
Another remarkable feature of the social democratic parties in their purest form is their ability to dominate the whole of the left wing of the political spectrum both politically and electorally. This position of left-wing hegemony – or even in some cases, of quasi-monopoly (e.g. the SAP, SPD or the LP) – enables them to maximize their influence within the working class and to be viewed as a credible force of government at the same time. In contrast, parties which had to compete with influential national communist parties until the 1980s – e.g. the French Socialist Party (PS), the Spanish Socialist Workers' Party (PSOE), the Italian Socialist Party (PSI), the Portuguese

Socialist Party (PSP) or the Panhellenic Socialist Movement (PASOK) – found it more awkward to combine left-wing policies and rhetoric, which would appeal to their domestic working classes, with more centrist stances, which would generate a suitably 'governmental profile'. Parties which did not have to struggle against other left-wing forces undoubtedly found it easier to adopt more centrist positions and consequently fared better against conservative rivals in the political competition for power. The 'working-class atavism' of some social democratic forces (i.e. a strong capacity to attract working-class votes due to the absence of any other serious competition on the left) is therefore characteristic of the 'pure type' of social democratic party. Hegemony of the left enables them to look towards the political centre secure in the knowledge that there is no serious challenge on the left. Conversely, the co-existence on the left of a social democratic party of a strong communist party makes any centrist orientation more risky in terms of electoral pay-offs.

Trade-off and Conciliatory Mode

One final underlying aspect of the social democratic model is that it is closely linked to a particular type of public policy, or even to a specific mode of co-governance of the economy between the state, the trade unions and the employers. After the Second World War, social democracy played a highly influential role in the shaping of a new set of socio-economic policies across Europe. With massive state intervention in sectors of society as diverse as health, education, work, transport and energy, social democratic governments implemented what would later be referred to as 'welfare state reforms'. In the late 1940s, state intervention in capitalist European societies took advantage of the poor reputation of capitalism in large segments of European populations to nationalize certain key industries or services. Economic reforms were largely influenced by the ideas of the liberal John Maynard Keynes and were consequently labelled 'Keynesian policies'. By and large, Keynesian policies advocated a method of managing the economy which depended on reinforcing internal consumption through a more equitable distribution of income and wealth within a political environment where the state was more economically and socially active. The cornerstones of these policies were public financing of investment and stimulation of demand through the state budget. Social democratic governments were thus able to kill two birds with one stone: (1) they could stimulate and sustain households' demand and consumption and consequently achieve economic growth; (2) they could redistribute wealth more equally and so satisfy aspirations for social justice. The British LP, in particular, was regarded as an exemplary model for this trend. Like many of its sister parties, the LP implemented vast reforms such as the creation of a National Health Service, the rebuilding and modernization of the infrastructure and policies to ensure economic growth, higher salaries and full employment.

The social democratic pattern of post-war welfarism originally relied on a system of social bargaining between employers and trade unions under the supervision of the state which was later described as the 'social democratic compromise'. According to this arrangement, employers, trade unions and the state work as partners to negotiate socio-economic policies without major social conflict. The key words for such a pattern are therefore 'social compromise' and 'bargaining'. In most cases, the social democratic trade-off suggests that the trade unions and the working class accept the capitalist logic of market forces and profit. In return for the guarantee of a peaceful social climate, employers are committed to providing their employees with social pay-offs such as full employment, salary rises and enhanced social rights and working conditions within the enterprise. Most analysts have pointed out that from the aftermath of the Second World War up to the mid-1970s, social democracy proposed a double compromise between the state and market forces and between Capital and Work. Furthermore, this system enabled social democratic forces in office at the time to set the socio–economic agenda for the capitalist system as a whole. The continued existence of such a system was guaranteed by representative and strongly organized trade unions with a capacity both to articulate the demands of the working classes and to make workers accept this culture of compromise and moderation. But while parties such as the SAP, LP, SPD or SPÖ were structurally able to implement such a system (although with varying levels of intensity), most parties of the south (e.g. PS, PSP, PASOK and to a lesser extent PSOE) were never actually able to do so because of their two traditional 'handicaps': (1) insufficiently strong links with rather weak trade unions and (2) strong political competition on the left from communist parties. As a consequence, the political culture of these countries was always confrontational in its attitudes and practices, a fact which made any social bargaining between employers and trade unions all the more uneasy.

PERSISTENT FEATURES AND RECENT CHANGES

The End of the Social Democratic Paradigm?

The so-called 'crisis' of the social democratic pattern is often dated from the mid-1970s. The deep structural and sociological changes which have affected most social democratic forces since the late 1970s have revealed the relative failure of the traditional social democratic model to adapt to the new socio-economic situation in western capitalist societies.

From a purely electoral point of view, the last twenty years have been relatively less favourable towards social democracy in Europe, particularly so in the 1980s when some of the parties which most closely corresponded to the social democratic paradigm received a significantly lower share of the vote than they had done in previous decades (e.g. SPD, LP and, to a lesser extent, SAP). The LP and SPD, two important parties with substantial governmental experience in the 1940s, 1950s and 1960s, were even condemned to long periods in opposition from the late 1970s or early 1980s. The broader picture reveals that between the 1960s and 1990s most other social democratic parties which have become governmental forces, either in social democratic-led cabinets or as part of a coalition, have known quite uneven electoral fortunes, especially in the case of parties with very few 'social democratic features' (PS, PASOK, PSP). The PSOE appears to be the exception which proves the rule with its continuous exercise of power from 1982 to 1996. The peculiarity of the Spanish case can be explained by the structural and ideological weakness of the Spanish conservative forces – in the wake of Franco's dictatorship, the majority of Spaniards did not trust them to consolidate the new democratic régime. The conclusion to be drawn from this is that the time spent in office is not necessarily synonymous with political popularity and does not necessarily help strengthen social democratic forces – quite the contrary. Over time, governmental experience seems to weaken social democratic parties in the short term and, with the exception of the PSOE, leads to defeat, or at best constant electoral decline.

Changes in Party Electorate

One major change in the voting structure of all social democratic parties – initiated in the 1950s and accelerated from the 1970s onward – is that they have all entered a cycle of 'de-proletarization' – that is, a decline in the level of the working-class vote. This decline has been largely due to the decreasing proportion of working-class people in the overall population. The change in the traditional voting pattern has been particularly spectacular for the LP and the SD. This general trend has led to a profound re-shaping of the overall sociology of social democratic forces whereby definite overtures have been made towards the middle classes in order to compensate for the loss of working-class suffrage. Electoral gains among the middle classes, although steady in most countries, have proved to be problematic for some. In countries where new political forces, such as Green parties (e.g. the Greens in Germany or Denmark), have attracted a wide range of middle-class voters (especially the young, educated and urban segments of the middle stratum), social democratic parties have clearly lost out. The other major feature of the evolution in voting patterns is the development of a more consistent middle-class vote among employees working in the public sector – that is, the people who are most keen to keep a high level of state intervention in the economy. By contrast, non-salaried workers and farmers have remained adamantly hostile to social democracy (with the exception of some parties of southern Europe such as Greece, Spain or, to a lesser extent, Italy).

The above observations reveal that the social basis of the social democratic electorate has been eroded progressively since the late 1950s: from being massively working class, it has clearly become interclassist since the 1970s as a result of a significant increase in the proportion of middle-class votes.

Changes in Party Sociology

As a reflection of the increasing influence of the middle-class vote, social democratic party membership and leadership have been steadily dominated by professional middle-class activists endowed with significant cultural capital. This trend has become evident even in parties with a traditional working class membership such as the SPD or the SPÖ. The LP is also an interesting case study: from the late 1990s, it has committed itself to reducing its 'working-class dependency' by adopting a series of measures designed to reduce the level of financial and political support from the TUC. It has also launched a massive campaign aimed at attracting new middle-class members with neither political background nor trade union links. Shifts such as this in the traditional working-class profile of social democratic forces in northern Europe have radically put their very identity in question. As 'catch-all-parties' on an electoral level, they have now become structures in which the élite plays an underlying role and the party policy-making process is heavily influenced by the party leader. Inversely, the 'politicization' and 'integration' of rank-and-file activists is no longer a concern. Party members and structures at local level tend, for most parties, to be active only in the run-up to elections where activists are asked to canvass voters on the doorstep, or distribute party leaflets. The end of working-class dominance in party culture has often hastened the departure of numerous working-class activists who feel ill at ease in a new 'technocratic milieu', while newcomers, often endowed with high levels of economic and cultural capital tend to take the upper hand in matters concerning the internal life of the party. The reorganization of the LP exemplifies this trend as follows: (1) the decision-making process has been centralized around the most senior party officials; (2) the party is 'personified' through the actions and image of the leader; (3) media pundits ('spin doctors') participate actively in the party decision-making process; (4) party officials and their political actions are over-mediatized and (5) marketing techniques are regularly applied to politics in order to assess the 'collective mood' on which policies or party platforms might be based ('focus group technique').

The End of Post-War-Style Policies

With the end of the post-war cycle of economic growth, the 'social democratic compromise' based on conciliatory policies discussed and agreed by the state, the trade unions and the employers has been under pressure. As a consequence of the beginning of a deep economic crisis, the policies of the welfare state have been seriously challenged and both conservative and social democratic governments have been forced to make substantial cuts in welfare provision as a result. Keynesian policies involving the re-launch of the economy through stimulated interior demand or sustained investment have been gradually abandoned. Instead, policies of 'austerity' have been launched which have in turn produced high levels of unemployment throughout the European Union. From the 1980s, in all countries where social democratic forces have been in power, Keynesian policies have been replaced by neo-liberal policies (notably involving increased income for capital holders at the expense of salaried employees' income, the withdrawal of the welfare state from its traditional spheres of intervention such as health, education, or transport and the deregulation of employment protection for some salaried workers, such as the implementation of 'flexible working hours' in the hope of creating new jobs).

This new economic trend has not only undermined the political originality of the social democratic model considerably, it has also confused its identity. In most European countries today it has become difficult to identify the differences in economic orientation and choice between conservatives and social democrats. Increasingly, the social democratic paradigm of 'Social Capitalism' introduced in post-war Europe is being superseded by a new paradigm, initially advocated by conservative forces, which could be labelled 'Liberal Capitalism'.

New Social Democratic Trends

If, in the late 1990s, the 'social democratic pattern' as set out and analyzed in this Introduction is still proving to be effective for some parties (SAP and to a lesser extent SPÖ), other parties have largely evolved towards a mode of organization, a party sociology and policies which now have little in common with traditional social democracy (e.g. LP, PvDA and, to a lesser extent, SPD). This poses the question – and the problem for social democratic forces – of their political identity and of the nature of their policies when in power.

The dilution of the social democratic paradigm into a variety of new trends reveals the deep confusion into which social democratic parties have sunk over the past twenty years. New political orientations and drastic sociological changes within most parties have generated new patterns which reflect the diversity of socio-political issues each party faces in its own national context. The main debates revolve around questions such as the level of social protection which should still be guaranteed by the state in the health, education and work sectors. Some parties in office, such as the LP, have adopted stances or policies in which the state no longer features as a key actor in wealth redistribution. In this situation, the reduction of the welfare state is justified by the fact that the state can no longer afford to distribute the same level of welfare provision to the worse off in society. But it seems that there is more at stake than just the question of scarcity of welfare. Such new trends seem also to be grounded philosophically: parties such as the LP or the PvDA argue that even if the state could afford it, it should not be up to the government to provide individuals with the level of welfare protection which European societies have come to expect since 1945. Thus, if the state still has a role to play in rectifying the most blatant social injustices and disparities, it should nevertheless be up to the individual as the fulcrum of social action, in conjunction with intermediary and private socio–economic entities, to take his/her own initiative to create work and economic prosperity. This recent underlying thrust prevails to such an extent that it shows how radically, for some parties, the traditional social democratic values and policies upheld until the late 1980s have now been challenged.

Although some parties still have quite a long way to go to come to terms with such a philosophical strand (e.g. PS, SPD and the Italian Democrats of the Left [DS]), the fact remains that the political agenda of European social democracy has now been structured around this revised form of social democracy. All social democratic forces have therefore been debating whether or not it is politically acceptable to reduce the role of the state in the economy and if so, what kind of minimal competence it should preserve.

Yet the sociological changes within social democratic organizations (namely, the loss of working-class identity and support compensated for by middle-class voters and members, or the 'personification' of power around the party leader) as well as the abandonment of traditional welfare state policies have also served to narrow the political and cultural gap between the forces of northern Europe and those of southern Europe. Following on from this, 'social democracy' now seems a much more appropriate term to designate the non-communist or 'reformist forces' in the European Union than it used to be. In fact, the term is now accepted and used rather loosely, a fact which allows political commentators and political scientists to speak of a 'European social democracy' which encompasses all parties of the European Union (only ten years ago, such a typology would still have been quite hazardous). The narrowing of differences between north and south (where 'reformist forces' preferred to be labelled as 'socialist' rather than 'social democratic') is particularly remarkable in a country such as France. The history of the PS shows that the word 'social democracy' has been traditionally scorned because it was synonymous with 'excessive political moderation' and 'excessive compromise with capitalism'. As a result of its experiences in government during the 1980s and 1990s, the PS has become progressively more willing to consider the possibility that there is one 'European social democratic mould' of which the French are clearly a part. Thus, 'reformist parties' on the centre-left in European countries have more in common today than they did in the past. This does not mean that they have all become similar – cultural and political differences and oppositions in some cases remain strong – but it underlines the fact that more political convergences and sociological similarities are now to be found in all centre- left parties. The foundation of the Party of European Socialists (PES) in the early 1990s, of which the fifteen parties to this study are all members, corroborates this point. It also justifies a systematic study of these 'reformist forces' in the European Union and their supra-partisan structure, the PES, and their presentation as part of a 'European social democratic family'.

Select Bibliography

Bell, D. and Shaw E. (1994) *Conflict and Cohesion in Western Social Democratic Parties*, London and New York: Pinter.

Bergounioux, A. and Grunberg, G. (1996) *L'Utopie à L'épreuve. Le socialisme européen au XXè siècle*, Paris: De Fallois.

Esping-Andersen, G. (1985) *Politics Against the Markets: The Social Democratic Road to Power*, Princeton, NJ: Princeton University Press.

Gallagher, T., Williams, A. *et al.* (1989) *Southern European Socialism*, Manchester: Manchester University Press.

Giddens, A. (1998) *The Third Way: The Renewal of Social Democracy*, Cambridge: Polity Press.

Kitschelt, H. (1994) *The Transformation of European Social Democracy*, Cambridge: Cambridge University Press.

Lazar M. (ed.) (1996) *La Gauche en Europe depuis 1945. Invariants et mutations du socialisme européen*, Paris: PUF.

Lukes, S. (1985) *Marxism and Morality*, Oxford: Oxford University Press.

Miliband, D. (1995) (ed.) *Reinventing the Left*, Cambridge: Polity Press.

Moschonas, G. (1994) *La Social-démocratie de 1945 à nos jours*, Paris: Montchrestien.

Paterson, W. and Thomas, A. (eds) (1986) *The Future of Social Democracy: Problems and Prospects of Social Democratic Parties in Western Europe*, Oxford: Clarendon Press.

Sassoon, D. (1996) *One Hundred Years of Socialism: The West European Left in the Twentieth Century*, London and New York: I.B. Tauris.

Tudor, H. and Tudor J.M. (eds) (1988) *Marxism and Social Democracy: The Revisionist Debate 1896–1898*, Cambridge: Cambridge University Press.

Wright, T. (1996) *Socialisms: Old and New*, London: Routledge.

1 The Social Democratic Party of Austria
Kurt Richard Luther

HISTORY

Unification and the Struggle for Political Rights, 1860s–1918

The roots of Austrian social democracy were originally nourished less by trade unions than by workers' educational associations. Created in part to circumvent the Habsburg Monarchy's restrictions upon 'political' organizations, they embraced both Lassallian principles of state help and Schulze-Delitsch's emphasis upon the intellectual and moral development of the working class. Workers' organizations were legalized in 1867, yet attempts to develop a single social democratic party throughout the multinational Empire were repeatedly frustrated by continued state repression, the late and uneven process of industrialization, national tensions, but above all by personal and ideological enmity, which in the 1870s led to the establishment of two hostile camps. Whilst Heinrich Oberwinder's 'Moderates' advocated co-operating with reform-minded liberals to bring about democratization, Andreas Scheu's Marxist 'Radicals' supported social revolution. The intense disputes between them reflected the contemporaneous conflict in Germany, from whence several of the early leaders of Austrian social democracy originated. The countries shared many key social democratic protagonists (e.g. Karl Kautsky), and significant elements of the German SDP's 1869 Eisenach Programme were incorporated into the 'Neudörfler Programme' adopted in 1874 by the new Austrian Social Democratic Workers' Party (SDAP).

The enduring economic crises of the 1870s increased the Radicals' popular support, yet unity remained elusive and conflict even escalated, leaving the divided labour movement incapable of effectively promoting workers' interests. Unity was finally achieved at the Hainfeld conference of 30 December 1888 – 1 January 1889 (widely held to mark the birth of the SDAP) and largely resulted from the efforts of Viktor Adler (1852–1918), the united party's first leader. A middle-class doctor of Jewish origin who had been a prominent German national, but had left that party because of its anti-Semitism, Adler persuaded the Radicals to accept the pursuit of parliamentary representation, which the Moderates in turn conceded was incapable of bringing about socialism on its own, but

16

merely offered a useful potential arena for political agitation. Hainfeld marked the beginning of a tendency to place party unity above ideological purity. Thus the party's 1901 'Vienna Programme' advocated specific reforms, whilst continuing to use Marxist rhetoric about the class struggle. Moreover, the turn of the century saw the beginnings of the 'Austro–Marxist' school, which aspired to offer a 'third way' between reform and revolution.

During the 1890s and 1900s, the labour movement fought for universal manhood suffrage and having achieved this, obtained 23 per cent of the vote and 83 (of 516) seats at the 1907 election. Second, it sought to build up a mass party organization based predominantly upon the industrial proletariat of areas such as Vienna, Bohemia, Styria, Lower Austria, Moravia and Silesia. The SDAP's growth was closely linked to the now rapidly expanding trade union movement and owed much to a cadre of trained 'activists' (*Vertrauensmänner*), to whom the party has since 1894 allocated a key organizing role. By 1909, the Austrian half of the Dual Monarchy contained over 100,000 SDAP members.

The SDAP's multinational character was threatened by the escalating conflict between the Empire's constituent nations. The nationalities issue was addressed in numerous programmatic initiatives (most notably in the 1899 Brünn Programme, which proposed the Empire's transformation into a democratic federation of nations), as well as in the writings of key social democratic theorists such as the reform-minded Karl Renner (1870–1950) and the more radical Otto Bauer (1881–1938). Foremost among the intraparty critics of the SDAP's German–Austrian leadership were the Czechs, who eventually seceded in 1911. After the general election later that year, tensions between the SDAP's national sections resulted in the formation of three separate social democratic parliamentary groups. By the time the First World War broke out in 1914, the pan-Austrian SDAP had effectively dissolved into its constituent national parties.

The war brought pressure from the party's 'Left' for a reassertion of Marxism and internationalism. However, the 1917 party conference agreed with leadership figures such as Adler and Renner that the SDAP should eschew civil unrest that might undermine the war effort and it approved Renner's plan to reform the Empire into a federation based upon national self-government. Inasmuch as these proposals sought to maintain the Habsburg state, they indicate the extent to which the SDAP had become a pillar of the Monarchy. By 1918, however, war weariness, mass strikes, military defeat and revolution abroad had fundamentally changed the situation, so that the party now adopted the Left's principles of national self-determination, internationalism and class struggle.

The First Republic, 'Austrofascism' and Nazi Rule, 1918–45

In October 1918, the SDAP found itself the largest party in the German-speaking rump of the Empire. Renner assumed the leadership of an all-party provisional government and remained its head after the SDAP's success in the election of February 1919 (69 of 170 seats). Like its competitors, the SDAP strongly favoured union with the German Reich. Though Austria was universally considered unviable, the Allies forbade an *Anschluß* and the SDAP grudgingly proceeded to play a key role in framing the centralized federal constitution of the First Austrian Republic, which came into force in October 1920. Despite its sizeable electoral following (Table 1.2, p.25), the SDAP had by then been permanently relegated to an opposition role at the national level and felt very alienated from the new state, the machinery of which was largely in conservative hands.

Much of the SDAP's pre-war industrial heartland was now incorporated within the Empire's successor states. Yet not withstanding deep and lasting economic crises, the party quickly achieved an unparalleled level of organizational density (Table 1.1, p.23). At its peak, its anti-clerical and predominantly proletarian membership included one in six Austrian adults. Over 60 per cent was located in 'red Vienna', where the SDAP embraced more than half of all blue-collar male workers. 'Island' strongholds were located in industrialized areas of Lower Austria and Styria, while rural western Austria was in the hands of the party's Catholic–conservative opponents. The SDAP used its hegemonic position in Vienna's municipal authority (simultaneously a province of the Austrian federation) and its resulting patronage opportunities to build up a young and vibrant movement. It pursued a radical social reform strategy and was especially active in the provision of municipal housing. Together with the trade union and co-operative movements, the party enmeshed members in a tight network of occupational, cultural and educational associations that ensured an ideologically committed and socio–politically encapsulated social democratic counter-culture.

In view of the SDAP's strength, the Austrian Communist Party (*Kommunistische Partei Österreichs* – KPÖ) was not a serious threat, though its presence after 1918 helped ensure the SDAP's retention of Marxist rhetoric, as demonstrated most clearly in its 1926 'Linz Programme', the embodiment of 'Austro–Marxism'. Using the language of scientific socialism, it proclaimed the SDAP's willingness to countenance force and even civil war to defend the Republic against any capitalist attempts to establish a monarchical or fascist dictatorship. Though the SDAP was *de facto* reformist, the programme's radical discourse incensed the party's clerical–conservative opponents and contributed to a radicalization across the political spectrum. The SDAP set up the paramilitary 'Republican Defence League' (*Republikanischer*

Schutzbund), which got embroiled in increasingly violent clashes with analogous bourgeois and Nazi groupings.

In March 1933, the government unconstitutionally suspended parliament and thereafter banned first the KPÖ and then the Austrian Nazis. Confrontation with the socialists peaked in a short civil war in February 1934, after which Engelbert Dolfuß Christian Social government banned all socialist organizations, executed some of their leaders and imprisoned others. Bauer fled to Brünn, where he established *Alös* (the Austrian Socialists' Foreign Bureau), whilst in April 1934, Dolfuß proclaimed the '*Ständestaat*', a one-party authoritarian dictatorship. Within the underground SDAP, younger activists were increasingly critical of the failed reformism of the older party leaders. In part to avoid losing support to the KPÖ, the party name was in March 1934 changed to 'Revolutionary Socialists' (RS) and Bauer drafted a radical declaration of principles. Conflict between the *Alös* and Austria-based elements of the RS intensified, but by late 1937, large parts of the RS leadership had been arrested. When in March 1938 Hitler's troops marched into Austria, many remaining social democratic activists were either immediately arrested by the Gestapo, or forced into exile. Some allied with communists and others in resistance activity, whilst the exiled party leaders remained divided in London, New York and elsewhere.

The Second Republic: From Sub-Cultural Defence to Establishment Party

In 1945, the Allies initially licensed only the reconstituted Socialist Party of Austria (*Sozialistische Partei Österreichs* – SPÖ), the Austrian People's Party (*Österreichische Volkspartei* – ÖVP) and the KPÖ. The latter threatened to be a formidable rival for the SPÖ, but its proximity to the occupying Soviets helped ensure that the SPÖ was soon the unchallenged party of the left. Renner headed the first, all-party post-war government (April–December 1945). Unlike during the First Republic, co-operation persisted, however, not least because Austria remained occupied until 1955 and because the experience of their inter-war predecessors meant the SPÖ and ÖVP were now committed to accommodation. After the KPÖ's 1947 departure from the coalition, Austria was until 1966 ruled by a succession of ÖVP-led 'grand coalitions' that controlled over 90 per cent of votes and seats. Consensual politics was further underscored by corporatism and *Proporz*, the proportionate division between ÖVP and SPÖ of positions in the extensive state sector, as well as of shares of other state resources. In part, *Proporz* was designed to militate against the alienation from the state which the social democratic movement had felt during the ill-fated First Republic.

Another effect was to provide the SPÖ with an extensive range of patronage opportunities. This facilitated the rebuilding of a self-contained socialist sub-culture comprising a dense network of party organization and auxiliary associations. Having discarded its revolutionary rhetoric, the SPÖ initially mobilized its supporters and maintained the mutual suspicion between it and its Catholic–conservative counterpart by appeals to class solidarity and by frequent allusions to the responsibility of inter-war bourgeois parties for the collapse of the First Republic.

A poor SPÖ election result in 1966 allowed the ÖVP to form the Second Republic's first single-party government. In 1967, the SPÖ elected Bruno Kreisky (1911–90) as its new leader. A key figure in post-war Austria, Kreisky was the son of a wealthy, assimilated Jewish family and had in 1938 been forced into exile in Sweden, where he was influenced by Scandinavian ideas of social democracy. He returned in 1949 and as Under-secretary of State for Foreign Affairs (1953–9) participated in negotiations leading to the 1955 Austrian State Treaty. From 1959 to 1966, he was Foreign Minister. After becoming party leader, he launched a raft of policy reviews and revitalized the party. In 1970, he headed an SPÖ minority government supported by the parliamentary FPÖ (*Freiheitliche Partei Österreichs*), the liberalization of which he promoted in order to help divide the bourgeois vote. From 1971 to 1983, Kreisky presided over three single-party majority governments, which mark the height of the SPÖ's post-war success.

The party's electoral setback of 1983 was followed by Kreisky's replacement by Fred Sinowatz (1929–) and a short coalition with the FPÖ, then under liberal leadership. With the election of Jörg Haider (1950–) as FPÖ leader in September 1986, Chancellor Franz Vranitzky (1937–), who had replaced Sinowatz in June 1986, terminated the coalition. Since January 1987, the SPÖ has been the senior partner in a series of coalitions with the ÖVP. In January 1997, Vranitzky resigned the chancellorship in favour of Viktor Klima (1947–), who in April that year was elected party leader. Since 1945, the SPÖ has been progressively transformed – not least by virtue of *Proporz* and 49 years in national government (the last 28 under SPÖ chancellors) – from a party of sub-cultural defence to an establishment party. In 1991, it renamed itself the Social Democratic Party of Austria.

ORGANIZATION AND PARTY PROFILE

Party Structure and Organization

The SPÖ has reformed its organization on four main occasions, the last being in 1993, but its underlying territorial structure has remained fairly constant. The party's basic building blocks are its over 3,000 local units (*Ortsorganizationen*). They combine into district organizations (*Bezirksorganizationen*), which then constitute the nine provincial parties (*Landesparteiorganizationen*) that in turn make up the national party. Each level elects its own assembly and leaders. The statute provides for a number of social democratic groups (*Referate*) and affiliated organizations. These include the party youth (*Junge Generation*); associations of SPÖ communal politicians organized from the *Land* level upwards; a section concerned with the education and training of party members and activists (*Bildungsarbeit*); one dedicated to youth work; the affiliated social democratic caucus (*Fraktion Sozialdemokratischer Gewerkschafter* – FSG) of the Austrian Trade Union Federation (*Österreichischer Gewerkschaftsbund* – ÖGB) and womens' sections (*Frauenkomitees*), which are organized at all levels of the party.

The biennial national party conference (*Bundesparteitag*) comprises numerous 'guest' and over 600 'ordinary' (i.e. voting) delegates. Some 350 of the latter are elected by SPÖ district party committees and 30 by *Land* party executives. They are joined by over 160 delegates from the SPÖ's many affiliated 'socialist organizations'. The largest such contingent is made up of 50 FSG representatives, whilst the Austrian Rentpayers' Association and the Austrian Workers' Choir each send just one delegate. Finally, there are *ex officio* delegates such as the party manager (*Bundesgeschäftsführer*) and the members of the 'full party executive' (*Bundesparteivorstand*). The party conference is responsible for approving changes to the party programme due to be updated in October 1998 and to the party's statute, as well as for considering reports and policy proposals.

The most significant party organ elected by the conference is the full party executive, which then immediately proposes from amongst its midst a party leader (*Parteivorsitzender*) and his/her deputies to the party conference. Once elected, this group constitutes the 'inner party executive' (*Bundesparteipräsidium*). There is also an 'extended' party executive (*erweitertes Bundesparteipräsidium*), which includes the leaders of the *Land* parties, two trades union representatives and two from the women's committee. All must be drawn from the full executive. Notwithstanding the formal primacy of the party conference and declarations regarding internal party democracy, it is within the party's executive organs (and in particular in the inner party executive) that the SPÖ's most important political decisions are made, or at least prepared. For the day-to-day conduct of party business, the SPÖ still relies greatly upon its designated 'activists', who currently comprise about 12 per cent of the party membership. The hierarchical and disciplined nature of internal party life has much to do with the SPÖ's virtually unbroken presence in government.

Auxiliary Associations and Interest-Group Links

The SPÖ has an enormous number of auxiliary associations. They include groups oriented to the youth; students; pensioners; stamp collectors; graduates, intellectuals and artists; cyclists and naturalists. Their total membership has risen from about 1.5 million in the mid-1960s to circa 2.4

million by the early 1990s. Though these figures contain multiple member-ships, they illustrate the extent to which the SPÖ and its auxiliary associations penetrate civil society and for many years helped ensure that members of Austria's socialist subculture could live their lives womb-to-tomb within their own milieu. Yet the greatest membership increases have been within the least politicized associations. For example, the 'Workers' Sport and Fitness Association' (in 1971 renamed the 'Working Group ...') grew by c. 150 per cent and the 'Workers' Automobile and Cyclists' League' (which in 1962 also ditched the label 'Workers' and in 1968 disaffiliated from the SPÖ) increased by over 500 per cent to about 1.2 million members. When these two largest socialist associations are discounted, gross membership peaked at c. 1.2 million in 1975, and has since declined.

The SPÖ also has unusually close interest group links. Of the five main actors in Austria's extensive and hitherto very influential corporatist system, the FSG dominates two: the ÖGB and the Chamber of Labour (*Arbeiter-kammer*). There are also social-democratic factions in the Chambers of Business and of Agriculture (both ÖVP-dominated). Though the SPÖ's relationship to the trade union movement has predictably been close, the trades unions are not corporate members of the SPÖ, which maintains its dominant position in the socialist movement. Indeed, since the party's adop-tion of a more market-oriented set of policies from the mid-1980s, there has regularly been conflict between it and the ÖGB.

Party Membership

The SPÖ has been Europe's most densely organized social democratic party. For most of the post-war period, it embraced 14–15 per cent of Austria's electorate and despite Austria's small population, the absolute number of individual SPÖ members has exceeded than that of many of its sister parties in larger European countries. The SPÖ remains especially strong in the capital, which in 1951 provided 45 per cent of the party's members and 32 per cent of its *Vertrauensleute*, or 'trained activists'. Though this imbalance has since declined, the figures for 1993 were still 30 and 18 per cent respectively (see Table 1.1). Other strongholds are the industrial areas of Lower Austria, Styria and Carinthia. In conservative western Austria, the party is compara-tively weak. SPÖ membership has been predicated upon not only political partisanship, but also instrumental considerations. Given the extensive party-politicization of post-war Austrian society, party membership has often been perceived as an indispensable prerequisite for jobs in Austria's extensive public sector, as well as access to public housing and other state-controlled resources.

The SPÖ's membership is still about two-thirds male, but its occupational profile has changed radically. Between the mid-1950s and early 1990s, the proportion of blue-collar workers fell from c. 40 to about 33 per cent, whilst

Table 1.1 SPÖ absolute membership and membership density in election years, (1913–97)

Year	Members	D*	Year	Members	D*	Year	Members	D*	Year	Members	D*
1913	89,628		1945	357,818	10.4	1964	717,624		1981	713,104	
1919	332,391	9.4	1946	500,181		1965	707,972		1982	702,414	
1920	335,863	9.0	1947	570,768		1966	699,432	14.3	1983	694,598	13.1
1921	491,150		1948	616,232		1967	702,926		1984	690,533	
1922	553,022		1949	614,366	14.0	1968	705,926		1985	685,588	
1923	514,273	13.4	1950	607,283		1969	716,196		1986	669,906	12.3
1924	566,124		1951	621,074		1970	719,389	14.3	1987	654,397	
1925	576,107		1952	627,435		1971	703,093	14.1	1990	637,469	
1926	595,417	16.3	1953	657,042	14.3	1972	696,438		1994	617,163	
1927	669,586		1954	666,373		1973	687,375		1990	605,493	10.7
1928	713,834		1955	691,150		1974	687,650		1991	585,063	
1929	718,056	16.9	1956	687,972	14.9	1975	693,156	13.8	1992	561,338	
1930	698,181		1957	683,249		1976	700,146		1993	535,446	
1931	653,605		1958	716,208		1977	703,624		1994	512,838	8.9
1932	648,497		1960	727,265	14.5	1978	706,039		1995	487,490	8.5
			1962	698,705		1979	721,262	13.9	1996	457,605	
			1963	724,955		1980	719,881		1997	434,281	

* Membership density as percentage of electorate, calculated using source of Table 1.2. Assuming an even trend between 1958 and 1960, density at the time of the 1959 election would have been 15.4 per cent.

Sources: Bundesgeschäftsstelle; Hollmann, E., 'Die Organization der Sozialdemokratie in der Ersten Republik', pp. 93–167 (here p.149), and Müller, W.C., 'Die Organization der SPÖ, 1945–1995', pp. 195–356 (here pp. 332ff), both in Maderthaner, W. and Müller, W.C. (eds), Die Organization der österreichischen Sozialdemokratie 1889–1995 (Vienna: Löcker, 1996).

that of white-collar workers more than tripled, rising to c. 27 per cent. This change broadly reflects overall demographic trends, so blue-collar workers remain over-represented within the SPÖ's membership. Since the mid-1980s, the SPÖ has experienced a large fall in its total membership and become unattractive to young Austrians. Thus whilst the over-60s made up only about 15 per cent of members in 1947, they now constitute nearly 30 per cent. Conversely, the under-30s have declined from about 17 to only 10 per cent. Membership decline has numerous causes. Demographic and socio–cultural change has weakened socio–political encapsulation and thus also the party's control over political socialization and communication. Potential supporters have been alienated by the SPÖ's hierarchical and bureaucratic style, as well as by a number of high-profile cases of political corruption. The rise of postmaterialist orientations led in the 1980s to the establishment of a Green Party, which now competes to the SPÖ's left and attracts in particular well educated young Austrians. Meanwhile, Haider's populist FPÖ appeals especially to blue-collar workers unsettled *inter alia* by the economic down-turn of the last ten years. Finally, among the effects of the latter have been substantial redundancies in public sector enterprises and cuts in public subsidies. Together with EU regulations against sectoral preferment and growing public disenchantment at the use of patronage, these developments have reduced significantly the SPÖ's scope for providing the material incent-ives that traditionally promoted membership.

Electoral Performance and Sociology

The SPÖ's post-war electoral performance can be divided into three phases. During the first, it consistently won fewer seats and (with two exceptions) fewer votes than the ÖVP. During 1970 to 1983, Kreisky added to the SPÖ's core of loyal voters sufficient numbers of the still very small pool of 'floaters' to enable the party to win first a relative and then an absolute majority of votes and seats. Since 1983, the SPÖ's vote has declined significantly, reach-ing an all-time low in 1994. Notwithstanding its slight revival in 1995, there is as yet little evidence that the SPÖ has found a long-term solution to its problems (See Table 1.2). Though the SPÖ remains the largest party (by some 10 points in 1995), votes have been lost to the Greens and to the Liberal Forum (formed in 1993), but above all to the protest-oriented FPÖ. Since 1987, the SPÖ has governed with the ÖVP and repeatedly ruled out coales-cing with Haider's FPÖ. A 'traffic-light' coalition of SPÖ, Greens and Liberal Forum has to date not proved viable, but is not inconceivable in future.

Until the 1960s, about three-quarters of SPÖ voters lived in blue-collar households, four out of ten were blue-collar workers and most exhibited low levels of religious activism. Religiosity has remained low, but only half of the party's voters now live in blue-collar households, a sure sign that the socialist

Table 1.2 SPÖ vote share at all general elections 1919–95 (%)

Year	Vote	Year	Vote	Year	Vote	Year	Vote
1919	40.8	1945	44.6	1966	42.6	1986	43.1
1920	41.8	1949	38.7	1970	48.4	1990	42.8
1923	39.6	1953	42.1	1971	50.0	1994	34.9
1927	42.3	1956	43.0	1975	50.4	1995	38.1
1930	41.1	1959	44.8	1979	51.0		
		1962	44.0	1983	47.6		

Source: Bundesministerium für Inneres (ed.), Nationalratswahl vom 17. Dezember 1995 (Vienna: Bundesministerium für Inneres, pp. 107–9).

Table 1.3 Social structure of SPÖ electorate, 1986 and 1995 (%)

	1986	1995	Change
Men	46	45	−1
Women	54	55	+1
18–29 years	22	18	−4
30–44 years	28	27	−1
45–59 years	23	23	0
60–69 years	12	15	+3
70+	15	16	+1
Self-employed/professionals	2	2	0
Farmers	0	1	+1
Civil servants	7	9	+2
White-collar	18	18	0
Blue-collar	30	21	−9
Housewives	12	12	0
Pensioners	28	31	+3
Obligatory education	32	29	−3
Vocational education	52	47	−5
Qualified for university entrance/graduates	16	24	+8

Sources: Plasser, F. and Ulram, P, 'Major Parties on the Defensive', in Plasser, F. and Pelinka, A, (eds), The Austrian Party System (Boulder, CO: Westview, 1989, pp. 69–91, here p. 75) and Plasser, F., Ulram, P., Neuwirth, E. and Sommer, F., Analyze der Nationalratswahl vom 17. Dezember 1995 (Zentrum für Angewandte Politikforschung Vienna, 1995, p. 41).

subculture's traditionally high level of cohesion has declined (Table 1.3). Particularly concerning for the party are the ageing of its electorate, as well the declining proportion of blue-collar voters, many of whom have moved to the FPÖ, the electoral profile of which is now no less working class than the SPÖ.

GOVERNMENT ACHIEVEMENTS AND CURRENT POLICIES

During the first period (1945–66) of its almost unbroken record of pragmatic government participation, the SPÖ was the junior partner in a series of ÖVP–SPÖ 'grand coalitions', whose initial priority was post-war reconstruction. They presided over rationing, price regulation and above all an extensive programme of nationalization, which established Austria as the western democracy with the largest state sector. Yet nationalization was motivated not by ideological considerations, but by the desire to avoid former German Reich property passing into Allied hands and by the paucity of domestic investment capital. From the early 1950s, the government developed a bipartisan 'Austrokeynesian' economic policy involving currency stability; fiscal promotion of capital formation; corporatist structures (*Sozialpartnerschaft*) in which representatives of capital and labour agreed price and incomes policy; and deficit spending. After some initial problems, the Austrian economy became very successful, with high rates of growth and low unemployment and inflation. On the foreign policy front, the government's major achievements were the 1955 Act of Neutrality and State Treaty, which ended Allied occupation and re-established Austrian sovereignty.

From a systemic perspective, however, the grand coalitions provided the necessary framework for the consolidation of Austrian democracy. Especially when compared to its predecessor, the Second Republic has been characterized by consensus, domestic peace and political stability. It has also sustained levels of economic prosperity which compare favourably with the post-war experience of most western states. Finally, prosperity and growing trust in the political opponents' commitment to democracy facilitated the development of the overarching national identity Austrians had hitherto lacked. Crucial components thereof have been *Sozialpartnerschaft* and neutrality.

After its only ever experience of opposition (1966–70), the SPÖ's second post-war period in government was the 'Kreisky Era' of 1970–83. It coincided with accelerated socio–economic change, including secularization; a new wave of industrialization; increased tertiary sector employment; and a growth of the women's liberation and ecological movements. Kreisky's SPÖ presented itself as the party promoting not only working-class interests, but also those of Austria's growing 'new middle class'. The 'social–liberal consensus' usually associated with the Kreisky Era meant, *inter alia* a strong commitment to full employment; liberalization of divorce and abortion; greater tolerance of sexual 'deviancy'; a significant expansion of and widening of access to higher education; as well as the promotion of women's legal equality via changes to family, employment and taxation law. There was also a considerable extension of the welfare state – with increases in, for example unemployment benefits and pension payments, as well as the introduction of the 40-hour week (already agreed by the 1969 government) and of a minimum four-week holiday (1976).

Meanwhile, *Sozialpartnerschaft* guaranteed wage and price stability and thus contributed to ensuring that, by international standards, the economy continued to thrive. During the 1970s, annual growth averaged 4 and unemployment only 1.9 per cent. Despite the 1970s' oil price shocks, inflation averaged only 6.1 and never exceeded 9.5 per cent per annum. Understandably, many SPÖ supporters regard the Kreisky Era as the 'golden age' of the SPÖ (and indeed of the country). In the early 1980s, however, growth slowed (1981: 0.3 per cent), unemployment increased (1983: 4.5 per cent) and the costs of more generous welfare spending and habitual budget deficits came home to roost, particularly in the form of a rapidly expanding public debt. It also became increasingly clear that a significant proportion of Austria's numerous public sector industries had become uncompetitive. Growing concern regarding the economy's structural problems and the unpopularity of the SPÖ's tax-raising proposals for addressing the budget deficit (the *Mallorca-Paket*) contributed to the SPÖ's 1983 loss of its electoral majority.

The third phase of SPÖ government participation started with an SPÖ–FPÖ 'coalition of losers' (1983–7), which tried to tackle economic and structural problems, making limited progress in terms of budget consolidation. However, the SPÖ was weakened by repeated allegations of misconduct and financial impropriety, as well as by criticism from the strengthening ecological movement of its energy and environmental policy (e.g. the 'Hainburg' issue). Moreover, it was not until the re-establishment in 1987 of an SPÖ–ÖVP coalition in which the SPÖ could share with the ÖVP the political odium of introducing unpopular measures that significant progress started to be made on the economic front. The SPÖ has since became much more market-oriented, accepting (and indeed promoting) privatization and deregulation. Some uncompetitive industries were restructured, but others were sold off or closed down, as the party's previous commitment to full employment at almost any price has been replaced by the perception that Austria cannot buck the international market.

There has also been a fundamental shift in the context and direction of Austria's foreign relations. First, the collapse of Eastern European communism and the war in former Yugoslavia led to a significant inflow of refugees and illegal immigrants, and giving to popular xenophobia. The populist FPÖ effectively mobilized voter concerns against the governing parties, which initially refused to respond by tightening immigration policy. A related issue has been Austrian security policy, where first the FPÖ and more recently the ÖVP have questioned the continuing relevance of neutrality and advocate NATO membership. The ÖVP tried to force the issue in government, but on 3 September 1997 the SPÖ full party executive responded with a statement reasserting the advantages of neutrality (still supported by a majority of Austrians) and rejecting NATO membership for the present. Though the governing parties undertook to agree a joint statement on Austria's security policy options by March 1998, they failed to do so and the NATO issue has been placed on the backburner until at least after the 1999 general election. Yet even if neutrality is not formally abandoned in the short term, its future days are probably numbered. The second major area of foreign policy subjected to fundamental change in recent years concerns Austria's relationship to the European Union. Under Vranitzky's leadership, the party formally moved from a position of considerable scepticism regarding membership (not least because of its alleged incompatibility with neutrality) to one of full acceptance. The European flag was incorporated into the party's logo and at the June 1994 referendum, SPÖ supporters proved to be disproportionately in favour of European integration. Thus whilst some 66.6 per cent of Austrians voted for accession, the proportion of SPÖ partisans who did so stood at 73 per cent.

Prioritizing budget consolidation (whether for domestic reasons or in order to comply with the Maastricht convergence criteria and allow Austria to be in the first wave of monetary union) has at times severely strained relations with the ÖVP, as well as with the trade unions. It has also heightened overall public discontent with government policy and helps explain why a majority of Austrian are now sceptical of the benefits of European Union membership. At present, a major concern relates to the implications for Austria's labour market of EU eatward enlargement, and these apprehensions are being mobilised by Haider's FPÖ.

Such problems help explain why the SPÖ has lost support not only from educated, post-materialist voters, but also from disgruntled blue-collar protest voters (many of whom were employed in the SPÖ-controlled state sector industries) seeking a return to old certainties and job security. As yet, there is little evidence that the SPÖ has an effective strategy to attract these two groups back to the party fold. Yo be sure, the party appears at long last to be about the replace its 1978, programme, which it has been seeking to renew since the 1980s. If the current draft programme is approved in October 1998, it will mark a significant departure from the SPÖ's classic ideological profile. For one, it abandons the SPÖ's traditional aspiration to a classless society. Second, rather than seeking to 'overcome' capitalism, it accepts the market as a wealth creation mechanism and concerns itself instead with promoting a more equitable (re-)distribution of wealth. Third, it abandons the notion that labour and capital are 'irreconcilable' classes, arguing instead that it is necessary to support in particular small and medium-sized businesses, which help generate jobs. The draft programme thus marks a radical departure from the SPÖ's traditionally radical rhetoric and has predictably generated considerable hostility from amongst more left-wing party members (in particular within the SPÖ's youth wing, but also in the unions). On the other hand, the draft programme can be regarded as but a very belated accomodation of the party's rhetoric to the fact that, after half a century of nearly unbroken government participation, the SPÖ has been transformed from the defender of a seemingly embattled proletarian subculture to an establishment party that had lost most of its radical edge. The extent to which the new programme will help revive the SPÖ's electoral fortunes remains to be seen.

Select Bibliography

Cap, J. (1989) *Sozialdemokratie im Wandel,* Vienna.
Fröschl, E., Mesner, M and Zoitl, H. (eds) (1990) *Die Bewegung. Hundert Jahre Sozialdemokratie in Österreich,* Vienna.
Jeffrey, C. (1995) *Social Democracy in the Austrian Provinces, 1918–1934: Beyond Red Vienna*, London: Leicester University Press.
Knapp, V. (1980) *Austrian Social Democracy, 1889–1914,* Washington DC: University Press of America.
Kreisky, B. (1986) *Zwischen den Zeiten. Erinnerungen aus fünf Jahrzehnten*, Berlin: Goldmann.
Maderthaner, W. and Müller, W. C. (eds) (1996) *Die Organization der österreichischen Sozialdemokratie 1889–1995*, Vienna, Löcker Verlag.
Pelinka, P. and Steger, G. (eds) (1988) *Auf dem Weg zur Staatspartei. Zu Geschichte und Politik der SPÖ*, Vienna: Löcker.
Rabinbach, A. (1983) *The Crisis of Austrian Socialism. From Red Vienna to Civil War 1927–1934*, Chicago: University of Chicago Press.
Schell, K.L. (1962) *The Transformation of Austrian Socialism*, New York: State of New York Press.
Sully, M. (1982) *Continuity and Change in Austrian Socialism: The Eternal Quest for the Third Way*, Boulder Co: East European Monographs.

Contact Information

Address
Sozialdemokratische Partei Österreichs
Löwelstraße 18   Tel: 43 1 535 47 17
1014 Wien   Fax: 43 1 534 27/336

SPÖ Web Page on the Internet: http://www.spoe.at

The SPÖ publishes a monthly magazine called *Zukunft*

Centres of Research on the Austrian Socialists and Labour Movement
Stiftung Bruno Kreisky Archiv
Rechte Wienzeile 97   Tel: 43 1 545 75 35/32
1050 Wien   Fax: 43 1 545 30 97

Verein für Geschichte der Arbeiterbewegung
Rechte Wienzeile 97   Tel: 43 1 545 78 70/27
1050 Wien   Fax: 43 1 545 30 97

2 The Belgian Socialist Party
Pascal Delwit

The Creation of the Belgian Workers' Party

The Belgian Workers' Party (*Parti ouvrier belge* – POB), created on 5–6 April 1885, emerged from the combination of several currents, the main ones of which were a minority socialist movement in a rural and catholic Flanders and the Walloon workers' movement. The first current was essentially established in the city of Ghent and was mainly influenced by the German social democrats. The second was characterized by traditions of conflicts marked by a-political if not anti-political anarchism (Liebman, 1979).

From the beginning, the POB organized itself on the basis of a network of economic or professional institutions. Beyond certain verbal declarations, all activity of the party and the mobilization of its members aimed for two objectives: the supervision and incorporation of Walloon workers and the conquest of universal suffrage as the central means of intervention in Belgium. From the end of the nineteenth century, the forms and nature of mobilizations demonstrate a rejection of any revolutionary strategy – often negatively connoted (Delwit, De Waele and Marquès-Pereira, 1989) – and the reformist ambition of this young party. Through the articulation of these two objectives, the POB distinguished itself from the entire international socialist movement by organizing – often under pressure – three general strikes: in 1893, in 1902 and in 1913.

An absence of interest in theoretical or ideological questions was confirmed by the fact that it was only after obtaining the right of suffrage tempered by the plural vote (1893) that the POB sought to attribute to itself – nine years after its creation – a declaration of principles that remains the same today.

At the party conference held at Quaregnon in March 1894, a charter was adopted, referred to as the *Charte de Quaregnon*. Although it was poor in terms of ideological sophistication, it was much more elaborate than the first constituent texts of POB. This was a rare attempt to give a perspective to the daily fight. It remains today a valuable document due to its longevity and also because of the symbolism it represents for numerous socialist militants.

Rapidly, the POB's focus on Parliament – as the working class representative – changed from merely a means into its main objective. Through parliamentary action, the POB would act in favour of the oppressed in Belgian society. But questions as essential as perspectives on the conquest of state power or a reappraisal of the power exercised by the upper middle class were not addressed, or else very rarely tackled. The POB would exercise power as soon as the opportunity occurred. In the meantime, once the voting system became proportional (1899) and thus parliamentary action had become a defining part of party life, only the exercise of power by the POB had yet to be attained.

Despite the fact that universal suffrage had not yet been achieved at the eve of the First World War, the integration of POB in Belgian political life was already well advanced. The vote on war credits at the beginning of August 1914 and participation in the government 'sacred union' definitively marked its realization.

The Inter-War Period

The lack of theoretical perspective in the POB was a well known fact within the international workers movement at the beginning of the twentieth century. Eminent socialists, such as Karl Kautsky, taunted the POB with this fact. Asked about the position of Belgians on the debate over revisionism, he answered that he did not see what the party should have to review (Mabille and Lorwin, 1979). This dimension was never denied, whether between the two wars, or since 1945.

The only notable exception to the lack of theoretical sophistication resides in the works of Henri De Man during the 1920s and 1930s. Representative of the Marxist wing before 1914, De Man had been deeply affected by the start of the war. Based upon experiences in Germany and the United States, he developed a body of work marking him as an innovative thinker in the Belgian context.

In the 1920s, during an economic growth period, new theoretical revisions of socialism began to take shape. Among them, De Man's *Beyond Marxism* played a major role. Published in 1926 in Germany, he stated that his contribution was meant to be a revision, if not an actual supplanting, of Marxism, based on an individualistic point of view. He rejected the idea of a proletarian struggle founded on economic and political oppression by the upper middle class in the framework of the capitalist production system. De Man contradicted the perspective of a separation of classes according to economic criteria and to the situation in production relations. In this way, he discarded the proletarian-type community and, to show the invalidity of Marxist analysis, gave instead as an example the United States. For De Man, it is less the objective situation than the one felt by the workers themselves that is the heart of the problem. Based on this observation, he introduced a sophisticated analysis of the social psychology on which workers' reactions are no longer conceived on the basis of class relations and exchange methods, but on the basis of an 'auto estimation instinct', that would lead to a 'social inferiority complex'. As important as *Beyond Marxism* was, it should be noted, this work made more of an impact outside Belgium.

Another development at the beginning of the 1930s, after the onset of the economic crisis, involved the pressing demands of the trade union commission of the POB, which was worried if not panicked about the absence of a social or economic perspective. In response, De Man wrote the *Working Plan*, adopted by the POB at the Christmas conference of 1933. The call for state intervention for reflation was simultaneously made in the United States. The *Working Plan* had a double significance: the introduction of a new role for the state and as a formidable means of mobilization around concrete objectives in order to counter the growing influence of the Belgian Communist Party (*Parti communiste de Belgique* – PCB).

1945: A New Party

After the Second World War, five important turning-points occurred during which the party re-positioned itself politically and ideologically. This re-positioning was more an adjustment than a new theoretical approach. The first event took place in May 1945, during the 'victory conference'. Two major modifications occurred: in the form of affiliation and name. The Belgian Workers Party became the Belgian Socialist Party (*Parti socialiste belge* – PSB; *Belgische Socialistische Partij* – BSP in Flemish). On the political front, the reformist perspective was made explicit: the transition from the capitalist economy to a socialist economy could be achieved only through a gradual process.

The second event took place between 1958 and 1959. Following a Liberal–Socialist government experience (1954–8) and the electoral failure of 1958, the leadership of PSB–BSP faced critics from its left wing. Subsequently, the party adopted a programme of structural reforms already approved by the union federation, the FGTB (*Fédération générale du travail de Belgique*) during its conferences of 1954 and 1956. These structural reform programmes had, according to its organizers, a planning vocation aimed at the development of an economic democracy.

Thirdly, in November 1974, the party held an explicitly ideological conference. Its continued role in opposition and the redefinition of its identity constituted the main motivations for the organization of these hearings. Generally speaking, the content of the resolutions and comments made at the conference represented an undoubted shift to the left. It is especially important to note that the enlargement of economic democracy appeared to be the *sine qua non* of this new identity.

In 1978, the Belgian Socialist Party (PSB–BSP) broke into two separate formations due to the process of federalization in Belgium: the *Parti socialiste* (PS) in the French Community and the *Socialistische Partij* (SP) in the Flemish one. Since then, French-speaking and Flemish-speaking socialists in Belgium have made autonomous choices and have had only minimal consultation.

The fourth event concerns the PS. It followed the electoral failure of 1981 – the PS was sent into opposition – the arrival in power of a new party president – Guy Spitaels – and the necessity to review the programme adopted eight years earlier at the peak of the period of economic growth. The Socialist Party gathered for an ideological conference on 27 and 28 March 1982, on the theme 'renovate and act'. If the conference of 1974 had been symbolic of the 'Golden 1960s', the one in 1982 entailed a re-focus on the economic crisis. Planning was left aside, and selective reflation was now in vogue, an idea and watchword defended by the PS from 1982 to 1985. At the same time, the *Socialistische Partij* opened itself to the christian workers' movement under the leadership of its president Karel Van Miert, later a commissioner of the European Union. This opening was in particular represented by the presence of Jef Ulburghs, a priest of Limburg, on the Flemish socialist list at the European elections of 1984.

Finally, Guy Spitaels initiated in 1990 a Forum-convention on social democratic identity. The functions of parties, the role of socialism and the nature of the socialist project had to be at the centre of concerns and of new reflection. The discussion addressed new problems, such as the demand for an ecological society, the necessity to confront new social movements and the need to reform certain forms of economy that had always characterized the Belgian workers movement. However, Spitaels especially contradicted the idea that ideology no longer mattered, and that the socialist movement had exhausted its functions. Three ways were explored to restore some vigour to Belgian social democracy: a reform of the 'ethics of solidarity', especially through taxation; an advance of democracy in Belgium through the feder-alization of the country; and a new policy of disarmament and co-operation. However, due to pressures as the result of conflict over the financing of education, these reforms were never implemented.

ORGANIZATION AND PARTY PROFILE

The Socialist Pillar

The Belgian Socialist Party has integrated and encapsulated the major part of the working class politically, socially and culturally, not only through partisan organization but also through multiple associated organizations, of which the most important are the mutual social insurance system and the trade union. This is how it became one of the 'pillars' of Belgian society, confronting the other 'pillar' – the Catholic world – through one party, one trade union, one mutual insurance system and many other organizations.

Until 1945, the socialist trade union – the union commission and then the *Confédération générale du travail de Belgique*, CGTB – was organically related to the party. At the Liberation, this link was officially undone. However, the FGTB, which succeeded the CGTB, remained profoundly linked to the Socialist Party especially after the creation of 'common action' in 1949. The workforce of the FGTB grew continuously after 1945 in line with a general increase in the rate of unionization until 1980. Even though a slight decrease has occurred, this rate remains today very substantial in comparison to the European average.

Until 1945, membership of the POB was constituted through union organizations. This situation changed during the 'victory conference' in May 1945. Collective membership was abandoned at the benefit of individual membership. The Belgian Socialist Party became therefore a 'direct party'.

Party Membership

The principle of individual membership has not undermined the mass character of the POB. This is shown by the evolution of the number of members in Table 2.1.

Table 2.1   Number of members of the PS and the SP, 1978–95

Year	PS	SP
1978	147,269	111,944
1979	144,852	112,883
1980	154,798	113,922
1981	167,087	116,730
1982	158,649	114,181
1983	149,829	111,798
1984	150,671	108,500
1985	140,462	108,223
1986	138,820	105,777
1987	145,919	103,778
1988	139,768	101,863
1989	131,897	99,112
1990	129,388	99,235
1991	126,795	97,919
1992	125,281	93,351
1993	125,073	89,085
1994	124,081	
1995	117,553	

Source: Author's own compilation.

Party Structure

According to its statutes, the goal of the PS is to 'organize in the midst of the class struggle, all the socialist forces of Brussels and Wallonia, without any distinction as to race, sex, language, nationality, religious or philosophical beliefs, in order to conquer power and consequently to realize the complete emancipation of the workers'. One can join the PS individually, with the required minimum age set at 16. Adhesion takes place at a local or company section.

The basic structure of the PS is the local section from which territorial limits and conditions of subsistence are determined by the federation of wards. The sections are approved by the communal entity in a USC (*Union socialiste communale*) which has competencies on political matters and on communal management. Even though adhesion to the PS is established at the place of residency, some company sections are created by the initiative or with the agreement of a wards' federation. The level superior to the local and company sections, as well as the USC, is the Federation, which covers the electoral district. The PS currently has fourteen such Federations.

At least once a year, the Walloon Federation on one side and the Brussels Federation on the other hold a regional congress having 'power of decision in the frame of the competencies that are attributed to the regions'.

The general instances of the PS revolve around the congress, the bureau, the forum and the college of federal secretaries. The congress is the supreme organ of the Party. It defines its political path – except for exclusive regional matters which are dependent on the regional congresses. It assembles every second year and on this occasion elects the members of the bureau. In between congresses, the bureau decrees the political decisions of the Party and makes all decisions regarding Federal competencies. Its missions and importance have therefore increased.

Since 10 May 1997, the bureau includes the president, the general secretary, six representatives of the Federation of Brussels as well as one 'by a slice of 5,000 affiliated starting from the 5,001st affiliated' and two representatives from every other Federation plus one 'by a slice of 5,000 affiliated starting from the 5001st affiliated'. The forum has a supple structure without any internal power. It constitutes a space for reflection and debate and is open to everyone. At least once a year, the Party must organize a forum on a theme chosen by the bureau. The college of Federal secretaries is a new body. It is competent on 'matters of organization and administration'. It is constituted by the fourteen Federal secretaries, the secretary of the interfederal committee of the company sections and the general secretary who presides the session. The president and the two vice-presidents may assist the session.

There are now four national positions for the Socialist Party: The president, the two vice-presidents and the general secretary. On 10 May 1997, the statutory congress adopted a major change concerning the presidency. In the future, the president will be elected by a direct poll of the affiliated for a mandate of four years, renewable once consecutively.

The Socialist Party has two vice-presidents, one from Brussels and one from Wallonia. Henceforth, the Walloon vice-president will be elected among and by the Walloon members of the bureau and the Brussels vice-president among and by the Brussels members of the bureau.

The general secretary is elected by the congress. He has responsibility in 'matters of organization and recruitment decreed by the instances of the PS'. For all the factions of the Party the PS has temporarily installed proportional quotas:

- No faction may count more than 80 per cent of representatives of the same sex.
- Every faction has to record at least 15 per cent of representatives under 30 years old.

The pyramidal structure of the Flemish Socialist Party is fairly similar. There are also proportional quotas for youth and for women. However, during the congress held on 9 and 10 December 1995, the Flemish Socialists introduced two statutory and very important innovations. Henceforth, the president of the Party will be elected by universal poll by the members. Moreover, the delegates at the congress of the Party will no longer be federation delegates but section delegates. The intermediate structure of the Party is therefore short-circuited.

Electoral Performance

Since its beginning, the Belgian Socialist Party has oriented all its action and energy toward the conquest of universal suffrage and the exercise of power. From this, three important moments can be highlighted: the obtaining of male suffrage regulated by the plural vote in 1893; the first governmental participation during the 1914–18 war; and the promulgation in 1919 of male universal suffrage (women have had the vote since 1948). With these advances, the Belgian Socialist Party became one of the main actors in the Belgian political framework.

From 1945 onwards, the Socialist Party experienced a spectacular electoral evolution, though with time a significant erosion has set in. In recent times, the PS and SP attained their best performance at the 1987 ballot, after six years of opposition to the Liberal–Social Christian government coalition. On the other hand, at the legislative elections of 1995, PS and SP fell to their lowest level since 1945. The 'socialist family' received only 24.42 per cent of the vote.

Since 1945, the Belgian Socialist Party, and then the PS and SP, were often present in the government; most often with the Social Christians from the PSC–CVP, an exception being the three-party Socialist–Liberal–Social Christian coalition and, between 1954 and 1958, one with only the Liberals. The PS and SP were absent from political power between 1981 and 1987. But since 1988, they have exercised power at federal and federated levels (Walloon, Brussels and Flemish regions, and the French community; see Table 2.2).

Just after the Second World War, the clerical–anti-clerical cleavage seemingly reasserted itself in two separate instances. The first concerned the return of King Leopold III. At the consultative referendum organized on 12 March 1950, the results maintained the picture of a Belgium divided between a Catholic Flanders and a liberal-socialist Wallonia. Admittedly 57.68 per cent of the voters declared themselves in favour of the return of the king. But in the Brussels region and even more in the Walloon area, the majority was 'no'. The second refers to the 'school war' that took place between 1954 and 1958. After difficult negotiations, a 'schools pact' was signed between the main formations of the country. The signature of this pact marks a very important moment in the political history of Belgium. The secular–Catholic cleavage lost, in a short period of time, the strong significance it had possessed from 1945 to 1958. In its place, class and linguistic cleavages emerged as the defining axes of conflict (especially during the 1960–1 conflicts).

The Belgian Socialist Party, however, did not acknowledge this turning-point, nor the structural modifications in the Walloon and Flemish economy. It paid a high price for this misunderstanding at the elections of 1965 when it experienced an unprecedented fall in support to the Democratic Front for French-speakers (*Front démocratique des Francophones* – FDF) in Brussels, to the People's Union (*Volksunie*) in Flanders and to those Walloon parties who anticipated the creation of the Walloon Rally (*Rassemblement wallon* – RW). The very mediocre results the Belgian Socialist Party received in 1968 encouraged its president Léo Collard to break with tradition and make an appeal, on 1 May 1969, to a 'progressive gathering', that would transcend philosophical cleavages. This invitation was not followed up for two main reasons. There was no real willingness to answer the call from President Collard, and little or no effort was undertaken to seriously draft concrete proposals in this direction. The Socialist Party never attempted to extricate itself from its position as the homogeneous party in the Walloon part of the country. To the party, any realignment had to be achieved through an integration of other progressives, especially Christians, into its ranks.

In the 1980s, an initiative aimed at a 'breakthrough' similar to the Dutch experience, was made by the SP towards Christian progressives. Despite the election of Jef Ulburghs as a member of the European Parliament, this

Table 2.2 Electoral performance of the Belgian Socialists, 1945–95

	Percentage of votes				Percentage of seats			
	Brussels–Hal–Vilvorde	Wallonia	Flanders	Kingdom	Brussels–Hal–Vilvorde	Wallonia	Flanders	Kingdom
1946								
PSB–BSP	33.33	36.34	27.47	31.56	33.33	39.47	27.08	32.67
Liberal–Socialist Cartel		2.05	1.75	1.59		2.63	2.08	1.98
1949								
PSB–BSP	28.00	37.82	24.48	29.74	28.12	39.47	25.96	31.13
1950								
PSB–BSP	38.37	44.56	25.97	34.51	37.50	45.45	25.24	34.43
Liberal–Socialist Cartel		2.44	1.84	1.76		2.59	1.94	1.88
1954								
PSB–BSP	42.25	47.66	28.62	37.34	43.75	50.00	28.84	38.67
Liberal–Socialist Cartel		2.81	2.26	2.09		3.94	1.92	2.35
1958								
PSB–BSP	40.01	46.17	27.68	35.78	40.62	50.00	27.88	37.73
Liberal–Socialist Cartel		2.61	2.41	2.09		2.63	2.88	2.35
1961								
PSB–BSP	39.21	46.42	29.71	36.72	40.62	51.31	30.76	39.62
1965								
PSB–BSP	25.74	35.20	24.65	28.28	27.27	38.88	25.23	30.18
1968								
PSB–BSP	15.03	34.51	26.26	27.09	15.15	34.72	25.23	26.88
Rode Leeuw	5.44			0.88	6.06			0.94
1971								
PSB–BSP	15.34	34.43	24.85	26.41	15.15	37.50	26.16	28.30
Rode Leeuw	5.18			0.82	3.03			0.47

1974								
PSB–BSP	15.14	34.43	20.81	21.86	17.64	37.14	21.29	23.11
PSB	4.26	2.39	1.87	3.12	2.94	1.42	1.85	3.30
BSP				1.65				1.41
1977								
PSB–BSP	11.79	34.59	21.13	22.14	14.70	40.00	21.29	24.05
PSB	4.62	2.66	1.85	2.61	2.94	1.42	2.77	2.83
BSP		1.75		1.69				1.88
PSB–RW				0.54		1.42		0.47
1978								
PSB	10.57	36.71	21.43	13.02	11.76	40.00	22.22	15.09
BSP	5.49			12.38	5.88			12.26
1981								
PS	9.54	36.21	21.11	12.72	11.76	44.28	22.22	16.50
SP	6.34			12.38	5.88			12.26
1985								
PS	11.27	39.45	0.05	13.76	12.12	44.92	26.36	16.50
SP	8.72	0.02	24.06	14.54	9.09			15.09
1987								
PS	15.48	43.94	24.56	15.64	18.18	49.27	26.36	18.86
SP	9.00			14.89	9.09			15.09
1991								
PS	11.49	39.16	19.86	13.48	12.12	44.92	23.63	16.51
SP	5.94			11.97	6.06			13.20
1995								
PS	11.49	33.70	20.71	11.87	9.09	39.58	22.50	14.00
SP	6.73			12.55	9.09			13.33

Source: Author's own compilation.

attempt did not last. In 1994, a further attempt was undertaken to establish a progressive cartel, aiming to unite, in the mind of its initiators, the Christian workers' movement, Agalev (the Flemish Green party), the progressive wing of the People's Union (*Volksunie*) and the SP. The crisis that shook the SP at the beginning of 1995 because of the alleged corruption of many of its leaders related to the Agusta and Dassault cases, as well as the elections of May 1995, effectively paralyzed this process, which has not been revived since.

On the French-speaking side, the PS remains slightly suspicious of any opening to include liberal Catholics or any other non-socialist progressive components of Belgian society. It remains closed off, due to its dominance in its geographical sphere and its almost hegemonic position on the left of the political spectrum (Delwit and De Waele 1997).

In the 1980s, the French-speaking PS made regionalism part of its identity, at the initiative of its new president, Guy Spitaels. A crucial and symbolic event was undeniably the presence of José Happart, hero of the 'Walloon combat', on the PS list at the European elections of 1984. He obtained 234,996 preference votes out of the 762 293 votes cast for the PS. Shortly afterwards, he joined the PS and was a member of its political staff until 1994 and remains one of the important personalities of the party. At the beginning of 1992, Guy Spitaels abandoned his position of president to become Prime Minister of the Walloon Regional Executive, a position from which he had to resign during the Agusta investigation. At the same time, Charles Picqué, an important socialist figure in Brussels, has occupied the position of Prime Minister of the Executive of the Brussels Region since 1989.

GOVERNMENT ACHIEVEMENTS AND CURRENT POLICIES

Since the return to power in 1988, socialists' priorities within government revolve around three main axes: the protection of the social security system, the federalization of Belgium, and the reduction of the public finances in order to meet the convergence criteria of the Maastricht Treaty. In the context of the economic deregulation that has been going on for nearly fifteen years, the PS and the SP have positioned themselves as the defenders of the existing social security system, even though there have been many cutbacks in the welfare state. It is therefore no surprise to note that the position of national, subsequently federal minister, of social affairs has been occupied by a socialist since 1988. The PS and SP have been two essential actors in the two state reforms of 1988 and in 1993 that led Belgium to become a Federal State.

Finally, as part of its continuous 'historic' position on Europe (Delwit, 1995), the PS and the SP have supported the Maastricht Treaty with conviction, if not always with enthusiasm. Both have found themselves confronted with its implications, especially budgetary ones, since the public debt reached 125 per cent of the Gross National Product (GNP). But they have maintained their support for the strategy to meet the criteria. The budgetary deficit of 1997 reached exactly 3 per cent, and that of 1998 is expected to be 2.4 per cent.

In recent times, it is important to note a difficult contradiction that Belgian socialists have had to face together with their European counterparts. At all times, the PS and SP have wanted to support further progressive social reform, while at the same time defending existing state social benefits, which they present as the social aspect of progress. This double ambition was realizable in a period of economic boom when the 'social benefits' did not really need to be defended, and when further reform was merely part of the party's 'general fight for progress'. Since the mid-1970s, however, this strategy has appeared untenable. During this period, the parties were faced with the following problem: how to combine the role of a progressive and reforming party while, at the same time, identifying itself as the guardian of the existing welfare state. Should the party, and Guy Spitaels' work in 1990 hinted at this, integrate more strongly values less related to labour? This would create a situation in which socialist leaders would still have to solve this contradiction, at the same time as finding a basis capable of holding new claims which might sometimes appear to be against the immediate interests of the majority of its members and socialist electors.

The current sociological composition of the party and the lack of will to reform policy shows the difficulty involved in trying to solve this contradiction, but it is possible, should the party have the will to do it. The attitude of Belgian Socialists towards the 'ecotax' case during the 1992–3 coalition negotiations testifies to this.

Select Bibliography

Delwit, P. (1995) *Les partis socialistes et l'intégration européenne (France, Belgique, Grande Bretagne)*, Brussels: Editions de l'Université de Bruxelles.
Delwit, P. and De Waele, J.-M. (1996) *Ecolo: Les verts en politique*, Brussels: Editions De Boeck.
Delwit, P. and De Waele, J.-M. (eds) (1997) *Les partis politiques en Belgiques*, Brussels: Editions de l'Université de Bruxelles.
Delwit, P., De Waele, J.-M. and Marquès-Pereira, B. (1989) 'La valeur de la révolution française dans la pensée du parti ouvrier belge', in *L'image de la Révolution française, Congrès mondial pour le Bicentenaire*, Oxford: Pergamon Press.
Lazar, M. (ed.) (1996) *La gauche en Europe depuis 1945. Invariants et mutations du socialisme européen*, Paris: Presses Universitaires de France.
Liebman, M. (1979) *Les socialistes belges. De la révolte à l'organisation. 1885–1914*, Brussels: Editions Vie ouvrière.
Mabille, X. (1997) *Histoire politique de la Belgique*, Brussels: Editions du CRISP.

Mabille, X. and Lorwin, V. (1979) 'The Belgian Socialist Party', in Paterson, W.E. and Thomas, A. (eds), *Social Democratic Parties in Western Europe*, London: Croom Helm.

Man, Henri de (1935) *Planned Socialism: The Plan du Travail of the Belgian Labour Party*, London: Gollancz.

Contact Information

Socialist Parties Addresses
Parti socialiste
Boulevard de l'Empereur 13   Tel: 32 2 548 32 11
1000 Bruxelles   Fax: 32 2 648 33 90

PS Web Page on the Internet: http://www.ps.be

Socialistische Partij
Keizerlaan 13   Tel: 32 2 548 32 11
1000 Brussel   Fax: 32 2 548 35 90

SP Web Page on the Internet: http://www.sp.be

Affiliated Centre of Research and Conference on the Socialist Movement in Belgium

Institut Emile Vandervelde
Boulevard de l'Empereur 13   Tel: 32 2 511 97 19
1000 Bruxelles

Archief en Musuem van de Socialistische Arbeidersbeweging
Bagattenstraat 174   Tel: 32 2 224 00 79
9000 Gent   Fax: 32 9 233 67 11

Publishes a monthly journal: *Brood en Rozen*

3 The Danish Social Democratic Party

Lars Bille

HISTORY

Since the mid-nineteenth century Danish society has been homogeneous in the sense that no ethnic, religious, linguistic or regional differences of any significance existed. The formation of political parties was consequently based on economic, social and ideological cleavages. Two political groupings dominated the period prior to the enactment of the first democratic constitution in 1849 as well as in the subsequent three decades: the conservatives and the liberals. In 1870 the various liberal factions and elements merged into The Liberal Party (*Venstr–v*). It was an agrarian party representing the interests of the farmers and organizing the rural population and it was the leading party in the struggle for equal and universal suffrage and parliamentary democracy. The party became the largest bourgeois party. The opponents of the Liberal Party in the constitutional struggle gradually organized in the right (*Højre*, renamed the Conservative People's Party in 1916). In the beginning the party was dominated by landowners, but as a consequence of increasing industrialization and urbanization this group lost influence and increasingly the party stressed general conservatives values appealing to business interests, middle-class values and national defence.

In 1871 The Danish Social Democratic Party (SD) was founded as a section of the First International and in the same year the tobacco workers organized the first trade union. The initiative to establish the SD was taken by Louis Pio, Harald Brix and Paul Geleff. In general, the founding fathers had some acquaintance with European socialist agitation and in particular of the German socialist movement and propaganda. None of them, however, had any knowledge of Marxist theory as such. Their driving motives were pure social and moral indignation and a desire to ameliorate the living conditions for working people, all mixed with a dash of a romantic approach to the project.

From 1872 to 1875 the leaders were imprisoned and in 1877 Pio and Geleff fled the country. The party was on the edge of dissolution when the second generation of founding fathers took over. They were all skilled workers with a practical approach to the professional and political organizing of the workers. P. Knudsen was chairman of the party (1882–1910), followed by T. Stauning (1910–42).

In the first seven years the Danish section of the International had encompassed both the political party and the trade unions. As part of the reorganizing of the party a formal separation between the two occurred in 1878, when an independent party responsible for the political organization and mobilization of the workers was established, leaving the trade unions to take care of their professional organization. In addition, and along with the political and professional organization, the workers gradually founded a number of co-operative firms, educational, social, and leisure organizations as well as a party press. Thus the Danish labour movement was composed of the party, the trade union, the co-operative movement, the press and a large number of affiliated organizations all of which were organizationally connected to one another, first and foremost by a reciprocal representation in the executive organs.

As indicated above the ideological roots of SD were not strictly Marxist. Reformism, not revolution, was and has always been the ideology of the party. Theoretical discussions of the ideological foundation of the party were almost absent in the nineteenth century. Thus, the first manifesto of the party adopted in 1876, the Gimle Manifesto, was a pure and simple translation of the German Social Democratic party's Gotha Programme. In the first two decades of the twentieth century the ideological debate intensified somewhat. One of the results was the adoption of the 1913 manifesto which was in effect until 1961. The 1913 programme employed a Marxist perception of society, used a Marxist-inspired vocabulary and analysis, and demanded among other things the seizure of the means of production by the state, but the gap between programme and day-to-day politics was considerable.

As a consequence of the increased support by the workers of various revolutionary and syndicalist groupings between 1910 and 1920, as well as the Russian and German revolutions, the left-wing opposition inside the SD gained in strength. In 1919 a section of the party's youth organization broke with the mother party and founded in 1920 together with other extreme left wing organizations the Danish Communist Party (*Danmarks kommunistiske Party*, DKP). The SD was no longer the sole political representative of the Danish working class.

The predominant position of the party was not affected by the split. The SD continued to increase its membership and electoral support and in 1924 became the largest party in parliament. The first SD minority government was formed and lasted from 1924 to 1926. In 1929 the party returned to office, this time in a coalition with the minor centre party, the Social–Liberal Party. The coalition held governmental power until it was forced by the German occupational power to step down. At the general election in 1935 the SD reached an all-time high in electoral support of 46.1 per cent. Since 1884 the party had increased its share of the vote at every single election, a fact that sustained the prevailing conviction at the party leadership that it was only a matter of time before it gained an absolute majority in parliament. Besides the increase of the party's 'natural' electorate, one of the reasons for the electoral success was a further downgrading of ideological distinctiveness. Thus in 1934 a new working programme 'Denmark for the People' (*Danmark for Folket*) was issued appealing to almost every segment in society. Furthermore, being in government, the party aptly compromised between simultaneously taking care of working-class interests and the national interest, incorporated the various interest organizations in the legislative process and initiated social reforms. The role of the state in society markedly increased as a result of the counter-depression policy of the social democratic-headed government.

The fundamental principles of the party's policy and strategy remained by and large unchanged after 1945. In one area, however, an important change occurred. Being traditionally an anti-militaristic party advocating a neutral foreign policy, the outbreak of the Second World War, the occupation of Denmark by the Germans in 1940–5, and the emergence of the Cold War convinced the leadership of the necessity to change policy. Thus, in 1949 the SD voted in favour of Danish membership of NATO and supported the ensuing build-up of the armed forces.

Keynesianism became the doctrine guiding the economic policy of the party after 1945. Regardless of other considerations, substantial economic growth was given top priority simply because growth as such was perceived as an indispensable prerequisite for achieving the ultimate goal: a further development and consolidation of the welfare state system. The main themes associated with the party in the 1950s and 1960s were the enlargement and improvement of the tax-funded and public-run social security, educational and health systems, along with a comprehensive unemployment benefit scheme.

Since the SD was not able to gain an absolute majority in parliament constitutive elements of the welfare state had to be enacted in agreements with one or two of the three other main parties, the Social–Liberal Party, the Liberal Party and the Conservative People's Party. The major and far-reaching reforms usually included all four of them. Denmark thus developed into a 'consensus democracy'. This was reflected in the catch-all-like manifesto adopted by the SD in 1961 in which, for instance, the clause stating the seizure of the means of production by the state was eliminated and Marxist vocabulary and analysis was absent. In the early 1970s the party tried to introduce economic democracy but failed due to the opposition of the bourgeois parties and lack of whole-hearted support of the rank and file of the trade unions. The economic recession of the 1970s and 1980s as well as the revival of neo-liberalism and monetarism forced the SD on the defensive, trying to preserve as much as possible the arrangements introduced in the heyday of the party.

ORGANIZATION AND PARTY PROFILE

The 125th anniversary party congress in 1996 enacted profound changes in the party rules. However, the basic structure of the party was maintained – i.e. a territorially defined hierarchial structure made up of local branches, constituency organizations, regional organizations, party congress, national committee (*hovedbestyrelse*) and national executive (*forretningsudvalg*).

The basic unit of the SD is the territorially defined *local branch*. Membership is direct and individual and to become a member one must join the local branch. Membership rights are exercised via the local branch. It registers members, periodically reporting their numbers to the party's central office. Only in 1988 did the party introduce central registration. The local branches determine and collect the membership subscription and send on the fixed amount stipulated in the party rules to the constituency and regional organizations and to central office. The local branches select candidates for municipal elections, conduct the municipal election campaign and function as backing group for the SD members of the municipal board. Furthermore the local branches elect representatives to the constituency and regional organizations and send delegates to the party congress. The most important functions of the *constituency organization*s are to select candidates for general elections and to conduct the election campaign for the local candidates. The constituency organization is the principal link between the party members and voters and their MP. The *regional organization*s are responsible for the selection of candidates and campaigning for the county elections and European Parliament elections and take care of the coordination with the SD members of the county board.

The *party congress,* convened every year (prior to 1996 every four years), is the highest authority in all matters. It elects the party chaiman and two vice-chairmen and adopts the party manifesto and policy statements. The highest authority next to the congress is the *national committee* (around 50 members) followed by the *national executive* (seventeen members) which takes care of the daily business. Prior to 1996, the party congress was composed of delegates from the local branches, the constituency and regional organizations, and by *ex officio* representatives from the affiliated organizations. The members of the national committee and the national executive were partly elected by lower-party bodies and were partly appointed *ex officio* by the affiliated organizations. The ratio of appointed *ex officio* members was higher in the executive organs (around one-third) than on the level of the party congress.

In 1996, the party decided to cut the formal ties with its affiliated organizations, most importantly to the trade unions and the co-operative movement. This was indeed a historic decision and a change of one of the deeply rooted and fundamental characteristics of the social democratic organizational tradition. Thus *ex officio* representation was eliminated, meaning that only representatives elected by party members were seated in the party bodies. However, even though formal reciprocal representation was abolished, *de facto* co-operation continued both on the national level and, especially, on the regional and local level. Furthermore, the party chairman is elected by a postal ballot among the party members unless a majority of at least three-quarters of the delegates support his or her election.

The explicitly stated purpose behind the fundamental changes was to 'modernize' the SD organization and to increase the influence of individual party members and thus create an incentive for a more intensive involvement by the rank and file. One of the reasons for this is to be found in the development of the numbers of party members. Since the 1950s the party had experienced a dramatic decline in membership (Table 3.1). Declining membership was not exclusively a social democratic phenomenon. Since 1960 all Danish parties have experienced a dwindling membership, but the decrease in the SD was dramatic and continued in the 1990s at a higher level than any other party.

Table 3.1   SD party membership, 1945–95

Year	Number of members	Member/party vote ratio (%)	Member/electorate ratio (%)
1945	243,532	36.25	10.22
1950	283,907	34.91	11.28
1955	278,229	31.09	10.32
1960	259,459	25.34	9.13
1965	223,977	20.29	7.25
1970	177,507	18.21	5.53
1975	122,394	13.40	3.52
1980	101,387	8.36	2.72
1985	90,739	8.54	2.37
1990	76,941	6.35	1.95
1995	62,452	5.43	1.57

Source: Official election statistics; party central office; Bille, L., *Partier i forandring. En analyse af danske partiorganisationer 1960–95* (Odense: Odense Universitetsforlag, 1997).

In Denmark no scientific and systematic research on voting behaviour was carried out prior to 1971, but some commercial opinion polls exist. Research exclusively on party members is still lacking, and hence data between 1945 and 1971 on the sociology of the SD membership and electorate are either scattered or not obtainable. Based on the available data Table 3.2 presents

Table 3.2	Sociology of SD membership, 1971 and 1990 (%)

	1971	1990	Population 1990
Occupation:			
Blue-collar workers	76	34	34
White-collar workers	22	58	53
Self-employed	2	8	14
Sex:			
Male	59	54	48
Female	41	46	52
Age:			
18–29	11	2	20
30–39	15	11	21
40–49	17	22	20
50–59	57*	19	13
60–		46	27
Education:			
>Nine years	92	65	48
Ten years	7	22	35
<Ten years	1	13	18

Note: * All above 49 years of age.
Source: Bille, L., 'Organization i bevægelse', in Callesen, G.,, Christensen, S. and Grelle, H. (eds) *Udfordring og omstilling. Bidrag til Socialdemokratiets historie 1971–1996* (Copenhagen: Fremad, 1996, p.155).

the composition of the SD membership in 1971 and 1990, and Table 3.3 presents a profile of the SD electorate in 1964–94.

Relations with other parties of the left has until recently been characterized by intense competition, certainly not by co-operation. It has always been a very strong conviction in the SD that it was paramount to the strength and success of the labour movement that it was completely united behind one party. Hence the SD has vehemently opposed all factions, groups or parties that deviated from the social democratic line. They were labelled 'splinter parties', damaging the cause of the labour movement. In general the SD has been quite successful in this respect. The social democrats dominated the trade unions almost completely except for a few strong footholds held by the communists, and in the parliamentary arena the SD was equally dominant (Table 3.4).

Table 3.3   Sociology of the Danish electorate: votes for the Social Democratic Party, 1964–94 (%)

	64	66	68	71	73	75	77	79	81	84	87	88	90	94
Blue-collar	64	59	53	54	41	46	52	52	46	47	41	41	56	45
White-collar	33	30	25	25	18	24	34	36	27	24	23	26	33	30
Self-employed	13	9	6	7	5	6	9	13	7	6	8	11	8	7
Private employed				27	19	22		36	24	20	17		25	21
Public employed				23	17	27		35	30	27	26		39	35
Female	43	39	37	40	29	30	38	39	34		31	32	39	33
Male	41	38	32	35	23	29	35	37	32		27	29	35	31
Age: 18–24				36		21		29		26	22		24	21
25–29	39			41		23		34		27			37	31
30–39	40			34		25		39		27	25		40	33
40–49	41			32		31		36		30	27		38	36
<50	44			41		35		43		37	36		39	39

Sources: Goul Andersen, J., 'Socialdemokratiets vælgertilslutning', in Callesen, G., Christensen, S. and Grelle, H. (eds), *Udfordring og omstilling. Bidrag til Socialdemokratiets historie 1971–1996* (Copehagen: Fremad, 1966, pp. 174–220). Goul Andersen, J. 'Konservatisme, vælgerne og velfærdsstaten', in Christensen, A.D. *et al.* (eds), *Velfærdsstaten i krise – sociale og politiske bevægelser* (Ålborg: Centre for Velfærdsstudier, 1986, pp. 169–203). Goul Andersen, J. *Kvinder og politik* (Aarhus: Politica, 1984, p. 79). Togeby, L., 'Politisering af kvinder og af kvindespørgsmålet', in Elklit, J. and Tonsgaard, O. (eds) *To folketingsvalg* (Aarhus: Politica, 1989 pp. 227–54). Borre, O., 'Politiske generationer', in Elklit, J. and Tonsgaard, O. (eds), *To folketingsvalg* (Aarhus: Politica, 1989, pp. 208–26). Borre, O. and Goul Andersen, J., *Voting and Political Attitudes in Denmark. A Study of the 1994 Election* (Aarhus: Aarhus University Press, 1997).

Similar to the situation in other European countries immediately after the Second World War and based on the actual strong position of the DKP and the relative weak position of the SD after the 1945 general election, the two parties entered into negotiations to merge. The negotiations were abortive, partly because it was impossible to bridge the ideological gap between the parties (the dictatorship of the proletariat was the main obstacle), partly because the motives behind the negotiations were driven by tactical considerations rather than by genuine desire to fuse, and partly because of a deep distrust of one another. The fierce battle and harsh accusations of the 1930s were not forgotten. This result and the outbreak of the Cold War meant a continuation of the competitive and strained relationship between the two parties. The DKP became more and more isolated.

Table 3.4   Distribution of Danish left-wing votes and seats at general elections, 1945–98

Year	Social Democratic Party	Communist Party	Socialist People's Party	Left Socialists	Other
1945	32.8 (48)	12.5 (18)			
1947	40.0 (57)	6.8 (9)			
1950	39.6 (59)	4.6 (7)			
1953	41.3 (74)	4.3 (8)			
1957	39.4 (70)	3.1 (6)			
1960	42.1 (76)	1.1 (0)	6.1 (11)		
1964	41.9 (76)	1.2 (0)	5.8 (10)		
1966	38.2 (69)	0.8 (0)	10.9 (20)		
1968	34.2 (62)	1.0 (0)	6.1 (11)	2.0 (4)	
1971	37.3 (70)	1.4 (0)	9.1 (17)	1.6 (0)	
1973	25.7 (46)	3.6 (6)	6.0 (11)	1.5 (0)	
1975	30.0 (53)	4.2 (7)	4.9 (9)	2.1 (4)	
1977	37.1 (65)	3.7 (7)	3.9 (7)	2.7 (5)	
1979	38.3 (68)	1.9 (0)	5.9 (11)	3.6 (6)	0.4 (0)
1981	32.9 (59)	1.1 (0)	11.3 (21)	2.7 (5)	0.2 (0)
1984	31.6 (56)	0.7 (0)	11.5 (21)	2.7 (5)	0.1 (0)
1987	29.3 (54)	0.9 (0)	14.6 (27)	1.4 (0)	2.2 (4)
1988	29.6 (55)	0.8 (0)	12.9 (24)	0.6 (0)	1.9 (0)
1990	37.4 (69)		8.3 (15)		1.7 (0)
1994	34.6 (62)		7.3 (13)		3.1 (6)
1998	36.0 (63)		7.5(13)		2.7 (5)

Source: Official election statistics.

In 1958, the DKP split. The expelled members, including the former party chairman, founded the Socialists People's Party (*Socialistisk Folkeparti* – SF) in 1959 and it gained represention in parliament at the 1960 election. Besides disagreements on the atttitude toward the USSR and ideological divergences, one of the reasons for the split was a wish to break the isolation of the DKP and to enter into co-operation with the SD. The SD, however, took its usual position: no co-operation with a splinter party, the SF were perceived as communists in disguise. The left wing of the SD, however, were less unsympathetic and saw opportunities to gain a majority of socialist votes. For the first time ever, this occurred in 1966. This forced the SD leadership to change its position. Negotiations between the two parties to form a government ended in the negative but close co-operation between the SD minority government and the SF was agreed upon in writing. The concessions to maintain the co-operation turned out to be more comprehensive than the left wing of the SF was willing to pay; the SF split in 1967 and the Left

Socialists (*Venstresocialisterne* – VS) was founded. Once again (1971–3), a SD–SF majority existed, but this time the two parties co-operated from issue to issue, not on the basis of a written agreement.

In the 1970s the competition between the three extreme left-wing parties (SF, VS, DKP) was keen and their opposition to the SD vehement. SD minority governments had to seek its support among the centre parties and one or two of the right-wing parties. When the conservative-headed minority coalition governments took over in 1982, the SD co-operated with the SF, the VS and the social–liberal centre party on issues related to national security and defence, environment, culture and justice, while disagreements on economic and social policy among the opposition parties still prevailed and blocked more stable and far-reaching co-operation. The 1994 election resulted in a SD-headed minority coalition government whose survival was supported by the SF and the Unity List (*Enhedslisten* – EL) at vital instances in parliament. This coalition continued after the 1998 election. In conclusion, SD relations with other parties to the left has gradually developed from fierce and uncompromising confrontation to an ordinary mixture of competition and co-operation between independent parties all of whom are operating on the basis of parliamentary democracy.

GOVERNMENT ACHIEVEMENTS AND CURRENT POLICIES

The SD has been in cabinet for the longest time of all Danish parties. Since the introduction in 1920 of a proportional representation system, it has been in office for a total of 50 years and each time it has been in government it has held the post of Prime Minister (see Table 3.5).

Even though the SD by far has been the largest party, it is important to stress that it has never gained an absolute majority of its own. The SD has always been forced to enter into compromises with other parties; hence it is difficult to isolate the main governmental achievements of the SD from the influence exercised by other parties in the legislative process. As mentioned above, Danish politics is and has for decades been characterized by a high degree of consensus. However, the SD has undoubtedly had a leading role in and a decisive influence on the construction of the tax-financed welfare state system and the public sector.

In 1982, the SD minority government resigned. The party wanted to recover in opposition, but none of the 1984, 1987, 1988 or 1990 elections brought the party back to office. This was a completely new situation for the party and it triggered a debate in the party on basic strategy. In 1977 a new manifesto was adopted. Compared to the manifesto of 1961, this new platform marked a distinctive move to the left. The seizure of the means of productions by the state was reintroduced in the platform. Concepts derived

Table 3.5 Party composition of national governments in Denmark, 1945–96

Dates	Prime Minister	Other Parties	Status
1945–7	K. Kristensen (V)[1]		Minority
1947–50	H. Hedtoft (SD)		Minority
1950–3	E. Eriksen (V)	KF	Minority
1953–7	H. Hedtoft/H.C. Hansen (SD)		Minority
1957–60	H.C.Hansen/V. Kampmann (SD)	RV, DR	Majority
1960–4	V. Kampmann/J.O. Krag (SD)	RV	Majority
1964–6	J.O. Krag (SD)		Minority
1966–8	J.O. Krag (SD)		Minority
1968–71	H. Baunsgaard (RV)	KF, V	Majority
1971–3	J.O. Krag/A. Jørgensen (SD)		Minority
1973–5	P. Hartling (V)		Minority
1975–7	A. Jørgensen (SD)		Minority
1977–8	A. Jørgensen (SD)		Minority
1978–9	A. Jørgensen (SD)	V	Minority
1979–81	A. Jørgensen (SD)		Minority
1981–2	A. Jørgensen (SD)		Minority
1982–4	P. Schlüter (KF)	V, CD, KRF	Minority
1984–7	P. Schlüter (KF)	V, CD, KRF	Minority
1987–8	P. Schlüter (KF)	V, CD, KRF	Minority
1988–90	P. Schlüter (KF)	V, RV	Minority
1990–3	P. Schlüter (KF)	V	Minority
1993–4	P. Nyrup Rasmussen (SD)	RV, CD, KRF	Majority
1994–6	P. Nyrup Rasmussen (SD)	RV, CD	Minority
1996–98	P. Nyrup Rasmussen (SD)	RV	Minority
1998–	P. Nyrup Rasmussen (SD)	RV	Minority

Note: 1. see pp. xiv ff for party acronyms.
Source: Folketingets Årbog.

from Marxist thinking were used in the description of the Danish, capitalistic society. The qualities of solidarity, equality, brotherhood and co-operation were frequently contrasted with the drawbacks of selfishness, individual competition, alienation and self-centred consumerism. The responsibility of the community to take care of the weak in society and the importance of a comprehensive state regulation of the free market economy was emphasized. The public sector was not the enemy but the tool to create an harmonious society.

A policy following these prescriptions apparently failed to bring the party back to power and the debate resulted in the adoption of a new manifesto in 1992. Ten years in opposition, less competition from the extreme left-wing parties, the fall of the Berlin Wall, the collapse of the communist regimes, and the revival of liberalism all made an impact. The 1992 manifesto must be characterized as a catch-all programme, phrased in very short sentences. Gone were Marxist-inspired vocabulary and lengthy analyses. Solidarity, community, and brotherhood were still mentioned in the programme, not as an end in itself but as prerequisites for individual freedom, the liberty to choose, pluralism and happiness. Public regulation was replaced by public service, public ownership of the means of production by co-operation between the public sector and private enterprise, welfare state by welfare society and so forth. In short, the programme was adjusted to a situation in which a liberal ethic prevailed.

At last the party succeeded in gaining governmental power in 1993 and managed to stay in office after the 1994 general election despite the loss of seven seats. This loss, decreasing support in opinion polls, the continuing decline in membership and the reform policy of the coalition government, aroused a continuation of the heated debate in the party between 'traditionalists' and 'reformers'. The 'traditionalists' claimed that liberalism was not the cure, but the disease. They wanted a stop to privatization and a build-up of the public sector instead of a cutback. Organizationally, they argued in favour of greater influence for party activists *vis-à-vis* the MPs and a retention of the formal ties, as well as a *de facto* strengthening of them, between the party, the trade unions and the co-operative firms.

It was precisely such standpoints the reformers considered as the main reasons for the weakening in electoral support. In their opinion, such views were old fashioned, totally out of tune and with no chance of appealing to the new generation of voters. Instead, the reformers recommended that the formal ties between the party, the trade unions and the co-operative firms be cut. To them, the public sector was not sacred and they had a more relaxed attitude towards privatization. What mattered was not who did the job, but how it was done, and that the public authorities laid down the general standards to be followed.

In 1996, at the 125th anniversary party congress, the debate was, for the time being, settled more to the advantage of the reformers than the traditionalists. But the debate continues. How should the party adapt to a situation in which the essential elements of its traditional goals have been achieved? How much state and how much market? What are the responsibilities of the public sector *vis-à-vis* the individual? What position should be taken regarding internationalization and European integration versus preservation of national sovereignty?

The position on the European Union has always been a problem for the SD; a schism exists between the party leadership and the rank and file. At the 1972 referendum a number of SD MPs for the first time ever in the history of the party was allowed by the party to explicitly organize a faction which recommended a 'no' vote to Danish membership of the then European

Economic Community (EEC). The EEC was perceived by opponents as a capitalistic construction favourable to multinational corporations threatening the independence of the Danish labour market model, central elements of the Danish welfare system, Danish sovereignty and Danish nationality. The supporters argued that membership was essential to maintain peace among the European states, to sustain economic growth and social security and to avoid unemployment. European integration would in the short as well as in the long run be beneficial to wage earners. Staying outside the EEC was, in the opinion of its supporters, a recipe for economic crisis and destabilization of the Danish welfare system.

By and large these attitudes have prevailed inside the party ever since. In 1986 the party, after severe internal disagreement, recommended a 'no' at the referendum on the Single Market. The party recommended a 'yes' at the referendum on the Maastricht Treaty and on the Edinburgh Agreement (with the four Danish exceptions) in 1992 and 1993, respectively. At both referenda, however, around 50–60 per cent of the SD voters voted no. The opposition against further political integration has been strong and stable among the rank and file of SD members and its voters, despite intense agitation by the party leadership. Even so, the government did succeed in May 1998 to have the Amsterdam Treaty approved in a referendum, 55.1 to 44.9 per cent.

Select Bibliography

Bertolt, O., Christiansen, E. and Hansen, P. (1954) *En bygning vi rejser. Den politiske Arbejderbevægelses historie i Danmark*, vols I–III, Copenhagen: Forlaget Fremad.

Bille, L. (1992) 'Denmark', in Katz, R.S. and Mair, P. (eds), *Party Organizations: A Data Handbook on Party Organizations in Western Democracies 1960–1990*, London: Sage.

Bille, L. (1994) 'Denmark: The Decline of the Membership Party?', in Katz, R.S. and Mair, P. (eds), *How Parties Organize: Change and Adaptation in Party Organizations in Western Democracies*, London: Sage.

Bille, L. (1997a) *Partier i forandring. En analyse af danske partiorganisationer 1960–95*, Odense: Odense Universitetsforlag.

Bille, L. (1997b) 'Leadership Change and Party Change: The Case of the Danish Social Democratic Party, 1960–95', *Party Politics*, Vol. 3, No. (3), 1997.

Borre, O. and Goul Andersen, J. (1997) *Voting and Political Attitudes in Denmark: A Study of the 1994 Election*, Aarhus: Aarhus University Press.

Callesen, G., Christensen, S. and Grelle, H. (eds), (1996) *Udfordring og omstilling. Bidrag til Socialdemokratiets historie 1971–1996*, Copenhagen: Forlaget Fremad.

Kitschelt, H. (1994) *The Transformation of European Social Democracy*, Cambridge: Cambridge University Press.

Krag, J.O. and Andersen, K.B. (1971) *Kamp og fornyelse. Socialdemokratiets indsats i dansk politik 1955–71*, Copenhagen: Forlaget Fremad.

Thomas, A. H. (1977) 'Social Democracy in Denmark', in Paterson, W.E. and Thomas, A.H. (eds), *Social Democratic Parties in Western Europe*, London: Croom Helm.

Contact Information

Central Office Address
Thorvaldsensvej 2
1998 Frederiksberg C

Other Addresses
Arbejderbevægelsens Bibliotek og Arkiv (The Labour Movement Library and Archive)
Nørrebrogade 66D
2300 Copenhagen N

Socialdemokratiets Nyheds Tjeneste (The Social Democratic Party's News Agency)
Christiansborg
1240 Copenhagen K

Secretariat of the Parliamentary Group
Christiansborg
1240 Copenhagen K

Web page on the Internet: www.socialdemokratiet.dk

4 The Finnish Social Democratic Party

Jan Sundberg

HISTORY

The labour movement in Finland was not organized as a party of collective working-class interest before 1899 when the Finnish Labour Party was founded. Until then, workers' issues were highlighted by liberal clubs inspired by the German social policy movement. The Finnish Social Democratic Party (SDP) is the youngest of labour parties in Scandinavia. In contrast to many other West European countries, industrialization of Finland came late. By the beginning of the Second World War half of the population was still tied to agriculture and forestry, and the lack of extensive industrialization oriented the party and its members to a rural radical socialist party. In 1903, the party adopted its present name and its programme was radicalized along the lines of the German Erfurt Convention of 1891.

The main political issues of that time were the struggle for better economic and social conditions for workers and landless cultivators. In addition, the party was the leading force in pursuing universal suffrage for Finland, which between 1809 and 1917 was an autonomous part of Russia. The Russian government strongly opposed it but after attempts of revolution in St Petersburg in 1905, universal suffrage was introduced in Finland in 1906. The SDP succeeded in winning 80 of the 200 seats and became the largest party in the first unicameral Finnish Parliament in 1907.

Once a trade union (Workers' Central Union – SAK) was founded in 1907 the division of labour between union and party became clearer. Previously the party had been a mix of a political party and interest organization. Soon frustration grew among the SDP as they failed to get their proposals of social and political reforms accepted either in the Finnish Parliament or by the Russian Government. Although the Parliament was elected by democratic means, the lack of parliamentarism and authoritarian Russian rule effectively stopped all their attempts at reform. When Finland became independent in 1917 the frustration culminated in a civil war between socialists and non-socialists. The outcome of the war was disastrous for the SDP; most of its MPs were imprisoned and the Communist Party was founded by former social democratic refugees in Moscow in 1918.

The Communist Party was banned and the SDP began a new era led by their reformist leader Väinö Tanner. As a result of the non-socialist victory in the civil war the SDP were under pressure from the right and by banned communists in the Socialist Worker's Party. After the Socialist Worker's party was banned as well, the SDP remained the only socialist party in Parliament. It received support from the Swedish People's Party (formed when the Swedish minority in Finland was threatened by the Finnish pro-fascists) and the Liberals. Democracy was in danger but survived, and in 1937 the SDP and the Agrarians formed a cabinet called the *Red Soil*. It was based on an agreement emphasizing the protection of democracy and economic reforms. By this golden hand shake Finland followed the same political route as Denmark in 1933, Sweden in 1933 and Norway in 1935 (Karvonen and Sundberg 1991, pp. 49–81). This was the political base for the well known Scandinavian welfare state and a definitive break with a radical past.

After the Second World War a new era began. Finland was pressed to accept a bilateral security treaty with the Soviet Union. The Communist Party and the related mass organization for supporters and adherents (Finnish People's Democratic League) rapidly grew to one of the strongest organizations after its legalization in 1944. Its electoral support grew to a level close to the SDP who lost many of their former voters, members and branches to the Communists. In addition, the Communist Party was supported by the Soviet Union and as a result the party garnered more political influence than its electoral strength implied. Plans were made to take over the Finnish government and make it a socialist satellite in 1948. It still remains unclear why the Communist cabinet members failed in their effort. The division between socialism and capitalism was not simply a demarcation between the socialist parties and the non-socialist parties; the demarcation divided the labour movement into two blocs, the Communist-controlled on the one hand and the social democratic on the other. This division affected partisan organizations, including the labour union and the socialist sports federation. The division resulted in deep conflict which lasted until 1966 when the Communists, together with the Agrarians, joined a coalition cabinet led by the Social Democrats. This coalition started a new era of consensualism in Finnish politics with the SDP and the Centre party (Agrarians) as main actors until the late 1980s (Jansson, 1992, pp. 143–69).

In 1982 the former prime minister Mauno Koivisto became the first social democratic elected president in Finnish political history. During his two mandate periods the consensus agreements between the SDP and the Centre Party were changed in an undramatic fashion to more active parliamentarism between the cabinet and the opposition. The SDP dropped the Centre Party from the 1987 coalition cabinet, and the Centre party did the same to the SDP in 1991. The conservative and urban National Coalition became the new coalition partner in 1987 and this was repeated in 1995. The Centre Party is critical of the European Union and European Monetary Union (EMU), whereas the SDP are strongly in favour. Perhaps this conflict is a renaissance of the old centre and periphery conflict where the Centre Party acts as the defender of rural interests against urban workers and managers.

ORGANIZATION AND PARTY PROFILE

The SDP is hierarchically organized at six different levels. The branch is the lowest unit. Every party member has to be a member in a branch. The branches are mainly geographically organized; in a few cases they are tied to a certain workplace. The branch is run by a board and led by a chairman. As a rule, three or more branches in one municipality are co-ordinated by a municipality organization. Its main function is to plan and run municipal election campaigns and to co-ordinate the municipal council party group. According to the SDP's annual report, in total 144 municipal organizations were registered in 1993.

At the sub-national level, the party is organized in fifteen districts, of which fourteen follow the geographic borders of the constituencies. The fifteenth district include all Swedish branches along the south west coast. *Finlands Svenska Arbetarförbund* (Swedish Confederation of Workers in Finland) was orginally independent but joined the party in 1906 keeping its autonomous right to assemble all Swedish Social Democrats and to nominate Swedish candidates in elections.

The Party Congress is formally the highest arena of decision in the party. However, as it meets only once every three years it functions more as an annual meeting of shareholders. One delegate is chosen per 200 members from the branches and municipal organizations. Congress meetings had been an important arena for delegates to receive information from the leaders and MPs. Meetings were dominated by the leaders who reported what the party had done in Parliament and informed them about future plans. In addition, the leaders had the opportunity to listen to grass-roots' members about party policy during the past three years. Today, congress meetings are well prepared by party bureaucrats who are inundated with motions from the branches, municipal organizations and the district organizations. Topics in these motions are spread over a wide area, as compared to earlier, when motions were few and concentrated on the main issues of the party. Between congress meetings some of its functions are delegated to the Party Council which meets once a year. As the Council is relatively large and meets seldom, the real power is concentrated in the executive which is chosen by the Congress for a three-year period. The executive comprises the party chairman, two vice-chairmen, the party secretary, one member from the *Finlands Svenska Arbetarförbund* and eight other members (Sundberg, 1996, pp. 44–69). As the executive is relatively small, it operates effectively and meets regularly.

Table 4.1 Party members in SDP, 1945–95 (selected years)

Year	SDP	Change (%)
1945	63,745	
1950	67,268	+5.5
1955	58,962	−12.3
1960	42,926	−27.2
1965	51,656	+20.3
1970	60,707	+17.5
1975	99,463	+63.8
1980	100,161	+0.7
1985	92,032	−8.1
1990	81,896	−11.0
1995	70,176	−14.3

Source: Sundberg (1996, pp. 88–9).

During the first decades after the Second World War the party suffered from Communist Party competition and an internal party split in the late 1950s. However, by the early 1960s party membership began to increase after years of stagnation (see Tables 4.1 and 4.2). The recruitment of young members culminated in the early 1970s when the party grew explosively as a result of the addition of many left-wing members who had been involved in the student revolt. Most of the left-wing enthusiasm faded in the late 1970s and the membership figures had peaked by 1980. During the 1980s, membership declined and this continued during the 1990s. No signs of change in the declining trend is visible as the natural recruitment via the youth organization, the workers' sport clubs and the union has more or less died out. The recruitment of youth is low, the sports clubs are no longer tied to the party and the SAK is no longer politically divided. The political ties between the union and the party still remain, but as the political intensity in the union is low, it is hard to recruit new members in this way.

In 1977, when the party still successfully recruited young members, slightly less than 40 per cent of the members were more than 50 years old. Since then the proportion has systematically increased and in 1996 70 per cent of the members were 50 years or older: in less than twenty years this proportion of older members has increased by 30 per cent. If this trend continues, half of the party members will have reached the age of 60 years by the year 2000. This trend is not exclusive to the SDP as the same problems are typical for the other established parties. As the membership has declined and the members have become older, the proportion of female membership has increased (to 38 per cent by 1993). The share of female candidates and those elected to Parliament has increased to a level over 40 per cent

Table 4.2   Party membership in SDP according to age groups, 1977–96 (%)

Categories of age	1977	1980	1983	1986	1992	1996
> 18	0	0	0	0	0	0
18–24	7	5	2	2	1	1
25–29	9	7	5	4	2	1
30–39	24	24	22	19	10	7
40–49	22	22	24	25	26	21
50–59	19	21	21	21	23	27
<60	19	21	26	29	38	43
Total	100	100	100	100	100	100
N =	101,388	99,484	95,785	90,115	78,247	70,279

Source: Sundberg (1996, pp. 117–18).

(Sundberg, 1995, pp. 83–111). As a result of changes during the past twenty years, the membership is now smaller, older and the share of female membership and the amount of female activity is higher than ever before in the party's history.

GOVERNMENT ACHIEVEMENTS AND CURRENT POLICIES

As discussed above the SDP has played a crucial role along with the Agrarian Centre Party in Finnish politics since the Second World War. Classical bloc politics where the SDP alone or together with other socialist parties compete against the non-socialist bloc is unheard of after 1945. The Communist ambition to integrate the SDP failed and after that a deep rift divided the labour movement. The share of seats between the parties is as in Table 4.3.

The intensive electoral competition between the communist umbrella organization SKDL and the SDP prevailed from 1945 to the early 1980s. In 1958, for the first time during Finland's independence, the socialist parties managed to win a majority of seats in Parliament. The electoral success was, however, overshadowed by the deep split between the communists and the SDP as well as within the social democratic labour movement. Therefore the socialist parties never managed to take advantage of their electoral victories. In 1966 the success was repeated and the communists were integrated in a cabinet coalition with the SDP and the Centre Party (the '*Folkfront*' cabinet'). This coalition was made possible because the majority of the communists rejected revolution as a political means in 1965 and adopted the 'peaceful' way to socialism, with respect for liberal democracy and human rights. Integration (in cabinet coalitions) was a means of deradicalization, and was

Table 4.3 Socialist seats won in the Finnish Parliament, 1945–95 (%)

Year	DA[1]	SKDL/VAS	TPSL	SDP	Total
1945	–	24.5	–	25.0	49.5
1948	–	19.0	–	27.0	46.0
1951	–	21.5	–	26.5	48.0
1954	–	21.5	–	27.0	48.5
1958	–	25.0	1.5	24.0	50.5
1962	–	23.5	1.0	19.0	43.5
1966	–	20.5	3.5	27.5	51.5
1970	–	18.0	0.0	25.5	43.5
1972	–	18.5	0.0	27.5	46.0
1975	–	20.0	–	27.0	47.0
1979	–	17.5	–	26.0	43.5
1983	–	13.5	–	28.5	42.0
1987	2.0	8.0	–	28.0	38.0
1991	–	9.5	–	24.0	33.5
1995	–	11.0	–	31.5	42.5

Note: 1. See pp. xiv ff for party acronyms.
Source: Author's compilation.

strongly supported by president Kekkonen who was the main architect behind the inclusion of the communists in government. The policy shift in the communist movement resulted in deep internal problems, which first led to open conflict between the majority and the orthodox minority supported by the Soviet Union. Then the conflict paralyzed party work, the party divided and finally the Communist Party vanished. In 1990 the remnants of the Communist movement was transformed into a totally new party, the Left-Wing Alliance (VAS). The party acquired a new egalitarian organization but retained its old communist members and adherents. The Social Democrats took advantage of the communist split and collapse. After years of Communist threat the SDP could begin to dominate the labour movement in terms of the labour vote in national elections as well as in the union movement which was united in the late 1960s. The small SDP League (TPSL) also merged with the SDP after some unsuccessful elections. The party had been formed in 1958 as a result of an internal conflict in the SDP. Although its electoral success was weak, its role in the labour union was important and the party kept close contacts with the communists.

During the period between 1945 to 1997, 37 cabinets in total were formed of which 13 were led by a social democratic as prime minister (Jansson, 1992) (see Table 4.4). Most of the 37 cabinets were short-lived but at the end of the period the cabinet office time had become regularized to four years (election period).

62   *The Finnish Social Democratic Party*

Table 4.4   SDP party leaders, 1899–1993

1899–1901 af Ursin, N. R.	1930–44 Harvala, Kaarlo
1901–3 Hellsten, K. F.	1944–46 Hiltunen, Onni
1903–5 Tainio, Taavi	1946–57 Skog, Emil
1905–6 Perttilä, Emil	1957–63 Tanner, Väinö
1906–9 Valpas, Edvard	1963–75 Paasio, Rafael
1909–17 Paasivuori, Matti	1975–87 Sorsa, Pertti
1917–18 Manner Kullervo	1987–91 Paasio, Pertti
1918–26 Tanner, Väinö	1991–93 Sundqvist, Ulf
1926–30 Paasivuori, Matti	1993– Lipponen, Paavo

Source: Author's compilation.

The Centre Party and the SDP were included in cabinet more often than any other party during this period. In addition, their political strength – measured in number of cabinet seats and government positions – clearly exceeded their political competitors. Today, however, it seems that the two former coalition partners have come to the end of their consensual relationship in terms of cabinet formations and foreign policy views. The Social Democrats are keen for deeper integration in the European Union and the party council signalled in September 1997 unanimous support for European Monetary Union (EMU). Like most other parties in Finland the SDP continue to hold a careful position regarding military integration. NATO membership seems so far not to be an issue high up on the agenda in the SDP or in any other party at the moment.

Select Bibliography

Bondestam, A. and Helsing, A.-E. (1978) *Som en stubbe i en stubbåker*, Helsingfors: Finlands Svenska Arbetarförbund.
Fargerholm, K.-A. (1977) *Talmannens röst*, Bogå: Söderströms.
Jansson, J.-M. (1992) *Från splittring till samverkan*, Helsingfors: Söderströms.
Jutikkala, E. with Pirinen, K. (1979) *A History of Finland*, Espoo: Weilin & Göös.
Karvonen, L. and Sundberg, J. (eds), (1991) *Social Democracy in Transition*, Aldershot: Dartmouth.
Kettunen, P. (1986) *Poliittinen liike ja sosiaalinen kollektiivisuus*, Helsinki: Suomen Historiallinen Seura.
Laulajainen, P. (1979) *Sosialidemokraatti vai kommunisti, Mikkeli: Itä-Suomen Instituutti*.
Paavonen, T. (1984) 'The Finnish social democratic Party since 1918', in Mylly, J. and Berry, M. (eds), *Political Parties in Finland*, Turku: University of Turku, Political History.
von Schoulz, J. (1924) *Bidrag till belysande av Finlands Socialdemokratiska partis historia*, Söderström & Co.

Soikkanen, H. (1975) *Kohti kansanvaltaa I, II, III. Helsinki: Suomen sosialdemokrattinen puolue.*

Sundberg, J. (1995) 'Women in Scandinavian Party Organizations', in Karvonen, L. and Selle, P. (eds), *Women in Nordic Politics*, Aldershot: Dartmouth.

Sundberg, J. (1996) *Partier och partisystem i Finland*, Esbo: Schildts.

Contact Information

Party Headquarters
Saariniemenkatu 6 Tel: 358 9 77511
00530 Helsinki Fax: 358 9 712752
Web Page on the internet: http://www.sdp.fi/

Affiliated Education Institutes
Työväen Sivistysliitto
Paasivuorenkatu 5B Tel: 358 9 4762800
00530 Helsinki Fax: 358 9 47628680

The 'Party School'
Työväen Akatemia
Vanha Turuntie 14
02700 Kauniainen Tel: 358 9 5052406

5 The French Socialist Party
Robert Ladrech and Philippe Marlière

HISTORY

The Unification of the French Socialist Movement, 1905–20

The French Section of the Workers' International (*Section Française de l'Internationale Ouvrière* – SFIO), constituted in 1905, put an end to twenty-five years of chronic division and weakness. The SFIO welcomed various Socialist factions and small parties which had been organized in the aftermath of the Paris Commune: trade unionists, anarchists, reformists, independent Socialists all converged on the new party – the two most influential figures among them being Jules Guesde (1845–1922) and Jean Jaurès (1859–1914). The former, politically a 'workerist', was the uncompromising defender of party 'doctrinal purity' on the basis of a Marxist vulgate which he had introduced to France. The latter, a bright scholar and fine writer, was more open to a reformist approach and ready to accept the rules of the parliamentary system and liberal democracy. Furthermore, he regarded the Republican regime first installed by the 1789 Revolution as the cornerstone upon which a Socialist society could be built. Jaurès, a deeply committed pacifist, was assassinated in Paris by a French nationalist in July 1914, on the eve of the First World War.

Socialist unity lasted only until 1920. Then, following the Bolshevik revolution in Russia, the SFIO had to decide whether to join the Communist International. The majority of delegates were in favour and immediately left the SFIO to found the Communist Party (*Parti Communiste Français* – PCF). A minority led by the Jauressian Léon Blum (1872–1950) rejected Lenin's and Zinoviev's adhesion conditions. The PCF was born and a considerably weakened SFIO was left to re-organize itself again only fifteen years after the unification of all Socialist factions.

Reconstruction and Collapse, 1920–45

After the Tours congress in 1920, the SFIO was under the dual leadership of the General Secretary of the party, Paul Faure (1878–1960) and of the parliamentary leader, Léon Blum. Once the reconstruction was achieved, conflicts erupted again within the party: first, the PCF appealed to the left-wing group of the party (organized around the faction called *La Bataille Socialiste* and by Marceau Pivert); second, the alliance of the SFIO with the centre–left wing Radical Party was criticized by the left. These internal quarrels led to the first split within the parliamentary right-wing faction, the *néo-socialistes*, in 1933. Then in 1938 at the end of the Popular Front experience the Pivertist left-wing broke away to found the Socialist Worker Peasant Party (PSOP). In the meantime, however, between 1934 and 1938, the SFIO had enjoyed the most successful years of its existence.

In July 1934, the SFIO and the PCF signed a 'pact of joint action' to initiate a common fight against the Fascist factions in France. They also agreed to form electoral alliances for the 1934, 1935 and 1936 elections which meant that the PCF was no longer left in political isolation. This led to the 'Popular Front' alliance between the SFIO, the PCF and the Radical Party. At the 1936 general elections, the Popular Front rose to power and Léon Blum became the first Socialist Prime Minister in France to lead a government composed only of Socialists and *Radicaux*, the PCF having refused to take on any ministerial posts. This unusual governmental experience lasted less than two years, however, and Blum was Prime Minister for just a year, but was able to implement radical social reforms (the two most popular being the statutory annual two-week paid holiday and the reduction of the working week to 40 hours without reduction in salary). The Popular Front government rapidly fell into disputes over economic matters with the *Radicaux*. Furthermore, a crisis between the PCF and the SFIO was triggered by Blum's refusal to intervene in the Spanish civil war in favour of the Republican camp. The Popular Front ended in 1938 having achieved diverse results. From 1940 onward, during the Vichy regime and the German occupation, the SFIO became a clandestine movement under the leadership of Daniel Mayer (1909–96), participating in the resistance networks alongside mainly Communist activists.

Stagnation and Regression, 1945–71

In the wake of the Second World War, a neo-Guesdist coalition took control of the SFIO. The new party leader, Guy Mollet (1905–75), believed that the SFIO had to keep faith in its Marxist doctrine and should reposition itself on the left in order to counterbalance the growing influence of the PCF. The more reformist and 'revisionist' line proposed by Blum and Mayer was rejected by the party delegates at the Paris congress in 1946. In the 1945 general elections, the left won absolute majority and the PCF became the leading party of the left in terms of an electoral support and membership. Socialists, Communists and Christian Democrats of the Popular Republican Movement (*Mouvement Républicain Populaire* – MRP) formed a government and started to rebuild the French economy (1945–7). Before long, however, the beginning of the Cold-War period triggered an irreconcilable dispute over the USSR question and the brief period of unity was lost again. In 1947 Communist ministers were expelled from the government by the Socialist Prime Minister, Paul Ramadier.

This led to a long period of mutual distrust and even hatred between Socialists and Communists. The former, allied locally and nationally to the Centrists of the Radical Party and to the Christian Democrats of the MRP (the *Troisième Force* alliance), were portrayed as 'Social traitors' by the influential Communist press. The latter were reproached by the SFIO for their blind allegiance to a 'totalitarian regime'. Meanwhile, Guy Mollet's designation as Prime Minister of a coalition government (1956–7) coincided with the start of the Algerian conflict. In October 1956, Mollet decided on a military intervention in Egypt with the Israeli and British governments in reaction to Nasser's nationalization of the Suez canal. This action was criticized by some officials in the party (notably André Philip and Edouard Depreux). De Gaulle was called back to office in order to resolve the Algerian crisis and implemented the semi-presidential regime of the Vth republic in 1958. Following the departure of Mollet from office, the SFIO began a lengthy period of opposition to Gaullist governments and institutions (1958–69), during which the number of party activists and voters gradually dwindled.

Renewal and Heyday of French Socialism, 1971–97

The old SFIO, in constant decline since 1945, was replaced by the 'New Socialist Party' in 1969. The real re-launch of the party, however, did not take place until the Epinay congress in 1971 when the *Parti Socialiste* (PS) was given a new *élan* thanks to the arrival of younger activists from various left-wing groups and small parties which had opposed the SFIO. In particular, François Mitterrand (1916–96) joined the party and was elected PS First Secretary by making an alliance with the party right-wing (Pierre Mauroy, Gaston Defferre) and the Marxist CERES (*Centre d'Etudes, de Recherches et d'Education Socialistes*) in order to defeat the former Molletist majority. In 1974, the PS received a new influx of recruits from the far-left PSU (*Parti Socialiste Unifié*) led by Michel Rocard. Members of the CFDT union (*Confédération Démocratique du Travail*) also decided to re-group within the party as did left-wing Christian activists despite the strong anti-clerical tradition of the PS. In 1972, the PS, PCF and Radical Party signed a 'Common Programme' of government which set up in broad terms the measures which a left-wing government would take if it were elected. The 'Union of the Left' period (1972–8) was characterized by a clear radicalization of PS policies and ideology. Marxism was again the main point of reference in the rhetoric of both officials and activists. The sole candidate of the three main parties of the left at the 1974 presidential election, François Mitterrand was defeated by the conservative Valéry Giscard d'Estaing in the second ballot vote (50.6 per cent to 49.3 per cent). The united left also lost the 1978 general elections largely because of a public dispute between Communists and Socialists over the updating of the 'Common Programme'. Mitterrand was finally elected

President of the Republic on his third attempt in 1981. The Socialists won an absolute majority of seats at the general election which immediately followed the presidential ballot. After launching Keynesian-style policies and implementing a range of social measures at the beginning of his term (1981–3), Mitterrand decided on a 'pause' in the reforms given that economic performances were quite poor. 'Austerity' policies were launched by the Mauroy and Fabius governments in order to beat down rising inflation and the 1981 objective of a 'progressive rupture' with capitalism was replaced by the theme of 'modernization' of the French economy. In the ultra-liberal atmosphere of the 1980s, notions of 'market', 'enterprise' and 'profit', once strictly banished from Socialist rhetoric, began to gain credence. The Socialists were defeated at the 1986 general elections, but Mitterrand's re-election to the presidency in 1988 allowed them to return a minority government and Michel Rocard to form a new Socialist government only two years after losing power. The second seven-year term under Mitterrand was notably less reformist than the first. As a result of continued policies of austerity and economic orthodoxy (with the defence of the 'Strong Franc') and a series of corruption scandals involving socialist MPs and officials, the PS was massively rejected by the electorate at the 1993 general election when it suffered the worst defeat since the re-foundation of the party in 1971. Following President Chirac's dissolution of the national assembly in June 1997, however, the PS, under the leadership of Lionel Jospin (1937–), defeated the conservative majority and was able to form a left-wing government composed of Socialists, Communists, Radicals and Ecologists.

ORGANIZATION AND PARTY PROFILE

Political Tradition

The first Socialists in France espoused all the main concerns of the Radical Party, that is the defence of the Republican regime against the Monarchists and its presumed allies, the Catholic Church and the army élite. At the end of the nineteenth century, Freemasons, imbued with anti-clericalism and positivist Republicanism constituted an influential element within the party. Under the leadership of Jaurès, the Socialist doctrine was enriched by a reflection on the French Revolution and Socialism. For Jaurès, Socialism was the complete application of Republican objectives. Today, the 'Republican ethos' is still prominent in party life and can be observed in a number of the party's distinctive traits such as its persistent 'anti-clerical culture' and its defence of the secular 'School of the Republic' given that a large section of rank-and-file activists are state school teachers.

Marxism has always occupied a more ambiguous status in the party, standing as an official ideological cornerstone of the party until 1991. A

Marxist vulgate was imported to France essentially by the Guesdist faction and until the late 1970s it remained a common point of reference in party speeches and manifestos. The late use of Marxism by the PS can be seen as a mark of distinction and radicalism when compared with the clear reformist stances of all other social democratic parties in Europe. It also can be analyzed as a political weapon used by party delegates and officials engaged in internal party competition and who are aware that party battles have to be won 'on the left'. Finally, the Marxist and radical basis of the rhetoric also has its roots in the competitive relationship between the PS and the PCF on its left: the PS must maintain a 'genuine left-wing stance' with respect to its Communist rival.

Relations with Trade Unions

Although about 70 per cent of Socialist activists are trade union members, the PS has never succeeded in establishing close ties with any of the French trade unions. It follows quite paradoxically that although PS members are to be found in the three most representative French trade unions (*Confédération Générale du Travail* – CGT; *Confédération Française Démocratique du Travail* – CFDT; and *Force Ouvrière* – FO), none of them has ever developed any organic relationship. The clear-cut divide between Socialism and trade unionism in France stems from the very conditions of the birth of the SFIO in 1905. The following year at the Amiens congress the CGT delegates agreed on a strategy – the general strike – and a political objective – the complete emancipation of the working class – without the mediation of any political parties. This not only meant that there was no unity between trade unionism and Socialism, but also that there was political rivalry between two conceptions of working-class emancipation. Nevertheless, the political disunity of the left was reflected to some extent within French trade unions themselves. After the 1920 split the PCF was quick to secure close links with the CGTU (*Confédération Générale du Travail Unitaire*) a Communist splinter faction of the CGT. From then on the PCF was able to enhance its influence among the working class, whereas the PS' position in factories remained very weak. After the Popular Front the re-unification of the CGT and the CGTU was to the clear advantage of the Communists: the CGT had become a Communist-oriented trade union. Following the dispute between Communists and Socialists in 1947, a minority of the CGT left and formed FO. However, FO and the SFIO remained independent entities despite sharing the same uncompromising anti-Communism. The re-foundation of the PS in 1971 brought the CFDT closer: trade union officials such as Edmond Maire and rank-and-file members joined the PS at this time. The CFDT proved influential to Rocard's thinking and also represented a source of theoretical reflection (e.g. *autogestion*, self-management), but the relative 'honeymoon' between the PS and the CFDT ended abruptly in the early 1980s at the beginning of Mitterrand's first term.

Given the importance of teachers in the PS, a significant number of Socialists are members of the once very powerful and Socialist-oriented *Fédération de l'Education Nationale* (FEN). The FEN may be the sole union whose clear Socialist leanings have remained solid over time, even if they have become less pronounced since the mid-1980s.

Party Structure and Organization

The party basic structure is the *section*, which must have at least five members and is based on the lowest local government unit or the commune, in rural areas, the *canton* (shire). In large towns, there are many sections which cover the different quarters of the city. In theory workplace sections exist although, unlike the PCF, the PS has never been able to recruit many members on this basis. Each section has a Secretary and section officers and the average frequency for section meetings is once a month. Above the section is the *Federation* at the level of the *département* (county), which must contain at least 50 members and five sections. Federations in practice are not all of equal importance: the SFIO and the PS have been dominated by a few big Federations (Pas-de-Calais, Nord and Bouches-du-Rhône). Federations decide local party policy and send delegates to party congresses or party meetings at national level. Each Federation is run by certain party strands of opinion (e.g. Mauroy in the North, Defferre in Bouche-du-Rhône until the 1980s, or CERES in Paris in the 1970s). Presiding over the Federation is a 'First Secretary' who is the leader of the party for a given *département*. Each Federation has a vote at the congress and its delegation has the right to one vote for every 25 members. As a consequence, the votes cast by the big Federations are often crucial at party congresses.

Once every three years the party meets at its national congress. Between congresses, the National Committee (*Comité National*) – which is composed of 204 members, the 102 'First Secretaries' of all Federations and 102 representatives of trade unions and associations – is in charge of applying congress decisions and policies and meets at least four times a year. The National Bureau (*Bureau national*) is a more restricted and effective structure of 54 members which meets on Wednesdays. Above the National Bureau is a National Secretariat (*Secrétariat National*) composed of about 30 'National secretaries' dealing with different departments who run the party on a daily basis. This last structure is under the leadership of by 'First Secretary' who is effectively leader of the whole party. Since 1995, the First Secretary has been elected directly by all members of the party.

By and large, proportional representation applies to all levels of party organization so that each 'political sensibility' is represented in the party structure. It is also important to mention the role played by 'currents' of opinion (*courants d'opinion*) from Epinary in the new PS. Very active throughout the 1970s, the main currents were re-grouped around main Socialist personalities or clubs such as Mitterrand, Mauroy, Rocard or CERES and reflected ideological oppositions within the party. Progressively, and most notably from the 1980s onwards, they became groups serving the presidential ambitions of party leaders and were held responsible for the disastrous Rennes congress in 1990, which saw leaders of different currents fighting fiercely for positions of power within the party.

Membership

Unlike its electorate which has become nationally strong and interclass since the 1980s, the PS membership has remained limited and relies on a very narrow social basis. Less working-class (see Table 5.1) and male-dominated than the SFIO, the PS attracted younger activists from other political or associative groupings (*Convention des Institutions Républicaines* – CIR; PSU; CFDT) in the 1970s. The new PS has become the party of the middle classes – often state employees – together with a significant proportion of professionals and most notably teachers. The proportion of people traditionally associated with the SFIO – working-class people, peasants, small businessmen/traders and pensioners – has been in steady decline since 1971. More recent trends show a slightly ageing party but nonetheless with more female members than in the 1970s.

Table 5.1 Evolution of the occupational structure of French PS members, 1951–90 (%)

	1951 (SFIO)	1954 (SFIO)	1963 (SFIO)	1973 (PS)	1990 (PS)
Farmers	9	8	9.3	11	7
Small business, Traders	15	11.9	6.8	12	7
Professionals and managers	3	2.6	2	10	9
Teachers	15	–	–	17	18
White-collar workers	–	–	–	10	20
Salaried employees	11	21.6	20.1	19	27
Manual workers	43	33.6	27.2	19	12
Other	4	7.9	4.2	2	–

Sources: Bergounioux A. and Grunberg, G., *Le Long remords du pouvoir. Le Parti socialiste français, 1905–1992* (Paris: Fayard, 1992, p. 363); Sadoun, M. 'Sociologie des militants et sociologie du parti. Le cas de la SFIO sous Guy Mollet', *Revue Française de Science Politique*, no. 3, June 1988, p. 350.

It is also worth noting that the party is built like a social pyramid – that is, the higher one climbs in the party hierarchy (party officials, parliamentary groups) the higher the social status of its members (professionals, academics, but most notably élite civil servants from the *Grandes Ecoles* like ENA [*Ecole Nationale d'Administration*].

The PS is one of the weakest social democratic parties as far as its membership is concerned. Even in its best years (1937, 1946, 1981), the party never gained more than 355,000 members, which is well below the membership levels of nearly all other European sister parties (see Table 5.2). With no effective link and interaction with social movements or trade unions the PS has constantly suffered from a degree of isolation *vis-à-vis* left-wing and popular associations. It is above all a 'party of elected members' (*Parti d'élus*) – that is, a party which is predominantly composed of members who hold one or more local or national mandates.

Table 5.2   French PS membership, 1905–95

Years	Activists	Years	Activists	Years	Activists
1905	35,000	1946	355,000	1979	159,000
1910	69,000	1950	140,000	1980	189,580
1914	93,000	1955	108,000	1981	196,501
1918	16,000	1958	115,000	1982	213,584
1919	133,000	1960	100,000	1983	203,535
1920	180,000	1965	85,000	1984	189,282
1921	50,000	1970	70,392	1985	176,878
1925	111,000	1971	80,300	1986	177,284
1930	126,000	1972	92,230	1987	183,210
1935	120,000	1973	107,757	1988	202.083
1936	202,000	1974	137,000	1989	204,172
1937	287,000	1975	149,623	1990	165,186
1939	180,000	1976	159,548	1991	155,000
1944	100,000	1977	160,000	1995	112,000
1945	336,000	1978	180,000		

Sources: Maret, J. and Houlou, A., *Histoire des socialistes. L'Identité des socialistes des utopistes à nos jours*. (Paris: Pro-Edi, 1990, pp. 190–91); Bergounioux, A., Grunberg, G., *Le Long remords du pouvoir. Le Parti socialiste français, 1905–1992* (Paris: Fayard, 1992, p. 361); *L'Hebdo des socialistes*, no. 29, 8 August 1997, p. 23.

Sociology of the Electorate and Electoral Performance

The PS is 'interclassist': like the SFIO, it is particularly strong among the working-class, employees and lower-middle-class categories (minimum 40 per cent support). But unlike the SFIO, it has become attractive to a growing proportion of the middle-class and upper-class segments of the population. By comparison with the SFIO, the PS has two new features: it has more female members and attracts a more youthful following. Since the 1986 general election, more women than men have been voting Socialist whatever the election (with the greatest difference in the first round of the 1988 election when 37 per cent of women voted for François Mitterrand as compared with only 31 per cent of men). The PS electorate is also younger than that of the SFIO (more than 40 per cent of its voters are under 35) and its support has been declining among the over-65 and the retired population. Significantly the PS has also been able to appeal consistently to a Catholic element comprising mainly non-church-goers or irregular church-goers. In a party which was overtly anti-clerical and to some extent anti-religious until the 1970s, this is probably the clearest sign of the 'nationalization' of its electoral audience.

This said, the PS electoral performances once again appear remarkably weak and uneven when compared with most other European social democratic parties (see Table 5.3). This explains why, in order to form a government, it has to engage in left-wing coalitions with the PCF, Radical Party and, since 1997, the Ecologists.

Until 1971, the SFIO was electorally strong in Southern France, where it could rely on former bastions of the Radical Party, and also in rural parts of the North and of the Loire region, far away from urban and modern France. From 1973 onward the PS has progressed, first in the West (Brittany, Normandy, Loire), then in the East (Lorraine, Alsace) where it now receives between 20 and 30 per cent of the votes (compared with only 10 per cent under the SFIO). Since the 1981 and 1988 presidential elections the PS electorate appears equally consistent in the North and in the South as well as in the Paris region and, since the mid-1990s, in metropolitan Paris as well.

Table 5.3   PS share of the votes at French general elections, 1919–97 (%)

1919	21.2	1962	12.4
1924	20.1	1967	18.9
1928	18	1968	16.5
1932	20.5	1973	20.8
1936	27.5	1978	25
1945	23.8	1981	38.3
1946 (2)	21.1,17.9	1986	31.6
1951	14.3	1988	37.5
1956	15.2	1993	19
1958	15.7	1997	25.5

Source: Author's compilation

GOVERNMENT ACHIEVEMENTS AND CURRENT POLICIES

The achievements of the Socialist Party since the Second World War can be grouped into two periods. The first involves the SFIO in the various government coalitions of the Fourth Republic (1946–58), where it held the prime ministership several times. Although the achievements of the Fourth Republic are often overshadowed by what went wrong – e.g. the Algerian crisis and governmental instability – nevertheless impressive achievements were accomplished by these governments. It instituted the first national modernization plan for the economy; it initiated extensive social legislation, including paid holidays for all workers, comprehensive medical insurance and financial subsidies to families with children. The decolonization process began in Southeast Asia and Africa and the founding of the European Community and the North Atlantic Treaty Organization (NATO) took place during this time, with both decolonization and European integration extended during the 1960s under the Fifth Republic.

The second period of Socialist policy impact can be dated from the election of François Mitterrand in May 1981 and the subsequent election of a PS majority the following June. The policy goals of the new Socialist government were to be found in the party's *Projet Socialiste* of 1980 and presidential candidate Mitterrand's *110 Propositions* in 1981. This was the first left-wing government of the Fifth Republic, the last Socialist to hold the prime ministership being Guy Mollet in 1956. As mentioned above, the new PS had to rebuild its image with a powerful Communist party to its left. In so doing, throughout the 1970s the use of Marxist analysis together with a denunciation of the timidity of European social democracy led the party to promise a true 'break with capitalism'. It was in this context, then, that the election of the PS into full control of the French executive and legislative branches made the Socialist experiment a point of attraction by activists all over Western Europe. Efforts by an unencumbered and self-professed radical government to achieve democratic socialist policy objectives would perhaps reverse the growing neo-liberal influences of the Thatcher and Reagan governments.

The achievements of this first PS legislature – 1981–6 – were mixed to the extent that in 1983 the government abandoned an economic policy of reflation and thereafter pursued a tight monetarist policy in line with its EC trading partners. In light of this change of policy, other spending priorities were affected. Nevertheless, significant changes in social, civil and industrial policy were introduced by PS governments. Most notable were the decentralization reforms initiated by Interior minister Gaston Defferre. France has long held the reputation of being a highly centralized state. Upon taking office in 1981, the government presented the Law on the Rights and Liberties for Communes, Departments and Regions. Decentralization had three sets of objectives: to devolve central state authority to local officials; to transfer power at each level of administration from appointed to elected representatives; and enhancing opportunities for local participation in planning, etc. This reform was partially successful in that statutory changes were enacted, but the 'political culture' of the system was only relatively affected, demonstrated by the fact that old local élites simply adapted to the new rules of the game. Nevertheless, the new responsibilities of elected regional bodies to pursue planning and development has meant acquiring funds from sources in addition to Paris, most notably the European Union.

Other changes promulgated by the new Socialist government included the abolition of capital punishment, nationalizations (especially in the industrial and banking sectors), and increased spending on certain social policies. For example, the governments of Pierre Mauroy (1981–4) and Laurent Fabius (1984–6) were responsible for raising minimum pensions, reducing the retirement age from 65 to 60 years of age, and boosting the minimum wage (SMIC). Family allowances were raised, housing allocations for the low-paid were increased and health insurance benefits were made more widely available to part-time workers. The working week was reduced from 40 to 39 hours with no reduction in salary and the workforce was given a fifth week of holidays. Many of these redistributive measures occurred at a time (1981–2) when most other democratic welfare states were cutting back on transfer programmes and workforce privileges. For the PS, its policy orientation of 'going against the grain' in these matters reinforced the sense of providing real change in the nature of state–society relations. The subsequent 'U-turn' in economic policy, with its consequences for social spending, was therefore a deep disappointment to party activists, contributing in large part to subsequent militant demobilization and the exit from the Cabinet of Communist ministers.

The parliamentary elections of 1986 brought for the first time in the Fifth Republic a parliamentary majority opposed to the presidential incumbent. A UDF–RPR coalition and a Socialist president introduced 'co-habitation', in which the new conservative majority acquired its own prime minister (as opposed to the practice of the President appointing an individual from his own party or coalition). Jacques Chirac, the mayor of Paris and leader of the RPR, thus became part of a new dual executive in which a much more pronounced form of power sharing now existed between president and prime minister. In policy terms, this meant that the new government could pursue its agenda with only marginal (though sometimes critical) interventions from the president. This was particularly the case with a privatisation programme intended to reverse the nationalizations of the Socialists. In the end, a few companies were indeed privatized, though certain concerns deemed vital to the national interest by the president were left untouched. In 1988, the newly returned Socialist government made no significant efforts at re-nationalizing those companies privatized only a year or two earlier. Instead, the government announced a policy of no new privatizations or nationalizations.

The PS governments between 1988 and 1993 witnessed three prime ministers and the erosion of Socialist support among the electorate. Rocard, a long time rival of Mitterrand within the PS, was appointed prime minister and sought to create a centrist orientation, reaching out to non-PS deputies to pass legislation and in cabinet appointments. Rocard prioritized budget-deficit reduction and set about to enhance the profitability of the private sector, for instance by reducing taxes and social insurance on French corporations in order to raise private investment. There were some modest successes along the way, one in social reform, the other in relations with overseas territories. In 1989 Rocard introduced a Minimum Income for Reintegration (*Revenu Minimum d'Insertion* – RMI), a minimum monthly supplement to people at the poverty level seeking employment. As regards France's overseas territories, in 1988 Rocard scored a notable success in negotiating an agreement between the contending parties in New Caledonia, averting a civil war.

After three years in office, Rocard was replaced by France's first female prime minister, Edith Cresson. Her tenure was short-lived, however, and after one year she was succeeded by Pierre Bérégovoy. He continued Rocard's economic orientation, though his time in office was plagued by cases of fraudulent financing of the PS by private business. The years of austerity, growing unemployment, a fixation on keeping the franc aligned with the German mark (the so-called *Franc fort* policy), together with scandals contributed greatly to the disenchantment of the traditional PS electorate. This was evidenced in the massive rejection of the PS in 1993, when its score dropped to its lowest level since its re-foundation in 1971. This election defeat ushered in the second period of 'co-habitation', with a conservative government led by the Edouard Balladur (1993–5).

The European policy of the Socialists has been complex, to say the least. The Mauroy government had been forced to deflate the economy by mid-1982 in order to address a growing balance of payments deficit. The Finance Minister of the day, Jacques Delors, convinced President Mitterrand of the long-term benefit of keeping to the existing European Monetary System (EMS) guidelines, thus binding France to future developments of the Community in monetary matters. Subsequent efforts by the French to enhance the 'social dimension' to EU policies was a corresponding policy response. To a large extent the efforts of Jacques Delors as European Commission president (1985–95) may be seen in this light. The timing of the Maastricht Treaty on Political Union and Economic and Monetary Union (EMU), drafted in 1991, was largely inspired by President Mitterrand's desire to address the question of Germany's role in the European Union and Europe as a whole in the wake of German unification. The commitment to the convergence criteria necessary for the introduction of a single currency by 1999 affected the budgetary considerations of all subsequent governments. In particular, the requirement that budget deficits be no more than 3 per cent of GNP meant that governments were obliged to pursue aggressive reductions in spending. The spectre of conforming to a 'bankers' Europe' drove political wedges among the parties on the Left and also within the RPR. This was reflected in the French referendum on the Maastricht Treaty, carried out on 20 September 1992 (51 per cent 'yes', 49 per cent 'no'). Defections from the PS over its ratification led to the creation of the MDC (*Mouvement des Citoyens*) led by former PS minister Jean-Pierre Chevènement. The unpopularity of these measures, combined with growing unemployment and scandals led to the defeat of the PS in the 1993 parliamentary elections (and the ushering in of a second round of 'co-habitation'). The new conservative coalition continued with this policy, although campaign pledges by newly elected Jacques Chirac (1995) to reduce unemployment were apparently abandoned in favour of new austerity measures. Amid a still worsening employment picture, the government was surprisingly defeated in parliamentary elections in 1997, an election called a year ahead of time by President Chirac, ostensibly to renew the government's mandate before launching even more restrictive spending reductions by the 1998 deadline for monetary union.

The election of a left majority in the parliamentary elections of April–May 1997, and the appointment of PS leader Lionel Jospin as Prime Minister, resurrected the EMU issue for the Socialists. As part of his campaign pledges, Jospin promised both to meet the EMU convergence criteria and to not impose any further austerity measures. Upon taking office, Jospin set about furthering the Socialist call for a more 'social Europe', focusing on EU-wide measures to combat unemployment at the June 1997 EU Amsterdam summit. In order to keep his campaign pledge not to increase the burden upon average citizens and yet meet the single currency requirements, the Socialist government increased taxes upon the largest and wealthiest corporations and slashed military spending, announcing the scaling down of French troops stationed in various African states with which France has bilateral defence and base-siting agreements. Another significant promise the government immediately set about fulfilling was to create 700,000 new jobs within five years – half in the private sector, half in the public sector. In particular, emphasis would be given to employing young people under the age of 26.

The Jospin cabinet reflects the fact that it is a coalition government – there are thus ministers drawn from the PS, the PCF and Ecologists. In addition, a number of high-profile cabinet positions are occupied by women, demonstrating a recent PS requirement to boost the number of female deputies. The minister of the Environment is the leader of the Ecologists, Dominique

Voynet; the Justice minister is former MEP and minister for European Affairs in the Mitterrand government Elizabeth Guigou (PS); a new and larger Labour and Solidarity ministry is presided over by Martine Aubry (PS); the minister for culture as well as the government spokesperson is the former mayor of Strasbourg Catherine Trautmann (PS); and the minister for youth and sports is Marie-George Buffet (PCF).

Select Bibliography

Bell, D. and Criddle, B. (1987) *The French Socialist: The Emergence of a Party of Government*, Oxford: Clarendon Press.

Bergounioux, A. and Grunberg, G. (1992) *Le Long remords du pouvoir. Le Parti socialiste français, 1905–1992*, Paris: Fayard ('L' Espace Politique').

Castagnez-Ruggiu, N. (1997) *Histoire des idées socialistes*, Paris: La Découverte ('Repères').

Graham, B. (1994) *Choice and Order: The French Socialist Party, 1937–1950*, Cambridge: Cambridge University Press.

Hanley, D. (1986) *Keeping Left: CERES and the French Socialist Party*, Manchester: Manchester University Press.

Hazareesingh, S. (1994) 'Resurrection and Death: The Socialist Tradition', in Hazareesingh, S., *Political Traditions in Modern France*, Oxford: Oxford University Press.

Judt, T. (1986) *Marxism and the French Left: Studies on Labour and Politics in France, 1830–1981*, Oxford: Clarendon Press.

Kergoat, J. (1997) *Le Socialisme français*. Paris: La Découverte ('Repères').

Kesler, J.-F. (1990) *De la Gauche dissidente au nouveau Parti socialiste*, Toulouse: Privat.

McCarthy, P. (1987) *The French Socialists in Power, 1981–1986*, Westport: Greenwood.

Rey, H. and Subileau, F. (1991) *Les Militants socialistes à l'épreuve du pouvoir*, Paris: FNSP.

Sadoun, M. (1982) *Les Socialistes sous l'occupation. Résistance et collaboration*, Paris: FNSP.

Contact Information

Party Address
Parti Socialiste
10 rue de Solférino   Tel: 01 45 56 77 00
75 333 Paris cedex 07   Fax: 01 47 05 15 78

PS Web Page on the Internet: http://www.parti-socialiste.fr
The Socialist Party publishes a weekly magazine called *L'Hebdo des Socialistes*.

Affiliated Centres for Research
Fondation Jean-Jaurès
73 avenue Paul Doumer   Tel: 01 40 72 21 21
75 116 Paris   Fax: 01 40 72 21 39

Office Universitaire
de Recherche Socialiste
86 rue de Lille   Tel: 01 45 55 08 60
75 007 Paris   Fax: 01 45 55 66 33
Publishes eight times a year a journal called *L'OURS*

Independent Centre for Research
Centre National
et Musée Jean-Jaurès
2 Place Pélisson   Tel: 63 72 01 01
81 000 Castres   Fax: 63 71 59 99

6 The German Social Democratic Party

Johan Jeroen De Deken

HISTORY

From Origins to the Second World War

The origins of the German Social Democratic Party (*Sozialdemokratische Partei Deutschlands* – SPD) can be traced back to the General Workers' Association (*Allgemeiner Deutscher Arbeiterverein* – ADAV), founded in May 1863 by Ferdinand Lassalle, a former Liberal leader who had turned socialist but not Marxist. The new organization sought to extend the limited suffrage and called for the building of socialism through the creation of a network of state-supported producers' co-operatives, even if the stated end-goal was indeed the abolition of private ownership of land and capital.

In the same year the ADAV was established, a number of local workers' educational associations (*Bildungsvereine*) had merged into the Federation of German Workers' Associations (*Vereinstag Deutscher Arbeitervereine*) which was set up in competition to Lassalle's association. In 1869 at a conference in Eisenach, this organization was transformed into a political party, the Social Democratic Worker's Party (*Sozialdemokratische Arbeiterpartei*, SAP) under the leadership of two Marxist leaders, August Bebel and Wilhelm Lieb-knecht.

In spite of their differences, the two rival working-class parties decided to merge on the occasion of a unification congress held in 1875 in the city of Gotha. The new party was called the Socialist Workers Party of Germany (*Sozialistische Arbeiterpartei Deutschlands*).

In 1891, on the occasion of its congress in Erfurt, the party again changed its name into its current appellation, Social Democratic Party of Germany (SPD), and adopted a new programme drafted by Karl Kautsky and Eduard Bernstein. Kautsky contributed the Marxist theoretical component, referring to the growth of monopolies, the increasing exploitation of the workers and the gradual collapse of the middle class that would result in an intensified class struggle, which in turn would transform capitalist private property. Bernstein, on the other hand, is credited with calls for more practical reforms, such as universal suffrage, freedom of association, a progressive income tax, an eight-hour day, the creation of employment offices, and equal rights for women.

Around the turn of the century intra-party tension between orthodox Marxists and the so-called Revisionists became more pronounced. The latter, led by Bernstein, rejected some of Marx's predictions as inaccurate: the working class was improving economically rather than becoming impoverished; the middle class was growing rather than shrinking: major economic crises had not occurred; and the capitalist system seemed to be well entrenched. Hence, the 'Revisionists' called for gradual economic and political reforms although still with the intention of eventually realizing socialism. Bebel, on the other hand, representing the orthodox Marxist current in the party, continued to defend the idea that in the end capitalism would be defeated only by a social revolution that would result from an ultimate severe economic crisis.

In 1916, following a controversy over the approval by the SPD of war credits, a group of twenty dissidents established their own parliamentary group, the so-called Social Democratic Working Group (*Sozialdemokratische Arbeitgemeinschaft*). A year later, this group was transformed into the Independent Socialist Party (*Unabhängige Sozialdemokratische Partei Deutschlands* – USDP). Though the main issue of contention was the approval of the war credits, the party also attracted figures from the radical left such as Rosa Luxemburg and Karl Liebknecht. Though the USDP succeeded in capturing control of the SPD organization in cities such as Berlin and Leipzig, the party obtained only 7.6 per cent of the vote in the first post-war elections, whereas the rump SPD, now called Majority SPD (*Mehrheits Sozialdemokratische Partei* – MSPD), won 37.9 per cent. A year later, though, the USPD obtained almost as many votes as the MSPD: 18 per cent as compared to 21.7 per cent. By that time the new party had dramatically shifted to the left and was at the point of leaving the Social Democratic International to join the Communist Third International. In 1922, the left wing of the USPD merged with the German Communist Party (*Kommunistische Partei Deutschlands* – KPD), established by the Spartacists in 1918, and rather unsuccessful in elections, commanding 2 per cent of the vote in 1920, to form the United Communist Party of Germany (*Vereinigte Kommunistische Partei Deutschlands*). The reformist–pacifist rump of the USPD, which included prominent figures such as Kautsky and Bernstein, rejoined the MSPD. Within a year, the united SPD regained its pre-war strength, obtaining 36 per cent of the seats in the Reichstag and boasting a membership of more than 1.2 million.

The SPD did not emanate from the trade unions, and it was not until the so-called Mannheim Agreement of 1906 that formal relations with the labour movement were established. This agreement came about following the dispute over the use of a general strike to obtain suffrage reforms. The unions were wary of allowing the party to call for a general strike of the sort that had been used in Sweden and Belgium in the struggle for universal suffrage (see chapters 2 and 15). But in the Mannheim Agreement both the party and the unions committed themselves to joint action. On the other hand, it can be argued that long before this normalization, the sheer numerical strength of the trade unions (whose membership was more than 1.7 million) had given them a *de facto* veto power over SPD decisions inimical to their interests. In this sense, the unions proved to be a valuable support for the reformist wing of the party, as they too were more interested in reforms leading to immediate benefits than in orthodox Marxist theory.

Reconstitution after the Second World War

After the collapse of the Nazi regime, three centres of the SPD emerged: one in Hanover led by Kurt Schumacher, a veteran leader who survived the Nazi concentration camps; a second in London consisting of the party executive in exile led by Eric Ollenhauer; and a third in Berlin, consisting of a 'Central Committee' led by Otto Grotewohl. Even though this 'Central Committee' claimed to be the legal heir of the Weimar SPD, this claim was successfully opposed by SPD leaders in the Western zones. In April 1946, Grotewohl accepted the merger of 'his' SPD with the communist KPD, thereby creating the Socialist Unity Party of Germany (*Sozialistische Einheitspartei Deutschlands* – SED). While the Soviet authorities prevented a referendum in their Berlin sector, in the three western zones of the city, 82 per cent of SPD members voted against this proposed merger. Hence the SPD survived in West Berlin. Initially, many former SPD officials received posts in the SED, but it was not long before they were replaced by more reliable communists, and social democracy ceased to be a part of political life in the Soviet zone.

Soon afterwards, Schumacher became the undisputed leader in the West German SPD and directed the party on a strict anti-communist but also anti-capitalist course. At the first official convention in Hanover in May 1946, the party was reconstituted on the basis of the 1925 Heidelberg programme which, though abounding in Marxist rhetoric nevertheless did not prevent the party from adopting reformist practices in the cities and the states where it held power.

The SPD's hopes to become the governing party of the new West German Federal Republic were dashed in the 1949 election when the party was narrowly defeated by the Christian Democrats. One reason for the SPD defeat was that the party had lost some of its strongest areas of support that now lay in Poland or in the Soviet zone: Silesien, Sachsen, Thüringen and East Berlin. The party also failed to mobilize the Catholic working class in the Ruhr, which was wary of the leadership's neo-Marxist campaign speeches. And though the party did gradually increases its support during the subsequent elections, it could barely surmount the one-third barrier.

These relative electoral defeats convinced chairperson Ollenhauer (who had succeeded Schumacher on his death in 1952) that changes had to be made. In 1955 he set up a programme commission whose draft proposal was finally approved at the 1959 Bad Godesberg Convention. The so-called Godesberg Programme marked the apogee of a full turn to reformism of a party committed until then to Marxist ideology and reformist practice. The main purpose of the programme was succinctly described by one of its main architects Carlo Schmid: 'dumping ideological ballast'. This 'ballast' included not only such party symbols as the red banner or the use of the term 'comrade' (*Genoße*), but also the abandoning of nationalization as the major principle of a socialist economy.

The Godesberg Programme also signalled the acceptance of some post-war political 'realities' such as German rearmament and the integration of the country into NATO – measures that only a few years earlier had been fiercely opposed by the SPD. Finally, the party sought to open its ranks to religious circles by asking respect for and co-operation with the churches, and by trading its Marxist doctrine for an eclectic mishmash of democratic socialism, Christian ethics, classic philosophy and humanism. With a rather vague commitment to a set of 'basic values' (*Grundwerten*), freedom, justice and solidarity, the SPD also expected to extend its electoral appeal towards the new middle classes which were wary of any 'experiments' that might undermine the relative affluence recently delivered by the *Wirtschaftswunder* ('economic miracle'). In essence, the Godesberg Programme marked the apotheosis of the SPD's transition from a workers' party (*Arbeiterpartei*) into a people's party (*Volkspartei*).

The Brief Existence of the East German SPD

The resurrection of a social democratic party in the German Democratic Republic can be traced back to a group within the dissident movement. On 7 October 1989, the Social Democratic Party of the GDR (*Sozialdemokratische Partei in der DDR* – SDP) was established. Half of the executive committee of the new party were pastors and most of its members were academics, teachers, librarians and students. The lack of manual workers and salaried employees was a harbinger of the weakness the party would subsequently experience in elections.

After the collapse of the SED regime, the SDP grew rapidly but failed to attract the traditional clientele of a social democratic party. By the end of 1991, the new party had about 27,000 members, still only a fraction of the membership of its main competitors who had simply taken in the entire membership base of the satellite parties of the SED regime.

The first free elections of the Volkskammer in March 1990 were a dis-appointment, at least compared to the high expectations based on opinion polls that had predicted that the social democrats would gain as much as 50 per cent of the vote. The anticipation that the party would be able to recover what in the Weimar Republic had been its strongholds simply did not materialize and instead the SPD obtained only a little over 22 per cent of the vote. In anticipation of the parliamentary elections for a unified Germany, the social democratic parties of West and East Germany merged on the occasion of a joint party conference in Berlin in September 1990.

ORGANIZATION AND PARTY PROFILE

Organization

At the grass-roots' level, the party consists of some 11,900 local branches (*Ortsvereine*), situated in city districts and municipalities (*Gemeinden*). Membership in each branch varies between fifteen and 400. The executive decides on the admission of new members, prepares the yearly membership assemblies, communicates with the sub-districts and districts and provides a forum for discussing local politics. The membership assembly is the highest local organ. It is empowered to vote on resolutions, it helps to select the candidates for the municipal councils (*Gemeinräte*), and votes for the executive and delegates to the subdistrict convention.

The Districts and Sub-district Associations
The locus of organization of the SPD is at the district level (*Bezirk*). Currently there are some twenty five district or *Land* associations (for those states that are not divided into districts). The central person at the district level is the chairperson. This person attends party meetings in Bonn and coordinates activities with the national headquarters. Each district is subdivided into sub-districts (*Unterbezirke*) or county associations (*Kreisverbände*). The 350 sub-districts, normally encompassing cities or counties (*Kreise*), work closely with the local branches and are responsible for local election campaigns and must fulfil a mediating role between base and top party organs.

The Länder Associations
The SPD statutes require that a *Land* association (*Landesverband*) be created if more than one district association exists within a federal state (*Land*) and if each district within that state also consents. But even if a Land association is created, the district association tends to remain the key party unit. Though there are some regional variations, the Länder association are headed by an executive elected by the *Land* convention. The *Land* convention meets twice a year to deal with broad policy matters including

resolutions submitted by lower-level units. In election years it must approve the candidates for the *Land* lists and a programme submitted by the *Land* executive.

The Convention

According to SPD statutes, the biennial party convention (*Parteitag*) is the highest organ, even if in practice it is the Presidium (see below) that formulates policies. The number of convention delegates has fluctuated over time, but currently stands at about 480. The quota of delegates allowed for each district is based on the total of its enrolled party members.

The Executive

The party executive (*Vorstand*) consists of some forty-five members elected by the biennial party convention. It meets once a month to deal with basic policies, programmatic issues, organizational questions and personnel matters. Most of these issue are discussed and cleared in advance by the Presidium.

The Presidium

The 86-page statutes only devotes but one paragraph to this 'inner cabinet' of the party which is central in the formulation of policies. The Presidium is elected by the party executive and consists of a 'rump' including a chairperson (*Vorsitzender*), four deputy chairpersons (*Stellvertretende Vorsitzender*), a party secretary (*Bundesgeschäftsführer*), and a treasurer (*Schatzmeister*). They automatically receive their seats owing to their elected party offices. In addition to this seven-person core, the party executive chooses another six members. The Presidium meets every week and is formally responsible for carrying out the decisions voted on by the executive. In practice though, it is the Presidium that also makes the decisions that are later affirmed by the executive without much discussion.

The Control and Arbitration Commissions

The control commission (*Kontrollkomission*) serves as a watch-dog that controls the party's executive by examining the treasurer's financial reports and the secretary's report about party matters entailing expenditures. The arbitration commission (*Bundesschiedskommision*) deals with disputes over the statute and over the guide-lines of constituent groups.

The Party Council

The party council (*Parteirat*) consists of some 110 delegates from the district and *Länder* associations and co-ordinates the activities of the party at all levels. The council has to be consulted before the party executive arrives at its major decisions. But as it meets only four times a year, the council cannot really actively participate in policy-making. Instead, it channels information from the executive to lower levels of the party and offers regional spokespersons an opportunity to air their views on national policies.

Membership Developments since 1945

Membership has fluctuated considerably over time. At the onset of the First World War, it had passed the million mark; and during the Weimar Republic it ranged from an all-time high of 1,261,000 in 1923 to a low of 806,00 in 1926. During the first post-war years membership rose sharply, but during the 1950s the party seemed unable to break out of its opposition and failed to attract new members while older members died. When it again assumed power in the late 1960s, new members flooded in. A peak was reached in 1976, when the party again passed the million mark, but since that year membership has gradually declined. Since 1990, less than 30,000 new members from the former East Germany have entered the party (Table 6.1).

During the early 1970s the SPD managed to rejuvenate its membership, but towards the end of that decade the party lost the younger generation to the upcoming Green Party (*Grünen*), and the average age of its members started to rise again, a trend the party does not seem to have been able to reverse. The influx of young people into the party during the late 1960s and early 1970s boosted the average educational attainment of the SPD membership base. If in 1968 only 23 per cent of SPD members had at least a secondary educational degree (corresponding more or less to the national

Table 6.1   SPD membership, 1946–96

Year	Membership	% Women
1946	711,448	15.4
1950	683,896	18.8
1955	589,051	19.5
1960	649,578	18.9
1965	710,448	17.4
1970	820,202	17.3
1975	998,471	20.2
1980	986,872	23.1
1985	916,386	25.3
1990	919,129	27.3
1995	817,650	28.3
1996	792,773	28.5

Sources: *SPD Jahrbuch 1986–1987*, p. 667; and figures provided by the SPD *Parteivorstand*. All figures are for 31 December.

average), by 1977 as many as 37 per cent had such a degree or higher (Braunthal, 1994, p. 79).

During the post-war period, the SPD has become less and less a party of manual workers. Compared to the occupational structure of the population at large, blue-collar workers are no longer over-represented. Their role has been overtaken by salaried employees, and in relative terms even more so by civil servants. Thus, while in 1977 there were only 4 per cent civil servants among the population at large, as many as 13 per cent of SPD members belonged to this occupational category. Even though the party has improved its recruitment among homemakers, this category continues to be strongly under-represented (Table 6.2).

Until the 1960s, the SPD seemed unable to obtain more than one-third of the vote. But after the Godesberg reform the party saw a steady increase of its electoral basis to reach an all-time high in 1972. After that year a gradual decline occurred, apparently primarily to the benefit of the new Green Party (Table 6.3).

Throughout its existence there have also been important regional differences in the SPD's electoral performance. Traditionally, the party has been weak in the Catholic states in the South, and strongest in the Protestant city states of the North. However, during the post-war years, the party saw its hegemony collapse in Berlin, while it succeeded in replacing the Christian Democrats as the strongest party in the most populous state in the federation, Nordrhein-Westfalen (Table 6.4).

After the Bad Godesberg reform, the SPD considered itself a people's party seeking also the support of 'bourgeois' voters. By 1976, manual workers

Table 6.2   The Development of the occupational structure of SPD members, 1952–96 (%)

	1952	1966	1973	1991	1996
Salaried employees	17	19	21.9	26.6	28.0
Manual workers	45	32	26.4	25.5	22.8
Civil servants	5	8	9.0	10.6	10.9
Soldiers	–	–	0.8	0.6	0.6
Homemakers	7	16	9.9	11.8	11.2
Farmers	2	–	0.4	0.2	0.1
Pensioners	12	18	13.4	9.0	10.9
Students	–	1	5.7	6.6	6.8
Apprentices	–	–	1.2	1.8	1.7
Unemployed	–	–	–	1.5	1.8

Sources: For 1952 and 1966, Heimann (1983, p. 2183) for 1973 and 1996, Braunthal (1994); for 1996, figures provided by the SPD *Parteivorstand*.

Table 6.3   Electoral performance of the SPD in federal elections compared to its main competitors (percentage share of the (second) vote), 1949–94

	SPD	CDU/CSU	FDP	GRÜNE	PDS
1949	29.2	31.0	11.9	–	–
1953	28.8	45.2	9.5	–	–
1957	31.8	50.2	7.7	–	–
1961	36.2	45.3	12.8	–	–
1965	39.3	47.6	9.5	–	–
1969	42.7	46.1	5.8	–	–
1972	45.8	44.9	8.4	–	–
1976	42.6	48.6	7.9	–	–
1980	42.9	44.5	10.7	1.5	–
1983	38.2	48.8	7.0	5.6	–
1987	37.0	44.3	9.1	8.3	–
1990	33.5	43.8	11.0	3.8	2.4
1994	36.4	41.5	6.9	7.3	4.4

Source: Author's compilation.

Table 6.4   Electoral support for the SPD according to occupation, 1976–90 (%)

	1976	1983	1990
All respondents	43	38	34
Manual workers			
– unskilled	62	50	46
– skilled	49	52	42
Salaried employees			
– low and middle	44	34	37
– upper	28	24	23
Self-employed	32	26	17

Sources: Forschungsgruppe Wahlen e.V. 'Gesamtdeutsche Bestätigung für die Bonner Regierungskoalition' in Klingemann, H.-D. and Kaase, M. (eds). *Wahlen and Wähler. Analysen aus Anlaß der Bundestagwahl 1990* (Opladen: Westdeutscher Verlag, 1994, p. 643).

accounted only for one-third of the SPD electorate, and by 1990 the share of that class was under a quarter. And though the party still remains the main party for the manual working class, it also succeeded in securing for itself a substantial share of the middle-class vote.

Relations with the Trade Unions

Until 1933, the major trade union federation was socialist and institutionally linked to the SPD. But after the Second World War, the Weimar Republic's system of *Richtungsgewerkschaften* was abolished in favor of a centralized united federation, the so-called *Einheitsgewerkschaft*, which formally is independent of any political party or church. The German Federation of Trade Unions (*Deutsche Gewerkschaftsbund*, DGB) was thus founded in 1949 with Hans Böckler, a social democrat as its president. However, in spite of this formal neutrality, the DGB has maintained a close informal alignment to its social democratic ally.

According to a 1977 survey, 58 per cent of SPD members belonged to a union (47 per cent to the DGB) (Infratest survey quoted by Braunthal, 1994, p. 154). This penetration of the union by the party has been reciprocated by a 60 per cent SPD membership of DGB officials as surveyed in 1969 (Willey, 1974, p. 42), even if only few trade union officials occupy top positions within the SPD. The DGB indirectly supports the SPD during elections, but is also sympathetic to the CDU/CSU's modest labour wing. Former labour leaders have been appointed a cabinet seat in social democratic administrations, and throughout the 1980s about one-quarter of the SPD's members in parliament had a trade union background.

As long as the SPD was in opposition, the party and the union were in agreement and their co-operation was seldom punctured by discord. But when the SPD entered a coalition government with the Liberal FDP, the party and the union at times became sharp adversaries. In 1974 the DGB-affiliated public sector union ÖTV authorized a strike for a 15 per cent wage hike against the government's policy of wage restraint, and after the 1976 elections, the relations between the SPD and the unions further deteriorated after Helmut Schmidt appointed a new Minister of Labour without consulting the DGB. The union also sharply criticized the fact that the new government's programme failed to make full employment one of its main priorities. From 1980 to 1982, the DGB unions staged major demonstrations against the social democratic-led governments' turn to supply-side economics.

Even after the SPD returned to the opposition benches, its relationship to the DGB unions remained ambivalent. Though both organizations showed a strong solidarity in their resistance against the Kohl governments' plans to limit the right to strike, the party only hesitantly supported the DGB-affiliated Metal Workers Union plan for a 35–hour week without a corresponding pay cut.

Relations with the Greens and the PDS

The so-called new social movements of the 1970s absorbed the political energy of thousands of predominantly young middle-class activists. Critical of the perceived inability of the traditional political parties to solve a number of problems primarily related to energy, the environment, large infrastructural works and centralization of institutions, they formed a multitude of ad-hoc single-issue groups, the so-called 'citizens initiatives' (*Bürgerinitiative*). The SPD sought to win converts from these groups, but was rather unsuccessful, especially when some of them began to organize into a new party, the Greens (*Grünen*), and run slates of candidates in local and state elections. This competition on the left meant a severe drainage for the SPD's organizational and electoral basis. The party developed a series of initiatives to win over the Greens to the SPD banner, but these attempts failed, especially after the 1979 party convention did not adopt their anti-nuclear energy programme. After the SPD changed its policy on nuclear energy in 1986 and the 'fundamentalist' faction (*Fundis*) lost ground in the Greens, both parties began to enter coalitions at the state level. The right-wing of the SPD nevertheless continues to oppose collaboration with the Greens. They claim that merely considering a 'red–green' coalition at the federal level is bound to alienate not only conservative voters but also workers worried about their jobs if environmental issues are put ahead of economic growth.

After unification, another competitor on the left appeared: the Party of Democratic Socialism (PDS). This heir of the SED regime is a diverse party with a heterogeneous membership ranging from those who analyze problems from an orthodox Marxist–Leninist perspective, ex-reformists who previously sought to change the SED regime from within and conservative older members who were successful in the former GDR but are now often unemployed or have been forced into early retirement, to radicals close to the extra-parliamentary opposition. This odd alliance nevertheless successfully vocalizes the problems of the East and (at least in the new Länder) does pose a serious electoral challenge for the SPD. For historical reasons the social democrats decisively reject at the federal level anything resembling a formal coalition with the PDS; and even at the state or municipal level the SPD remains wary of formal cooperation with the SED successor party. This leads to the paradoxical situation that even if the PDS' success in state and federal elections increases the total 'left vote', this victory may actually undermine the chances of a red–green alliance replacing the christian–liberal coalition.

GOVERNMENT ACHIEVEMENTS AND CURRENT POLICIES

During the post-war era, the SPD has been in office only sixteen years: three years in a coalition government led by the Christian Democrats and thirteen years leading a coalition with the small Free Democratic Party (FDP). However, because of the German federal system the party also had a substantial influence upon national policy-making during its time in opposition:

the second chamber of the federal Parliament, the Bundesrat, consists of representative of the different state governments. The federal government needs the consent of the Bundesrat for all legislation that affects the financing of the states and this includes many aspects of taxation policies.

This very same federal mechanism also meant that the SPD was itself constrained during its years in government. In addition, it always had to water down or altogether abandon its major reform projects to please its junior coalition partner, the FDP. This obstruction was most clearly observable each time the SPD tried to reform the tax system, extend co-determination or establish schemes for collective capital formation. On the other hand, it should also be emphasized that the basic architecture of the socially regulated capitalism of the Federal Republic in part took its inspiration from the institutional structure of the Weimar Republic upon which the SPD had a decisive impact. In addition, some of the core features of the post-war 'Model Deutschland', while formally introduced by the Christian Democrats, were in fact concessions that probably would not have come about without pressure by the SPD.

Under Schumacher, the SPD had initially been engaged in an intransigent opposition that sought to provide a radical étatist alternative to the policies of the bourgeois governments, but by the time that the party assumed power at the federal level it had come to endorse modest pragmatic reforms. It had reconciled itself with an institutional and cultural environment which had been defined in the main by its Christian Democratic rival. Nevertheless, it still distinguished itself from this rival by its commitment to Keynesian economics and economic democracy, a more accommodating relationship with the East in foreign policy and a liberalization of the domestic social order.

The SPD in a Grand Coalition (1966–9)

In 1966 the German economy experienced a recession that led to a crisis within and the ultimate end of the Christian–Liberal coalition. This allowed the SPD to participate in government at the national level for the first time since 1930, albeit in a coalition led by the Christian Democrat Kurt Kiesinger. Among the nine SPD cabinet members were Brandt as vice chancellor and Foreign Minister and Karl Schiller as Minister of Economic Affairs.

Brandt initiated his *Ostpolitik* through which Germany re-established close relations with Eastern Europe. The resumption in 1967 of diplomatic relations with Romania effectively ended the Hallstein Doctrine of 1957. With the Moscow Agreement of 1970, the Federal Republic also recognized the Oder–Neiße as the Western border of Poland and thus for the first time no longer questioned the territorial changes that were brought by the Second World War.

With the so-called Stability Act (*Stabilitätsgesetz*) of 1967 Schiller launched a counter-cyclical economic policy, which was complemented two years later by the so-called Labour Promotion Act (*Arbeitsförderungsgesetz*) that was to stabilize full employment and optimize the functioning of the labor market by means of a more activist policy. These two laws exemplified the re-orientation of the economic policies of the Federal Republic away from the *laissez-faire* neo-liberal approach of Ludwig Erhard towards a Keynesian approach with a more interventionist role for the state.

Within the Grand Coalition, the SPD also was the driving force behind the so-called 'concerted action' (*Konzertierte Aktion*), an attempt to institutionalize tripartite negotiations between the Economics Ministry, the trade unions and the employers' associations with the purpose of co-ordinating the economy. This form of neo-corporatism had become possible after the trade unions at their conference in Düsseldorf in 1963 followed the SPD in trading Marx for Keynes. However, from the beginning the concerted action was undermined by the continued commitment of both capital and labour to the principle of freedom of collective bargaining (the so-called *Tarifautonomie*, one of the core features of the social order of the Federal Republic). Moreover, employers mistrusted the economic reform programmes of the subsequent social democratic-led governments, and it was due to the employers' resistance against government attempts to generalize co-determination that, in 1976, the trade unions decided to withdraw from the concerted action. But by that time this experiment in institutionalized corporatism had, to all intents and purposes, long ceased to function.

The Brandt Governments, 1969–74

The first social–liberal coalitions under Brandt implemented a number of important social policy reforms most notably the so-called *Lohnfortzahlungsgesetz* of 1972 which extended the right to enjoy a full wage during the first six weeks of sickness from salaried employees to manual workers. The Brandt government also initiated an overall reform of the educational system. Thus in 1971 the Occupational Qualification Promotion Act (*Berufsausbildungsförderungsgesetz* or *Bafög*) introduced a comprehensive system of means-tested educational grants that were to reduce unequal access to the educational system. Though the *Bafög* is not restricted to students enrolling in universities, it is at this level that the new system produced the most spectacular results. Thus, during the period 1967–79, the percentage of university students with a working-class background went up from 7 per cent to 14 per cent in. These educational reforms were continued by the Schmidt governments. The University Directive of 1976 (*Hochschulrahmengesetz* – HRG) was the culmination of a grand reorganization of the university system: it unified the admission criteria for universities in the different states and introduced federal standards for matters such as curricula and manpower structure.

The Schmidt Governments, 1974–82

The Schmidt-led governments increased the progressivity of the income tax system and realized various improvements in social welfare legislation such as the introduction of pension insurance for the self-employed, sickness insurance for students, special measures for the disabled, and a consolidation of the Tenants Protection Act (*Wohhraumkündigingsschutzgesetz*) (first introduced by the Brandt administration in 1971). Schmidt also successfully implemented a fundamental reform of marriage and divorce laws, and of the penal code concerning homosexuals. On the other hand, the partial liberalization of abortion as legislated in 1974 was repealed by the Constitutional Court and a far more restrictive compromise was legislated in 1976.

But typical of many of the successful reforms of the five Social Liberal cabinets is that either those reforms did not cost the treasury too much money, or they failed to challenge the existing balance between capital and labour. The only major reform of the latter character was the extension of co-determination. Already in 1972 the Company Statute Act (*Betriebsverfassungsgesetzes*) had been reformed, leading to a significantly improved participation in corporate governance for a majority of wage-earners. More important though was the Co-determination Act of 1976 (*Gesetz über paritätische Mitbestimmung*) which introduced equal representation in the supervisory boards of all enterprizes with more than 2,000 employees. Even if the SPD's Liberal coalition partner effectively used its veto power to water down the reform, the 1976 Act is clearly a landmark in social democratic institutional reform. The relative success of this reform can be contrasted with the failed attempt to establish comprehensive wage-earner funds (*überbetriebliche Ertragsbeteiligung*).

The SPD in Opposition

When the SPD moved to the opposition benches, the party opted for a policy of 'co-operative opposition', as it feared that a too competitive stance would alienate too many voters who still had an ambivalent attitude to political conflict and were still attached to the idea of social harmony. Most of the alternatives the SPD proposed during the Kohl years thus differed only in degree from those advanced by the government. Two important exceptions to this general trend were the reforms of the statute of political asylum (but even here the SPD in the end did give in to the demands of the christian–liberal coalition and approved in the Bundesrat a change of the Basic Law); and the conflict around NATO's plan to deploy 572 middle-range nuclear missiles in western Europe (which had already proved to be a divisive issue for the party during the last months of the Schmidt administration).

In December 1989, on the occasion of a special party conference in Berlin, the SPD adopted a new 'basic programme' (*Grundsatzprogramm*) to replace the Godesberg Programme of 1959. The Berlin Programme is an attempt to provide the basis for a reformist coalition between 'old' and 'new' social movements – i.e. between the traditional labour movement and the left-libertarian movements that developed out of the student protests of the 1960s. In order to cater to its 'traditional' labour movement clientèle the programme includes such proposals as the general reduction of working time to 30 hours a week; and in order to appeal to the left–libertarian voters includes a pledge to grant the same rights to homosexual couples as those already enjoyed by heterosexual ones, as well as a call for the environmental re-orientation of economic policies. In the party programme adopted for the 1994 elections, this re-orientation was made more concrete in the form of a proposal for an 'ecological tax reform' (*ökologische Steuerreform*) and the promise to start to phase out nuclear power generation.

The Berlin Programme includes a strong position endorsing European integration. It not only called for a harmonization of economic policies and the introduction of a common currency, but also pledged to launch a Euro-pean-wide activist employment policy, institute a systematic financial adjustment (*Finanzausgleich*) between weaker and stronger member states, and extend the German model of co-determination and works councils to other member-states. The SPD also seems to endorse the Christian Demo-cratic principle of subsidiarity as it wants to keep responsibilities as much as possible at the level of member states, regions and municipalities, and pledges to prevent what it calls a 'European over-bureaucratization'. On the other hand, the election programme also promises to extend the control and co-determining role of the European Parliament and urges that it be granted the right to initiate EU legislation.

In 1998, the SPD selected Gerhard Schroeder as their chancellor-candidate for the September 1998 general elections. Thus a dual leadership was created: Oskar Lafontaine as party leader and Schroeder as potential government leader. As minister-president of Lower Saxony, Schroeder had national public opinion support far outstripping the 'party-popular' Lafontaine. Schroeder was regarded as 'electable' due to his seeming 'pragmatism'. This strategy resulted in an SPD victory. With 41 per cent of the vote, an SPD-led coalition took over the reins of government.

Select Bibliography

Bickerich, W. (ed.) (1986) *SPD und Grüne: Das neue Bündnis*, Reinbek: Rowohlt.
Braunthal, G. (1994) *The German Social Democrats Since 1969: A Party in Power and Opposition*, Boulder, CO: Westview Press.
Heimann, S. (1986) 'Die Sozialdemokratische Partei Deutschlands' in Stöss, R. *Parteien Handbuch, Vol. 4*, Opladen: Westdeutscher Verlag.

Langkau, J., Matthöfer, H. and Schneider, M. (eds) (1994) *SPD und Gewerkschaften. Band 1. Zur Geschichte eines Bündnisses*, Bonn: Dietz.

Lösche, P. and Walter, F. (1992) *Die SPD: Klassenpartei, Volkspartei, Quotenpartei*, Darmstadt: Wissenschaftliches Buchgeschäft.

Miller, S. and Potthoff, H. (1981) *Kleine Geschichte der SPD*, Bonn: Verlag Neue Gesellschaft.

Rudzio, W. (1992) 'Partei im Spagat: Die SPD nach der Bundestagwahl 1990', in Eisenmann, P. and Hirscher, G. (eds), *Die Entwicklung der Volksparteien im Vereinten Deutschland*, Munich: Bonn Aktuell.

Rueschemeyer, M. (forthcoming) 'The Social Democratic Party in Eastern Germany: Political Participation in the Former German Democratic Republic After Unification', in Rueschemeyer, D., Marilyn Rueschemeyer, M. and Wittrock, B. (eds), *Participation and Democracy: East and West*, Armonk, NY: ME Sharpe.

Schmitt, H. (1992) 'Die Sozialdemokratische Partei Deutschlands', in Oberreuter, H. and Mintzel, A. (eds), *Parteien in der Bundesrepublik Deutschland*, Bonn: Bundeszentrale für Politische Bildung.

Willey, R.J. (1974) 'Trade Unions and Political Parties in the Federal Republic of Germany', *Industrial and Labour Relations Review*, 28, (1).

Contact Information

Address of the Party Headquarters
SPD Parteivorstand
Erich Ollenhauer Haus (the so-called 'Baracke')
Erich Ollenhauer Straße 1
53113 Bonn

From 1997, the headquarters are being gradually moved to Berlin to the following address:
Willy Brandt Haus
Wilhelmstraße 141
10963 Berlin

SPD Web page on the Internet: http://www.spd.de
e-mail address of the Party Executive: Parteivorstand@spd.de

Main Affiliated Research Association
Friedrich Ebert Stiftung
Godesberger Allee 149
53170 Bonn

7 The British Labour Party*
Paul Webb

HISTORY

Background

A frequently repeated, if anatomically unlikely, aphorism about the British Labour Party (LP) is that it grew out of 'the bowels of the trade union movement'. Coined by the former Transport union leader and Foreign Secretary in the Attlee governments, Ernest Bevin, this phrase graphically embodies the umbilical link which, constitutionally and organizationally, has tied Labour to its affiliated unions since the time of its birth nearly a century ago. Today this link seems, perhaps, more under-stated than at any time in its history, yet that it remains intact cannot be disputed.

In 1900 the Trades Union Congress (TUC) co-operated with the Independent Labour Party (ILP, founded in 1893) and various socialist bodies to establish the Labour Representation Committee (LRC). The LRC officially became the Labour Party in 1906, and was born chiefly out of frustration at the inability of working-class people to find parliamentary candidacies through the established parliamentary parties. Prior to 1900 trade unions had sought parliamentary representation primarily through the Liberal Party, though by the 1880s there were many who argued for independent labour candidacies.

Even after the foundation of the LRC some trade unions preferred to work for the election of working-class parliamentarians through the Liberal Party, though a significant juncture occurred in 1909 with the decision of the Miners' Federation to switch their allegiance from the Liberals to Labour. Up to 1914, the party's electoral progress continued to depend in part upon co-operation with the Liberals in that an informal agreement operated whereby the two parties sought to avoid running parliamentary candidates against each other wherever possible (the original 'Lib–Lab Pact').

Given its eclectic socio-political background, it is not surprising that the early Labour Party lacked a distinctively socialist profile or a nation-wide mass-membership organization. Ideologically, it drew upon a melange of traditions; broadly speaking, these can be divided into socialist and labourist influences, though there were various significant sub-divisions, especially within the former camp. Given the predominance of the trade unions within the party's structure in the 1900s (they collectively accounted for 94 per cent of the initial affiliated membership), it is obvious that they should have had a profound influence on the ideology and ethos of the developing party. While it would be inaccurate to suggest that a monolithic union 'ideology' ever existed, many commentators have suggested that a typical union outlook has nevertheless permeated the Labour party, typified by a 'labourist' approach to maximizing working-class gains within the economic structures and processes of capitalism, and within the political channels of parliamentarism (Leach, 1991; p. 134). Labour's socialist strand drew on a number of sub-traditions, including: Marxism (embodied in H.M. Hyndman's Social Democratic Federation which was among the party's founder-affiliates); Christian socialism (hence former party General Secretary Morgan Phillips' oft-cited observation that Labour 'owes more to Methodism than to Marxism'); and Fabian social democracy (exemplified by the middle-class intellectual radicalism of Sidney and Beatrice Webb).

Despite the modest progress of the early 1900s, nothing was at this stage inevitable about Labour's emergence as one of the two major parties in the country, as the Liberals were clearly still the electorally dominant reform-minded organization in Britain. However, Labour joined the war-time coalition government in 1915, and made great strides in the decade after the First World War. This progress derived in part from the sheer good luck of internecine Liberal Party factional strife (which endured into the 1930s), and the beneficial effects of the 1918 Representation of the People Act (which extended the electoral franchise to all males aged 21 or over, and to women aged 30 or over).

As important as either of these factors, however, was the decision to reconstitute the party with a definite socialist identity, a democratic constitution and a nation-wide individual membership structure in 1918. Prior to 1918 there had been no individual party members; rather, Labour was effectively a means by which a coalition of (to some extent) like-minded organizations could confederate to seek common political ends. At the end of the First World War the party created a national structure of local branches which individual activists could join. These members (along with the pre-existing affiliated organizations) were given defined roles and granted certain rights under the new party constitution. Equally importantly, a new policy statement (*Labour and the New Social Order*, drafted by the Webbs) committed the party to the pursuit of full employment with a minimum wage and a maximum working week, public ownership and democratic control of industry, progressive taxation and the expansion of educational and social services. In short, Labour was able to present itself as a democratic organization open to the common man and bent on a coherent programme of radical parliamentary reform which promised to benefit the newly enfranchized masses, many amongst whom had been radicalized by the experience of war and its aftermath. By the end of 1922 it had supplanted the Liberal Party as the official opposition to ruling Conservatives.

The Labour Party in Office

In January 1924, with Liberal support, James Ramsay MacDonald was able to form the first Labour government, though this minority administration only survived in office for less than a year. After five years of opposition, Labour emerged from the 1929 election as the largest party, though again it lacked an overall majority and formed a government with Liberal support. This administration experienced one of the severest internal political crises in the Labour Party's history when, in the summer of 1931, it was faced with demands for various public expenditure cuts as a condition of securing loans from foreign banks. These loans were required to stave off a currency crisis, but the proposed cut in unemployment benefit was regarded as unacceptable by the majority of the cabinet and the party in parliament. To the horror of most of his parliamentary colleagues, Ramsay MacDonald responded by forming a new coalition government (the National government) with Conservatives and Liberals. At the ensuing election which was called, Labour's parliamentary representation was reduced from 288 to 46, and the party remained out of office until 1940, when Labour ministers joined Winston Churchill's Second World War coalition government.

Labour achieved a famous election victory, and its first overall parliamentary majority, when it returned some 393 MPs to parliament in July 1945. Most commentators attributed this surprise rejection of Winston Churchill's Conservatives to the electorate's overwhelming desire for social reform and its determination to avoid any risk of a return to the inter-war era of economic depression and unemployment. Under the leadership of prime minister Clement Attlee, the Labour governments of the next six years set about building on the state's recent experience of wartime intervention to construct a new post-war political consensus based on a mixed economy, a much more extensive system of social welfare (including a National Health Service), and a commitment to the pursuit of full employment. The expansion of the public sector through the creation of a new set of nationalized industries (taking in *inter alia*, the Bank of England, coal mining, electricity, gas, iron and steel production, the railways, and airways) was central to the Labour government's conception of how it should fulfil the famous commitment laid down in Clause 4 of the party constitution to seek 'common ownership of the means of production, distribution and exchange'. By the time the second Attlee government met electoral defeat in 1951 it had effectively enacted the bulk of the first programme for socialist government expounded in *Labour and the New Social Order*.

After its ejection from office in 1951, Labour had to endure what its successful campaign strategists memorably referred to as 'thirteen wasted years' of Opposition until the narrow election victory of October 1964. While in Opposition Attlee's successor Hugh Gaitskell had sought to draw on the social democratic themes of his Shadow Cabinet colleague Anthony Crosland (Crosland, 1956) in leading a campaign to revise the party's constitutional commitment to public ownership of industry. A calculated attempt to adapt to the changing socio–economic realities of post-austerity Britain, and thereby create a new inter-class electoral appeal, this generated considerable internal tension. Central to Crosland's vision of gradualist reform was a willingness to acknowledge the importance of the market. While he recognized that common ownership of industry could combat problems of excessive monopoly power, consistent under-investment or the failure to utilize a resource in the best interests of the community, he was equally aware of its dangers, regarding complete state collectivism as incompatible with liberty and democracy.

This 'revisionist' perspective on British Labourism inspired Gaitskell to campaign for the reform of the party's constitutional commitment to public ownership (1959). In this he was unsuccessful. However, following Hugh Gaitskell's sudden illness and death in 1963, Harold Wilson emerged as the new leader who, despite an initially left-wing reputation, achieved notable electoral success as a catch-all strategist. His governments of 1964–70 attempted to resolve the problem of Britain's relative economic decline by pursuing a strategy of technocratic reform, indicative economic planning and a corporatist style of relations with business and union leaders. The party held power again from 1974 to 1979, first under Wilson and then (from 1976) under James Callaghan. Ultimately, however, the moderate social democratic approach exemplified by the Wilson–Callaghan years foundered on the twin problems of Britain's chronic external trade problems and worsening relations with the party's allies within the trade union movement.

On assuming office in 1964, Wilson and his cabinet quickly discovered that the country faced a severe balance of payments crisis. The new Cabinet swiftly moved to prioritize the protection of sterling's value; this could be achieved, however, only by deflating the economy (thereby reducing the demand for imported goods and reducing pressure on sterling), which undermined the expansionist technocratic ambitions of the new Department of Economic Affairs. In short, the British plan was stillborn (Opie, 1972, p. 171). Ironically, this strategy proved futile even in its own terms, as currency problems persisted until Chancellor of the Exchequer James Callaghan finally devalued the pound in late 1967. Callaghan was haunted by currency crisis a decade later when he was prime minister, obliged, with his Chancellor, Denis Healey, to plead for IMF funds with which to shore up sterling's precarious position. The conditions imposed by the IMF ensured a new commitment to prudent management of public finances by the Labour government. Under both Wilson and Callaghan, therefore, problems with trade, sterling and public finances produced a degree of fiscal constraint which hampered welfarist and interventionist aspirations.

Even more testing were the severe problems which both Labour premiers faced in relationships with trade unions. If it is true that Labour's arrival in power was greeted with warm enthusiasm from affiliated union leaders in both 1964 and 1974, it is equally clear that party–union relations became enormously fraught in each period. While the goal of these governments may have been the achievement of the kind of harmonious corporatism which typified a number of European social and Christian democracies during the period (especially those in Scandinavia and Germany), the essential foundations of such a model were lacking in Britain (see, e.g., Panitch, 1976;). Most importantly, perhaps, the trade union movement was never centralized and co-ordinated enough to deliver the long-term pay restraint desired by Labour governments. The various incomes policies of the period proved unstable as they fostered steadily growing resentment within the union movement, especially at grass-roots' level, and levels of industrial unrest escalated alarmingly throughout the 1960s and 1970s. The culmination of this was the notorious 'winter of discontent' in 1978–9, when the Callaghan government's pay policy collapsed in a welter of public sector strikes which few would deny contributed fundamentally to the electorate's rejection of Labour the following Spring.

The Labour Party in Opposition

After Labour's defeat by the Conservatives in the general election of 1979, the party experienced a period of considerable internal turmoil. Aided by the temporary allegiance of some major trade union leaderships, the party left expanded its influence at the expense of the usually dominant social democratic wing of the Parliamentary Labour Party (PLP), and succeeded in forcing through a number of internal organizational reforms. These enhanced the powers of grass-roots' activists and trade unions over matters of parliamentary candidate selection and party leadership election, and entailed a period of intense factionalism which culminated in the secession from Labour of a number of leading parliamentarians and supporters who founded the Social Democratic Party in 1981 (Kogan and Kogan, 1982).

Callaghan's successor Michael Foot oversaw these changes and the presentation of a radical left-wing manifesto at the 1983 general election. This proposed extensive nationalization of industry, economic planning, unilateral nuclear disarmament and British withdrawal from the European Economic Community, but – exacerbated by what was commonly perceived to be a shambolic and unprofessional campaign effort – this resulted in the party's worst national electoral performance in more than 50 years. Foot was replaced by Neil Kinnock, a politician with leftist credentials who set about re-establishing it as a credible national electoral force. This 'modernization' process encapsulated both programmatic and organizational changes, and was fundamentally driven by electoralist imperatives. This new 'electoral professionalism' was willingly continued by his successors as party leader, John Smith (1992–4) and Tony Blair (1994–), achieving its apogee under the latter (Webb, 1992; Shaw, 1994; Mandelson and Liddle, 1996).

Over the course of fourteen years following the traumatic defeat of 1983, the party systematically reviewed its policies so as to re-embrace the mixed economy in the tradition of the social democratic 'revisionists' of the 1950s and 1960s; return to a position of support for Britain's continuing role within the European Union; drop its pretensions to a unilateralist defence policy; jettison its historic commitment to the public ownership of industry; seriously consider a range of reforms in the fields of constitutional and social policy. While these measures are widely regarded as having contributed to Labour's electoral revival during these years, it was nevertheless unable to deprive the Conservatives of achieving governing majorities at the elections of 1987 and 1992. A number of factors explained the continuing attraction of the Conservatives for the British electorate during this period, despite the growing issue appeals of New Labour. Chief among these was the Tory party's reputation for economic competence, and its undoubted skill in manipulating the electoral business cycle; its perceived advantage over Labour as a harmonious and unified organization; and the personal appeal of its leaders over Labour's (Sanders, 1993). By 1997, however, the Tories' advantages in

Table 7.1 The major British parties, 1945–97: seats and share of the total vote (%)

Election	% share of total vote		Seats won	
	Lab	Con	Lab	Con
1945	47.8	39.8	393	213
1950	46.1	43.5	315	298
1951	48.8	48.0	295	321
1955	46.4	49.7	277	344
1959	43.8	49.4	258	365
1964	44.1	43.4	317	304
1966	47.9	41.9	363	253
1970	43.0	46.4	287	330
1974 (Feb.)	37.1	37.9	301	297
1974 (Oct.)	39.2	35.8	319	277
1979	36.9	43.9	268	339
1983	27.6	42.4	209	397
1987	30.8	42.3	229	375
1992	35.2	42.3	271	336
1997	44.4	31.4	419	165

Source: Compiled from official statistics.

each of these areas had disappeared: after 'Black Wednesday' in September 1992, when sterling crashed out of the EMS amid signs of desperate policy confusion, the party's enduring reputation for economic competence was left in tatters; similarly, the issue of European integration (and especially of EMU) produced the worst internal divisions the Conservative Party had suffered since the Tariff reform crises of the early 1900s; and in Tony Blair Labour at last found a leader with a personal appeal which consistently outstripped that of his Conservative rival. In short, Labour's strategy of modernization finally combined with the accumulation of Conservative woes to pay off, as Blair's 'New Labour' inflicted the most crushing electoral defeat of the century on John Major's embattled Conservatives (Table 7.1).

ORGANIZATION AND PARTY PROFILE

Structure and Profile

Since its foundation, the Labour Party has maintained a federal structure which accords rights of representation throughout its structure to its various affiliated components. These components include: the constituency Labour parties (CLPs) which have been responsible for recruiting and organizing its individual members (currently numbering 400,000) in each of the country's parliamentary constituencies; the affiliated trade unions; and a variety of small socialist groups (such as the Fabian Society). Since the constitution of 1918 was drawn up, the party's *annual conference* has formally been sovereign in policy making matters, with the *National Executive Committee* (NEC) overseeing party affairs on a day-to-day basis. Annual Conference comprises 1500 or more delegates sent by the affiliating organizations; each is permitted to send a certain number calculated to reflect the total number of members it affiliates to the national party. In addition, the party's various ancillary bodies (such as the women's and youth sections) are entitled to representation, and a number of individuals attend in an *ex officio* capacity, including the MPs, MEPs, parliamentary candidates, and the General Secretary. The NEC has traditionally been elected at conference, with places reserved for representatives of trade unions, local constituency parties, women, young people and affiliated socialist societies.

Notwithstanding the formal claim of conference sovereignty, it has been widely recognized that the reality of Labour's history has been one of domination by coalitions of parliamentary élites and major trade union leaders. These coalitions have shifted over time and although moderate parliamentary leaders have usually been able to rely on union support against radical sections of the CLP activists, this has not always been the case. Combined with the bouts of conflict between party and union leaders over industrial relations and incomes policy which have marked Labour's history, this has served to make the role of the unions within the party controversial. Since 1980 a number of organizational reforms have been instituted, many contentious and some concerned with the unions' role.

These reforms have affected a number of areas of the party's structure and operation. The first of these is the way in which the party leader is elected. The constitution of 1918 had given the PLP sole authority in this matter, but the left-wing *Campaign for Labour Party Democracy* succeeded in 1981 in persuading the party to change to a system whereby the leader and deputy leader were to be elected by a new electoral college, in which 40 per cent of the votes were controlled by affiliated trade unions, 30 per cent by the local constituency parties and 30 per cent by the PLP. (In 1993, this was amended so that the unions now only control one-third of the votes.) Moreover, the 'block vote' system by which all delegates of a particular affiliated organisation voted for the same candidate disappeared, as votes in the union and constituency sections of the college are now cast by individual members of these bodies.

The second aspect of the party's operation affected by post-1980 reform is parliamentary candidate selection. This had hitherto been the preserve of local party élites, but in 1987 a system of local electoral colleges was established in which 40 per cent of the votes were accorded to unions affiliated to a local party and the remainder were reserved for the CLP's individual membership. In 1993, this was amended so that selection is now simply by a ballot of the local constituency party membership. In addition, this aspect of party life was affected by the introduction of mandatory re-selection of Labour MPs between general elections, though this was rendered unnecessary after 1990 unless a ballot of local party members produced a majority demand for re-selection.

The third area of party life affected by reform concerns the role of affiliated trade unions at the party's annual conference. The voting power of unions here has traditionally been linked to the number of individual union members for which each union pays affiliation fees; this system resulted in a situation whereby more than 90 per cent of the votes at conference were controlled by union delegations (though it was rare for all unions to vote as a monolithic block). After 1990, the maximum percentage of the overall vote that unions were permitted to control was set at 70 per cent, and it was subsequently reduced further to 50 per cent. Moreover, the 'block vote' was formally abolished in 1993, in that union delegations were permitted to split their votes on a 'one-delegate-one-vote' basis (Webb, 1995).

The final, and most innovative, aspect of recent reform of the party structure is the *National Policy Forum*. This effectively downgrades further the role of party conference (which leaders have always been inclined to ignore anyway when drafting election manifestos). The Forum is split up into a number of smaller policy commissions, each working to a two-year cycle and producing reports for the Forum and the NEC to inspect and for conference to approve. Each commission is co-ordinated by a (shadow) minister, and conference can vote on the commission's proposals only *en bloc*, rather than item by item. Affiliated organizations cannot propose policy resolutions while issues are being deliberated by a commission. All of these factors, in combination with unelected membership of the Forum and commissions, probably serve to strengthen the hand of the leadership in controlling the party's grass-roots.

Overall, the organizational changes instituted since 1980 represent a some-what paradoxical blend of democratization and centralization. Since 1987 it has become apparent that the parliamentary leadership has sought to reduce the formal powers of the ever-controversial trade union component of the party, although care should be taken not to exaggerate the degree of change. The party remains heavily dependent on union funding, and the leadership has been able to achieve its desired reforms only because important union leaders have accepted and supported them. It is clear, moreover, that the party leadership has not yet completed its programme of modernization. In 1995 a 'Party into Power' project was initiated with a view to reconstituting the relationship between the parliamentary leadership and the rest of the party for a new period of Labour government. This resulted in the publication of a consultative document entitled *Labour into Power* in January 1997. The report proposes a number of things, including reform of the NEC's membership and functions, and the introduction of a two-year 'rolling programme' of policy formulation, in which national, regional and local policy forums, a Joint Policy Committee, sectoral policy commissions and party conference would all play tightly defined roles. Whether such changes will enhance or inhibit intra-party democracy is an open question.

Membership and Support

Labour's basis of electoral support prior to the Second World War rested largely on an amalgam of manual workers and middle-class socialists. This amalgam has changed somewhat since the 1960s, in that sections of the middle class who work in the public sector have now joined the coalition (Dunleavy, 1980). At the same time, there has been great debate among politicians and psephologists about the implications for Labour of socio-logical change in the country; much of this centres around the assertion that social class matters far less as a source of political identity than was hitherto the case. This debate goes back to the early 1960s at least, and for many it implies the need for the party to create a broader inter-class appeal. This notwithstanding, it is interesting to observe that in 1992 around 70 per cent of Labour's vote still derived from manual employees, while approx-imately 80 per cent of the party's vote came from electors who regarded themselves as 'working class'. After 1979, the party's geographical basis of support became heavily regionalized, in that it was closely associated with the most industrial parts of Britain (which were often afflicted by structural decline) in Scotland, South Wales and Northern England. That said, the avalanche of votes which swept over the Labour Party in 1997 went some way towards rectifying this regional bias, though it did not eradicate it. Similarly, the party extended its appeal greatly within all social classes, especially among routine non-manual employees. Thus, at the approach of the millennium Labour is able to portray itself as a catch-all party which nevertheless enjoys particularly heavy support within the working class (Table 7.2).

Table 7.2 The class basis of electoral support in Britain, 1950–97

		Labour	*Conservative*	*Other*	*Total*
Non-manual	1950	19	74	7	100
	1964	21	64	15	100
	1992	23	54	23	100
	1997	38	35	27	100
Manual	1950	73	23	4	100
	1964	60	31	9	100
	1992	49	34	16	99
	1997	58	23	19	100

Sources: Estimated from Denver, D., 'Elections and Voting Behaviour', in Robins, L. and Jones, B. (eds), *Half a Century of British Politics* (Manchester: Manchester University Press, 1997, p. 133); and Kavanagh, D., 'Voting Behaviour', in Jones, B. *et al. Politics UK*, 3rd edn (Engleword Cliffs: Prentice-Hall, 1997, p. 145).

Table 7.3 Labour party's individual membership since 1960, UK

Year	*Total*
1960	790 192
1974	691 889
1983	295 344
1987	288 829
1992	279 530
1997	420 000

Sources: Webb, P., 'The Iron Law Of Centralization? Party Organizational Change In Britain', in Katz, R.S. and Mair, P. (eds), *How Parties Organize* (New York: Sage Publications, 1994, p. 113); and Kavanagh, D., 'Labour's Campaign', in Norris, P. and Gavin, N., *Britain Votes* (Oxford: Oxford University Press, 1997).

It is interesting to observe a contrast between the social profiles of the party's voters and members, in that around two-thirds of the latter come from non-manual backgrounds; nearly half are employed in the public sector (Seyd and Whiteley, 1991). While the number of individual members generally declined after 1960, there is clear evidence of a significant revival in the 1990s, though whether this reflects transient political fortunes, or represents a longer-term secular trend is as yet unclear (Table 7.3).

GOVERNMENT ACHIEVEMENTS AND CURRENT POLICIES

On 1 May 1997 the British Labour Party ended its longest period of post-war exile from national government when it scored a resounding electoral victory over the Conservatives who had been incumbent for eighteen years. As we have seen, New Labour represents the culmination of a decade or more's intensive adaptation in party policy and organization. At the heart of this process lies a clear willingness to embrace both the market and European integration.

While the market remains the fundamental mechanism of resource allocation, Labour recognizes that such a system inevitably generates both social and economic disadvantages which it is the task of the state to rectify. Security, health, social services, environmental concern, education, training and research are all areas in which the state can play a proper interventionist role. What is interesting about Labour's approach, however, is that the state is regarded not only as a rectifier of social problems created by the market, but also as an 'enabling' mechanism which can smooth and facilitate the operation of the market. In particular, Labour regards the state as playing an important role in processes of individual and corporate adaptation – by, for example, providing education and (re)training services appropriate to the continually changing needs of the labour market. Central to Labour's analysis is the view that the British state has not done enough in the past to make firms and individuals in this country suitably adaptable to the conditions of international capitalist competition. That is why the party is now keen to emphasize the need to build a 'skills culture' that will underpin a 'talent-based economy'. Thus, while John Smith used to refer to education and training as the 'new commanding heights' of the economy, Blair placed education at the very forefront of the 1997 manifesto, describing it as his 'passion'. During the 1990s, Labour gradually dropped its traditional insistence on public ownership of major utilities (gas, water, electricity, public transport, postal and telecommunication networks). Indeed, in New Labour's lexicon, 'public ownership' has been replaced by 'regulation'.

While Labour continues to espouse the virtues of equality (ironically couched in the traditional Tory rhetoric of 'one-nation' communitarianism),

even this is now frequently stated in terms of the need to create 'opportunities' for individuals and groups to compete fairly and effectively in the
modern world. Indeed, the 1992 election manifesto seemed to have virtually
re-prioritized its values, given its prominent assertion (in the Foreword) that,
'at the core of our convictions is a belief in individual liberty'.

It should also be stressed that Labour has come a long way from its days of
anti-Europeanism in the early 1980s. Throughout the 1960s and 1970s, the
British Labour Party had displayed divisions on Europe which closely coincided with general left– right positions within the party. While the right saw
in the EEC a way of arresting Britain's relative economic and political
decline, the left regarded it as a capitalist club which purveyed liberal
economic orthodoxy and threatened to restrict the capacity of national
governments to implement socialist policies. It is no exaggeration to state
that one of the factors underlying the departure of the schismatic SDP in
1981 was the emergence of Labour's anti-European *Alternative Economic
Strategy* at the time. However, for Labour – as for social democrats across
Europe – the experience of the French *Parti Socialiste* during the early 1980s
(in combination with its own catastrophic election defeat in 1983, see Chapter 5) provided real food for thought. The French experience demonstrated
the virtual impossibility of operating national economic policy in isolation
from the rest of the industrialized world, and many left-of-centre observers
concluded that the European Community offered the best hope of launching
co-ordinated economic strategies which would enable governments to regain
greater control over market forces. Erstwhile Eurosceptics in the party (and,
it should be said, in the trade unions) were further persuaded of the merits of
Europe by the impact of EC Commission President Jacques Delors in creating a 'social dimension' to the integration project. In addition to all this, by
the late 1980s the growing disharmony of the British Conservatives on the
issues of European integration offered Labour an opportunity for party-
political advantage in adopting a more favourable position. By 1992 clear
majorities of the PLP and ordinary party members favoured further integration; for instance, while three-quarters of the party's MPs and prospective
parliamentary candidates wanted 'more integration', some 16.6 per cent
desired a 'fully integrated' European Union ($n = 344$). Similarly, 77 per
cent of the new PLP felt that the government should 'move towards a single
European currency' in 1997.

As the 1997 general election approached, and with it the real prospect of
national power for the first time in a generation, Labour sought to outline a
position which was critical of the Tories on Europe, without running the risk
of moving too far ahead of a public which remained in many respects
Eurosceptic. Thus, Labour criticized the Conservative government's often
fraught relations with EU partners, and argued that, as a result, Britain
risked being left behind in a two-speed Europe. On assuming office in May

1997, Blair and his new Cabinet were immediately faced with the realities of policy towards Europe as the culmination of the Inter-Governmental Conference (IGC) arrived with the Amsterdam summit at the end of the same month. With respect to institutional reforms, the extension of Qualified Majority Voting (QMV) in the Council of Ministers was readily agreed on a range of issues, including social, environmental and regional policy. Furthermore, Labour was happy to countenance an extension of co-decision rights to the European Parliament over all issues hitherto settled in council by QMV. The new government did insist on maintaining national vetoes over Common Foreign and Security Policy (CFSP), as it did national control over border controls and immigration. However, it reversed the Major government's 'opt-out' on the social chapter of the Maastricht Treaty.

With respect to the difficult question of European Monetary Union (EMU) which had so damaged the Conservatives, Labour is officially in favour and has few illusions about the loss of sovereignty. However, it is adamant that British entry will come only if the economic conditions are appropriate. These include not only the formal convergence criteria laid down at Maastricht, but also a further insistence on convergent labour markets and economic cycles. Blair has, moreover, committed the government to holding a referendum on entry to EMU, and Britain will not enter in the 'first wave' in 1999. Though this has been interpreted as pusillanimous in some quarters, it may prove a judicious move in the long run. Britain has already experienced the effects of popular backlash against policy decisions which clearly lack legitimacy – witness the poll tax protests at the beginning of the 1990s. EMU is a matter of far greater moment, and one which opinion research suggests lacks public support in the UK. A British government would probably stand a far better chance of convincing the electorate of EMU's merits by delaying entry until after the first wave, especially if it were then able to point to a successful initiation of the project. A further indication of the party leadership's serious intent about EMU was provided by the decision of new Chancellor Gordon Brown to hand responsibility for interest rate policy to the Bank of England.

These aspects of European policy apart, the Labour government also welcomes a co-ordinated strategy for fighting unemployment across Europe; the widening of the European Union to include new members from central Europe; reforms of the Common Agricultural Policy (CAP); and greater co-ordination of anti-fraud and crime efforts across the Union. All of these themes were articulated upon Labour's arrival in power, and were complemented by a Queen's Speech which prioritized: a new 'welfare-to-work' scheme to help the young and long-term unemployed to find subsidized jobs or training; a one-off 'windfall profits' tax levied on certain privatized companies as a means of funding welfare-to-work; a new scheme designed to help single parents find employment; a 'fast-track' system of administering justice for young offenders; the reduction of class sizes and an injection of extra funds into public sector schools; the abolition of the internal 'quasi-market' which the Conservatives had introduced into the National Health Service, and an increment in funding; a raft of constitutional changes including devolution of power to Scotland and Wales, and the incorporation of the European Convention on Human Rights into British law; a greater emphasis on consumer protection through regulation; and the continuation of the peace process in Northern Ireland.

Note

* I am grateful to the Data Archive at the University of Essex for supplying me with copies of the 1992 British Election Survey data set, the British Candidate Survey data (1992) and the Labour Party Membership Survey data (1989) from which figures in this chapter derive.

Select Bibliography

Crosland, CAR (1956) *The Future of Socialism*, London: Jonathan Cape.
Dunleavy, P. (1980) 'The Political Implications of Sectoral Cleavages and the Growth of State Employment: Part 1, The Analysis of Production Cleavages', *Political Studies*, 28, pp. 364–83; 'Part 2, Cleavage Structures and Political Alignment', *Political Studies*, 28, pp. 527–49.
Kogan, D. and Kogan, M. (1982) *The Battle for the Labour Party*, London: Fontana.
Leach, R. (1991) *British Political Ideologies*, Oxford: Philip Allan.
Mandelson, P. and Liddle, R. (1996) *The Blair Revolution: Can New Labour Deliver?*, London: Faber & Faber.
Opie, R. (1972) 'Economic Planning and Growth', in Beckerman, W. *The Labour Government's Economic Record 1964–1970*, London: Duckworth.
Panitch, L. (1976) *Social Democacy and Industrial Militancy*, Cambridge: Cambridge University Press.
Sanders, D. (1993) 'Why the Conservatives Won – Again', in King, A. *et al.*, *Britain at the Polls 1992*, Chatham, NJ: Chatham House.
Seyd, P. and Whiteley, P. (1991) *Labour's Grass Roots: The Politics of Party Membership*, Oxford: Clarendon.
Shaw, E. (1994) *The Labour Party Since 1979: Crisis and Transformation*, London: Routledge.
Webb, P.D. (1992) 'Election Campaigning, Organisational Transformation and the Professionalization of the British Labour Party', *European Journal of Political Research*, 21, pp. 267–88.
Webb, P.D. (1995) 'Reforming the Labour Party–Trade Union Link: An Assessment', in Broughton, D., Farrell, D., Denver, D. an Rallings, C., *British Elections and Parties Yearbook 1994*, London: Frank Cass.

Contact Information

Address
Party headquarters since the early 1980s have been at John Smith House

150–152 Walworth Road	Tel: 0171 701 1234
London SE17 1JT	Fax: 0171 277 3300

Web page on the Internet: http://www.labour.org.uk

email: labour-party@geo2.poptel.org.uk

During the election campaign of 1997, campaign operations were moved to a centre at Millbank Towers, on the Embankment of the River Thames, and near to the Palace of Westminster. After the election, it was announced that party headquarters would eventually move there on a permanent footing.

Millbank	
Westminster	Tel: 0171 277 3640
London SW1P 4GT	Fax 0171 277 3660

Web page on the internet: http://poptel.org.uk/media-centre;
email: millbank-media@geo2.poptel.org.uk

8 The Panhellenic Socialist Movement

Gerassimos Moschonas

HISTORY

Three families of parties structured the Greek party system of the post-civil-war period (1949–67): the right, an ideologically ultra-conservative force; the centre, the 'soft structure' of the system with a rather centre–right ideological orientation; and the third pole, the communist left, which emerged in a weakened state due to its defeat in the civil war. The distinctive trait of the politics of this period was the absence of a socialist or social-democratic pole. The left was identified to such a degree with the communist tradition that in the everyday political vocabulary the term 'left' clearly designated the communist left. The founding, therefore, of the Panhellenic Socialist Movement (PASOK) in 1974 and its dynamic presence on the Greek political scene constituted a significant change in the continuity of the Greek political arena. Modern centre for some (continuation of the old Centre Union), a prototype of a populist party for others, an idiosyncratic social democracy in Greek colours for yet others, PASOK was all of these in turn and simultaneously. At the same time it was more than their sum total: PASOK is in fact a party of many faces.

The period after the fall of the dictatorship (1967–74) through perhaps 1985 was one of the great constitution-making moments of the modern Greek political history. In 1974, PASOK, a party without a 'reserved' electoral and social territory, attempted to 'establish' itself as an entirely new party with an unambiguously distinct identity and no ties with the past (Mavrogordatos in Clogg, 1983, p. 76). Its roots, nonetheless, are to be found in the radicalism of the centre–left wing of the pre-dictatorship Centre Union. This tendency made its presence felt, primarily after 1963, under the leadership of Andreas Papandreou, son of the leader of the Centre Union Georgios Papandreou. PASOK's roots are also to be found in the anti-dictatorship resistance organizations, chiefly that of PAK (Panhellenic Liberation Movement), founded by Andreas Papandreou in 1968, committed to armed struggle to overthrow the Colonels' régime – something quite alien to the Centre Union tradition (Featherstone in Featherstone and Katsoudas, 1993, p. 119).

It is nevertheless certain that PASOK's antecedents should not be sought in the weak and fragmented labour movement in the interior of which the

110

communist left had been playing the leading role, though not always an institutional one – due to the regime of 'reduced democracy' of the period 1949–67 (see Clogg, 1987, p. 128).

Continuity between PASOK and the old Centre Union is only partly true (mostly at the parliamentary level; the Central Committee, which is the group exercising crucial power in the interior of the party, are in the majority newcomers).

In the particularly radical founding document of PASOK, the 'Declaration of the 3rd September' of 1974, the relationship between socialism and anti-imperialism was presented as central and was expressed through the emphasis placed upon 'anti-imperialist' goals (withdrawal from NATO, ousting of American bases, rejection of the European Community). A typical example of this osmosis was the position of PASOK with regard to the European Economic Community (EEC). PASOK rejected the accession of Greece into the EEC which it considered a 'club of monopolies' and an impediment to an independent national economic policy.

The Marxism explicitly adopted by PASOK was eclectic, 'non-dogmatic' and 'non-consistent with Leninism'. The opposition 'centre–periphery' was dominant in the Marxist analysis and in the political discourse of PASOK. According to such an analysis, Greece was a country in the periphery of the world capitalist system, a 'peripheral appendage' of western monopoly capitalism. As a consequence, Greece's economy, notwithstanding a significant part of the country's political class' (the right), were subordinate to the economical and political 'metropolitan decision-making centres'. Hence the emphasis on 'national liberation' and 'anti-imperialistic' objectives.

In a sense, through the adoption of the 'centre–periphery' scheme, PASOK managed to express in a Marxist jargon and to integrate within the party ideology a significant element of the Greek political culture: the widespread perception of a 'small' and 'threatened' nation. This perception was reinforced by the American support for the military regime and by the Turkish invasion of Cyprus. It formed the theoretical and cultural basis of PASOK's nationalism.

In the same vein, PASOK placed itself in opposition to European social democracy. The 'third road' of PASOK rested upon decentralization, collectivization and self-management and was presented as more radical than social democracy and more modern, democratic and participatory than soviet socialism. This stand was of utmost significance because it enabled PASOK to outdo the communist left – the 'traditional left' as it was called in PASOK's discourse – in radical rhetoric.

Essentially, PASOK developed its electoral dynamics upon a fundamentally ambivalent strategy which its leadership handled masterfully to the advantage of the party. On the one hand, it constituted an 'anti-capitalistic' and an 'anti-imperialistic' party in a position to compete with the communist left on its own privileged terrain; on the other, it was a 'democratic', 'modernizing' and 'anti-right' party in a position to claim the traditional centre. In the period 1974–1981, PASOK managed to function as the primary vehicle of challenge and radicalism within the political system, touching with its rhetoric the limits of an anti-systemic party, while at the same time remaining at the centre of the system.

It is important to note than not even the major crisis and the split of 1975 were able to hinder PASOK's electoral dynamic. The organizational question was the prime focus of a major conflict within PASOK, during which two main poles were opposed: on the one hand, the 'hardcore' tendency of PAK in alliance with the party cadres of centrist origin and on the other, the majority of 'Democratic Defence' members (a resistance organization generally recognized as leftist). The proposals of this 'second pole' aimed at establishing a democratically structured mass organization, to undercut the further concentration of power in the hands of Papandreou and to promote some level of autonomy between PASOK and PASKE (Panhellenic Militant Trade Union Movement), the labour front organization of PASOK. This conflict, which Andreas Papandreou resolved in an authoritarian manner, provoked a mass defection of some 2,000 active members of the party, among which some prominent figures of the resistance.

The factor which 'tied' and consolidated the 'centrist' and the 'left' facets of PASOK in an electorally effective way was, beyond the catalytic role of Andreas Papandreou, the 'anti-right' rhetoric and ideology. The regime of limited democracy and the authoritarian control of the state imposed by the ultra-conservative right following, and as a consequence of, the civil war, had by the 1960s contributed to the development of a widespread anti-right attitude throughout abroad stratum of the population. The painful experience of the dictatorship (1967–74) bolstered the imposition of the cleavage 'democratic forces–right' as the central division in Greek politics from 1974 onwards. PASOK employed the anti-right rhetoric and mobilization, systematically and persistently, as a means not only to delegitimize the New Democracy party but also as an *instrumentum regni* in the 'democratic anti-right' area. PASOK's use of an aggressive anti-right rhetoric had two functions. First, it reinforced its catch-all nature as it enabled the party to address both the centrist part of the electorate and fringes of the communist left. Secondly, it allowed PASOK to remain faithful to the aggressive discourse of its founding period and to minimize the electoral cost of moderation (or of rightward shift), a moderation which was connected with the rise of the socialists to power and the abandonment of the original 'anti-capitalist' and 'anti-imperialist' goals.

Indeed, the initial 'ultra-radical' strategy (1974–7) was gradually replaced by a complex and more moderate one, turned towards the centre, a strategy which would characterize the period of PASOK's approach to power

(1977–81) as well as the governmental phase (1981–9). Insistence on an aggressive – and, quite often, extremely demagogic – anti-right rhetoric, systematically accompanies 'moderate' and 'responsible' politics, and functions as a kind of safety-lock for PASOK's base (Spourdalakis, 1992, p. 116).

ORGANIZATION AND PARTY PROFILE

Membership and Party Structure

In its genetic phase, PASOK belongs to the category of 'charismatic parties'. The 'pure' charisma of Andreas Papandreou contributed decisively to the formation of a centralized organization in which the principle of 'loyalty to the leader' prevailed absolutely. Within PASOK, the freedom of action available to the leader was extremely great, greater for example than that of François Mitterrand in France, or of Felipe Gonzales in Spain, leaders with large margins of manoeuvrability within their parties.

PASOK was formed – both with regard to its 'formal' structure and the number of its members – as a mass party, a kind of party which, with the exception of the communist left, was absent from the Greek party system. The increase in the number of its organized members in the period 1974–81 took place by leaps and bounds, just as did the increase in its electoral strength. However, in the period in which PASOK approached and gained power, these increases took extreme and unprecedented dimensions (from approximately 75,000 members in 1980 to between 220,000 and 250,000 in 1984, more than two-thirds of whom became members after the victory in 1981). The expectations of 'individual gains' seem to have influenced this 'invasion' of new members to a significant degree, while the 'huge public sector was recruiting exclusively from within the Movement's ranks' (Spourdalakis, 1988, p. 249). The dynamic of the recruitment of this period gives PASOK the character of a charismatic–clientelistic mass party. In the 1988–93 period, one of tremendous political and ethical crises within PASOK, and also a period of its return to the official opposition, the PASOK membership decreased dramatically. The observed recovery in 1992 which is connected chronologically, as is that of the 1980s, with the return to government, falls far short of the peak at the beginning of the 1980s. The generalized crisis of reliability of the Greek parties, the weakness of the socialists in providing a convincing and socially-oriented economic policy, in addition to the fiscal crisis of the state, explain this development (Table 8.1).

The basic organizational units of the party are the local sections, the workplace sections and the local branch sections (relative to the same branch of economic activity). The most important intermediate party structures are the Departmental Committees and the Departmental Council at the level of

Table 8.1   PASOK membership, 1974–96

1974–5	8,000	1987	220,000
1977 (Early)	17,426		
1977 (July)	27,000	1991	97,880
1980	75,000	1993	112,088
1981	110,000	1994	156,868
1982	140,000	1995	155,642
1983	200,000	1996	155,642*
1984	220,000		

Note: * In 1996, there was no renewal of card-holding membership.
Sources: 1974–80–see Achimastos, M., 'Le mouvement socialiste panhellenique et l'implantation de l'idéologie populiste dans un régime pluraliste', in Lazar, M., *La Gauche, en Europe depuis 1945* (Paris: PUF 1996); 1981–7–see Sotiropoulos (1996, pp. 63, 65); 1991–5: Organizational Office of PASOK.

the *Nomos* (county). The Departmental Council meets twice a year. It is constituted, among others, of (1) the Co-ordination Committees of each Section of the *Nomos*; (2) the members of the Departmental Committees of both the Party and its youth Organization; (3) the members of the Central Committee as well as those MPs who come from the Department. The National Congress is held once every three years. The party president and the Central Committee (150 members) are selected by a secret vote cast by the member's representatives at the National Congress. The Central Committee elects the party Secretary and the Executive Bureau composed of nineteen members (including the secretary and the party president).

The selection of MPs is carried out through preliminary elections in all sections at electoral – constituency level and usually is approved, with few exceptions, by the Central Committee.

Institutionalization of the Organization

If the charismatic leader contributed to the formation of PASOK as a mass party, at the same time, he hindered the development and the culmination of the mass characteristics of the party. The unrestricted power of Andreas Papandreou hampered the formation of a hierarchical party structure within which the 'internal leaders' and the lower ranks could limit, in a real way, the strength of power of the party 'Centre'. The recruitment of élites, the opportunity structure for the 'ambitious members', definitely relied absolutely upon the centre. It is characteristic that the first congress of PASOK took place as late as 1984, ten years after the founding of the party, and that in twenty-three years PASOK held only four congresses (1984, 1990, 1994, 1996).

The parties with very autonomous leaders, with an 'anaemic' bureaucracy and a limited role of the party base, are often more flexible, have quicker 'reflexes', adjust better to new conjunctures – provide, in other words, greater tactical and strategic flexibility. The case of PASOK perfectly illustrates the above tendency. The great autonomy and freedom of action of Andreas Papandreou, combined with the absence of effective equilibrating and controlling mechanisms, both within and without the organization (for example, trade unions), contributed decisively to the successful process during the 1980s of the significant and 'abrupt' programmatic and ideological shift of the party towards moderation (acceptance of the EEC, non-withdrawal from NATO, maintenance of the American bases, the policy of 'competitive austerity' in the period 1985–7). A more rigidly mass and collectively functioning organization would have had difficulty undertaking this shift with such speed and ease.

The strength of the 'power of one' began to be moderated only after the illness of Andreas Papandreou (1988). During the 1988–95 period, the functioning of the organization became by necessity more collective, the role of the leadership group surrounding Papandreou, in whatever concerned the management and the everyday direction of the organization, became more autonomous, the internal questioning stronger. The formation of an 'ordinary' administration gradually liberated from the leader – functionally but not, however, politically – performed under the Papandreaou's shadow and did not of course question his solid primacy. Nevertheless, the total overlap of the leader's image and party identity, *sine qua non* of charismatic power, had unquestionably been restricted.

The election (January 1996) of Kostas Simitis, leader of the modernizing wing of PASOK and opponent of Andreas Papandreou, as prime minister by the parliamentary caucus (in place of the seriously ill Papandreou), was the starting point for the overturning of internal party relations. It led to the election of Simitis as president of the party at the Fourth Congress (July 1996), only a few days after Papandreou's death. The intense and passionate but democratic confrontation over succession between the 'modernizing' and the 'traditional' factions during the Fourth Congress symbolically 'liberated' the organization from its past. The 'age of Simitis' marks a shift in the organizational tradition of PASOK. The end of the cult of leadership, the legitimization of internal dissent and the logic of the majority and of the minority shape the new organizational culture of the party. The party's executive bodies function more collectively. The same holds true, at the governmental level, for the Ministerial Council (the cabinet) and the various collective governmental organs, the role of which in a system of 'prime minister-centrism' has obviously been strengthened. In addition, the victory of PASOK in the elections of September 1996, after a catch-all leader-focused electoral strategy, contributed to the stabilization of the new internal 'power bloc' of the party. PASOK now appears to belong to those charismatic parties which have successfully completed the difficult process of the routinization of charisma and the subsequent institutionalization which it entails.

Sociology of the Electorate and Electoral Performance

The large and successive waves of increase in the strength of PASOK (13.58 per cent in 1974, 25.34 per cent in 1977, 48.07 per cent in 1981) are due in large part to its ability to gradually attract a significant portion of the old Centre Union vote. This justifiably strengthened the view that PASOK was a new party, built however on the old centre terrain, 'the true reincarnation of the old centre' (Mavrogordatos, in Clogg, 1983, p. 79).

In 1981, the year of the triumphant rise of PASOK to power, the genuinely amazing geographical balance of influence of the party and the remarkably strong 'interclassist' nature of its electorate appeared to be, for a majority of analysts, the expression of a 'spectacular catch-allism'. However, this was in part an artefact, related to the doubtful 'operationalization' of definitions of the socio–economic groups on the part of the research institutes of public opinion. In 1981, in the municipalities and surrounding areas of Athens and Piraeus, the largest urban centre of the country, one can clearly determine three levels of PASOK's strength, which were indicative of the class logic which governed its electoral dynamic. The lowest level of strength is found in the more bourgeois districts and suburbs (the influence of PASOK is significantly lower than the national average), the middle level constitutes the *petit bourgeois* districts and suburbs, (its influence approximates the national average) while the highest level of strength is found in the working-class/popular districts (where the influence of PASOK, despite the strong competition of the communist Left, unambiguously exceeds the national average, see Mavris, 1997). PASOK of 1981 was unquestionably a particularly disparate electoral coalition with a large, by European standards, impact on the swelling traditional *petit bourgeois* class and on the extensive agricultural sector. In this sense, it was clearly more catch-all than the parties of the social-democratic type. However, its social penetration was not uniform and indistinguishable along class lines. It differed significantly from that of the old Centre Union: to some degree, PASOK built its original penetration upon the electoral body of the centre, but this penetration was, on the one hand of a more popular nature and, on the other, extended itself slowly but surely in the historical areas of influence of the communist left.

This so-called 'catch-allism' gradually declined in the 1980s. The structure of votes after 1985 clearly became more classbased. PASOK declined significantly among the higher social strata (this reached a peak in the 1988–9 period). These strata turned towards New Democracy, the conservative party with a more centre–right ideological orientation. PASOK maintained its influence among the lower social groups (within which the influence of the Communist Party is also high), while in the politically uncertain middle classes it displayed significant losses. It is characteristic that the relationship between bourgeois and working-class/popular suburbs was transformed from less than 60:100 in 1981 to less than 40:100 in 1989. At the same time, PASOK held out to a greater degree in the agricultural areas than in the urban centres. In the electoral results of 1989, 1990, 1993 and 1996, the penetration of PASOK – impressive for a socialist party – was larger in the agricultural areas. PASOK, at the end of the 1980s, was particularly weak among the higher social strata, weakened among the middle strata, of limited influence among the intellectuals. It was a people's party, a heterogeneous multi-class 'movement' of which its sources of electoral strength corresponded to a great degree to the Greece of the 'non-privileged' which the programmes of PASOK so insistently appealed to. This kind of multi-class social impact is often considered as a demonstration of and a dimension of the populist nature of the party.

It is worth noting that after 1984 the increased popular rooting of PASOK was accompanied by the most significant strengthening of its position in local government (particularly among the working-class constituencies) and in the unions, where it imposed itself through PASKE as the strong pole within the union movement. Indeed, throughout the 1970s and 1980s, PASOK succeeded in constructing a powerful union organization within an organizationally united, yet politically fragmented, trade union movement (in Greece every organized interest down to the smallest has become a mini-replica of parliament and a real arena of party competition). PASKE maintains close ties with PASOK and, despite a certain autonomy from it, is largely controlled by the party. This local government and union rooting not only gives a greater organizational and sociological depth to PASOK's influence, but it delineates more clearly the distance which separates it from the centrist tradition.

The electoral results of 1993 (46.88 per cent) which brought PASOK once again to power show that it remained very strong among the farmers, the traditional *petty bourgeoisie* and of course among wage-earners. Its penetration reached a peak among those employed in the public sector (a tendency which appears in all the countries of Europe, but which is strengthened in Greece by the extensive clientelistic mechanisms of PASOK) and among the less well trained, lower-paid working-class and employee strata of the private sector, as well as the low-income pensioners (Table 8.2).

Table 8.2   Social penetration of PASOK, 1993–6

Occupation	1993	1996
Farmers	46.6	38.3
Merchants, craftsmen and independent employees	48.0	38.5
Self-employed	36.4	36.2
Public sector wage-earners (primary and high school)	58.0	53.7
Public sector wage-earners (University educated)	48.8	46.1
Private sector wage-earners (primary, high-school education)	51.0	43.2
Private sector wage-earners (College educated)	37.1	35.1
Unemployed	46.0	38.9
Students	36.7	37.0
Housewives	47.2	41.5
Pensioners (at most, primary school)	54.3	49.0
Pensioners (some high school education and more)	40.6	36.2
National percentage	46.88	41.49

Note:
* *For 1993: Exit Poll MEGA-BVA Opinion. Unpublished data.*
*Source*s: For 1996, Exit Poll MEGA-BVA Opinion in Nikolakopoulos, E., ' "Decided" and "Undecided": The Contribution of Exit Polls in the Analysis of the Vote', *Greek Review of Political Science*, 9 (April 1997, p. 206).

PASOK's victorious electoral results of 1996 marked a turning point in the dynamic of its social penetration. The decrease in its influence relative to 1993 was clearly greater among the lower-wage-earning categories in both the public and the private sector, among the farmers and the traditional *petty bourgeoisie* class. Its losses were in contrast very small among the self-employed and the well educated, in particular among those upper-echelon wage-earners in the public and private sectors. At the same time, the impact of PASOK increased significantly in the more bourgeois districts and suburbs (despite the fall of 5.39 per cent of its national impact relative to 1993), decreased in the petit bourgeois areas and shrank intensely in the working-class and popular areas. The strict policy of austerity of the period following 1993, the retreat of Andreas Papandreou and the creation of the Democratic Social Movement by D. Tsovolas (the former minister of the Economy under PASOK), a populist party which displayed its greatest popularity in the working-class neighbourhoods and suburbs, explain this development. The 'European pragmatism' of PASOK under the leadership of Papandreou from 1993, and more markedly from 1996 under the leadership of the modernizer Simitis, improved the credibility and the appeal of the party among the higher social strata but alienated a portion of the poor and non-privileged strata of the urban areas (Table 8.3).

Table 8.3 PASOK electoral performance, 1974–96

Year	(%)	Seats (total 300)
1974	13.58	12
1977	25.33	93
1981	48.07	172
1985	45.82	161
1989 (Jun.)	39.13	125
1989 (Nov.)	40.67	128
1990	38.61	123
1993	46.88	170
1996	41.49	162

Source: Compiled from official statistics.

In short, PASOK, from its foundation until the present day, has been a party of high 'catch-allism', more so than the social democratic parties of western Europe. This catch-all texture weakened after 1981. In the period 1985–93, PASOK became a multi-class popular party: very strong among the 'non-privileged' wage-earning working-class and employee strata of the cities, strong among the extensive agricultural class and in the traditional *petty bourgeoisie* class, relatively weak among the higher social strata. 1996 marked a turning point in the structure of the social appeal of PASOK, as the 'popular' face of the movement weakened.

GOVERNMENT ACHIEVEMENT AND CURRENT POLICIES

On civil rights ground, PASOK took a series of measures to modernize and democratize public life and civil society which became accepted, or at least not seriously questioned, by all the political forces in the country. These measures of political modernization either brought an end to the last remaining effects of the civil war (1946–9) and of 'limited democracy' (1949–67) or were measures of political and cultural liberalism which the modernized but always conservative right was not in a position to pursue in depth.

Most notably, the PASOK took laws recognizing the communist Resistance against the forces of the Axis and favouring the repatriation of political refugees, in addition to the abolition of laws relating to the civil war climate. The police and the army, fundamental institutions of the pre-dictatorial regime which characterized political and cultural extreme conservatism, were modernized and the systematic exclusion of communists and fellow-travellers from public administration posts (a consequence of the civil war) was stopped. In the same vein, the running of higher education was democratized and the trade unions were granted new rights. Civil marriage was institutionalized and new legislation stating the equality between men and women and the 'liberalization' of divorce procedures was introduced.

These measures of political democratization and cultural liberalism allowed PASOK, particularly during its first four years of government (1981–5), to establish itself as a modernizing and democratizing force within Greek society. The winds of democratic rejuvenation which were blowing in the country stabilized PASOK electorally and allowed it to politically exploit the anti-right 'syndrome' of a large part of Greek society.

Secondly, on economic grounds, PASOK, during the period 1981–3, and in a more hesitant and prudent fashion during the period 1984–85, followed an expansionist Keynesian-type policy which was accompanied by measures to strengthen the institutions of the welfare state (wage and pension increases, price controls, the establishment of the National Health System in 1983). These policies strengthened the 'social profile' of PASOK, and in combination with the inflow of funds from the EEC, and with the creation of an extensive clientelistic network, stabilized the hold of the party on the popular strata, shaping an extensive 'belonging' vote. This facilitated its electoral dominance in the elections of 1985. Nevertheless, the unfavourable economic conjuncture and the uncontrolled remittances, which enlarged the clientelistic nature of the Greek state, decisively undermined PASOK's social ambitions. Confronting the large public deficit and the lack of competitiveness of the Greek economy, PASOK was obligated to adopt a severe restrictive austerity policy, which led to an intense confrontation with the unions. However, PASOK's economic policy changed once again in the light of the elections of 1989: during the 1988–9 period, PASOK undertook a lax economic and fiscal policy which quickly led the fiscal deficits to an explosion.

The 'macroeconomic populism' of PASOK between 1981 and 1985 and between 1988 and 1989 was a series of policies which, at an unfavourable economic conjuncture, combined extensive redistributive measures of Keynesian inspiration, extensive clientelistic remittances and a lack of a taxation policy capable of increasing the income of the state through the limitation of very widespread tax evasion (which in Greece functions as a basic mechanism for the redistribution of wealth among the middle classes). In essence, during the period 1981–9, PASOK refused to make a clear choice about the intended beneficiaries of its policies. The main beneficiaries of this policy mixture were not the poor social strata, who lost in the 1985–7 period what they had gained previously. Those who benefited the most, were 'the strata that the tax man failed to reach', primarily strata which belonged to the traditional *petty bourgeoisie* and to the self-employed, including those portions of the population who benefited from the clientelistic remittances and the political favouritism, some of whom belong unquestionably to the popular strata, part of which also belongs to the 'privileged' groups of Greek society. Finally, in the pre-welfare Greek society of 1981–9, the difficult task of constructing an effective welfare state was undermined, on the one hand by the limitations of the economic conjuncture and on the other by the non-cohesive and unorthodox populist policy of the socialists.

The return of PASOK to government in 1993 under the leadership of Andreas Papandreou and the renewal of the mandate in 1996 under Simitis, marked a new phase in PASOK's policies. The goals of lowering inflation and the public deficit in order to meet the terms of the Maastricht Treaty are central, and are being pursued consistently and effectively. The governments of Papandreou (1993–5) and of Simitis (from 1996) managed to reduce the high inflation rate (from 13.7 per cent in 1993 to 5.2 per cent in 1997), to dramatically reduce the public deficit (from 14.2 per cent of GNP in 1993 to 4 per cent in 1997), to increase GNP (from –1 in 1993 to 3.5 in 1997) and to keep unemployment, which remains on an upward trend, in check (from 8.6 per cent in 1993 to 10.3 per cent in 1997). Given the above-mentioned record, the PASOK governments in the 1993–7 period are, in a technocratic sense, the most effective of all the governments of the 1974–97 period and fall short only of the Karamanlis government of the 1977–9 period.

In conclusion, PASOK has been a party without a stable course along which to navigate. During the 1974–97 period, PASOK has changed faces many times, often giving the impression of a political chameleon. The dominance of radicalism, gave way to the 'national populism' of the 1980s and the domination of European pragmatism after 1993, and primarily in 1996, under Simitis' leadership. PASOK has been a party of many faces: faces that, paradoxically, shape through their complementarity and opposition, through their succession and co-existence, a strong – and not a pallid – identity.

Select Bibliography

Clogg, R. (ed) (1983) *Greece in the 1980s*, London: Macmillan
Clogg, R. (1987) *Parties and Elections in Greece: The Search for Legitimacy*, London: Hurst.
Clogg, R. (ed). (1993) *Greece 1981–89: The Populist Decade*, New York: St Martin's Press.
Diamantopoulos, A. (1997) *Greek Political Life: The Twentieth Century*, Athens: Papazissis (in Greek).
Elefandis, A. (1991) *In the Constellation of Populism*, Athens: Politis (in Greek).
Featherstone, K. and Katsoudas, D. (1987) *Political Change in Greece*, London: Croom Helm.
Kariotis, T. (ed.) (1992) *The Greek Socialist Experiment: Papandreou's Greece 1981–89*, New York: Pella.
Mavris, G. (1997) 'The Restructuring and Reformation Tendencies in the Post Dictatorship Party System', *Greek Review of Political Science*, 9 (April 1997) (in Greek).

122   *The Panhellenic Socialist Movement*

Moschonas, G. (1994) 'The "Right–Anti-Right" Cleavage in the Post-Dictatorship Period (1974–1990)', in Demertzis, N. (ed.), *The Greek Political Culture Today*, Athens: Odysseas (in Greek).

Papadopoulos, I. (1986) *Dynamique du discours politique et conquête du pouvoir. Le cas du PASOK (1974–1981)*, Berne: Peter Lang.

Sotiropoulos, D. (1996) *Populism and Bureaucracy: The Case of Greece Under PASOK, 1981–1989*, Notre Dame and London: University of Notre Dame Press.

Spourdalakis, M. (1988) *The Rise of the Greek Socialist Party*, London: Routledge.

Spourdalakis, M. (1992) 'A Petty Bourgeois Party with a Populist Ideology and Catch-All Party Structure: PASOK', in Merkel, W. *et al.*, *Socialist Parties in Europe II: Of Class, Populars, Catch-All?*, Barcelona: ICPS.

Tzannatos, Z (ed.) (1986) *Socialism in Greece: The First Four Years*, Aldershot: Gower.

Contact Information

Address of the Party Headquarters
50 Hariliaou Trikoupi St
106 80 Athens

Tel: 301 360 9831
Fax: 301 360 6958

PASOK Web page on the Internet: http://www.hol.gr./pasok

Main Affiliated Research Institution
ISTAME (Institute of Strategic and Developmental Studies)
4 Academias Avenue
106 74, Athens

Tel: 301 363 1745–8
Fax: 301 362 5616

9 The Irish Labour Party
Michael Holmes

HISTORY

The Irish Labour Party was officially founded in 1912, when the Irish Trade Union Congress declared 'the independent representation of Labour' as an objective. However, it took some time for any party organization, policies or politicians to emerge. The party did not fully enter the electoral arena until 1920, and did not contest a general election until 1922. In these first elections in an independent Ireland, Labour came third with less than a quarter of the vote.

However, during the 1920s Labour played a disproportionately important role in establishing democratic practices. First, Labour was the *de facto* leader of the opposition between 1922 and 1927, because a number of *Teachtaí Dála* (TDs, that is members of the Irish parliament) refused to take their seats. Under the leadership of Tom Johnson, Labour helped establish the basic rules of parliamentary practice. Second, Labour played a part in facilitating the first democratic transition of power, after the abstentionist TDs formed the Fianna Fáil party (a right-of-centre nationalist party) and took their parliamentary seats in 1927. In the short term, this almost catapulted Labour into power at the head of a minority coalition. Then, when Fianna Fáil won the 1932 general election, though still five seats short of an overall majority, Labour gave it the necessary external support to form a government.

This loose alliance gradually cooled during the 1930s. In 1936, Labour made a tentative move to the left, with the introduction of a new party constitution which called for the creation of a workers' republic. Under pressure from the Church, that phrase was soon recanted. But the party's electoral fortunes did pick up, and the early 1940s were a period of considerable promise, with Labour's vote growing to 15.7 per cent in 1943. However, at that point an inter-union dispute spilled over into the party and caused a damaging split, with the break-away National Labour Party being formed.

By this time, Labour was firmly set against any further deals with Fianna Fáil, and in the post-war period it twice joined coalition governments led by Fine Gael (a right-of-centre party). This was Labour's first taste of government, but the experience also confirmed that Labour was at best the third party in the system, and reinforced the image of Fine Gael as the leading opposition party. As a consequence, Labour's vote slumped, and in 1957 it chose to stay out of coalitions (Table 9.5).

Table 9.1 Labour Party leaders in Ireland, 1922–97

1918–27	Thomas Johnson
1927–32	T. J. O'Connell
1932–60	William Norton
1960–77	Brendan Corish
1977–81	Frank Cluskey
1981–2	Michael O'Leary
1982–97	Dick Spring
1997–	Ruarí Quinn

Source: Coakley and Gallagher (1993, p. 273).

After twenty-eight years as party leader, William Norton resigned in 1960 and was replaced by Brendan Corish. The party gradually moved leftwards during the 1960s, and a number of high-profile intellectuals joined. In 1966, Labour openly declared itself to be a socialist party, and in the following year it affiliated to the Socialist International. At the same time, electoral fortunes picked up again. In the 1965 election, the party equalled its best-ever return with twenty-two TDs. The party approached the 1969 election full of confidence, talking optimistically of becoming the second largest party in the state and with the manifesto detailing what a Labour government would do. The slogan of the era was 'The Seventies will be Socialist'.

The resulting electoral setback ended hopes of a socialist break-through, and led to a reappraisal of the party's opposition to coalition. Labour returned to government on a joint platform with Fine Gael in 1973, and was to more in and out of coalition with them until the late 1980s. Under Michael O'Leary's leadership, there was a short-lived coalition in 1981–2. That was followed by a conference decision to avoid pre-electoral pacts and to rely instead on special post-election conferences to decide whether or not to join coalitions. O'Leary resigned over this decision, and was later to join Fine Gael. But the new party leader, Dick Spring, was able to persuade such a special conference to agree to another coalition with Fine Gael after the second election in 1982. Labour was eventually to pull out of that government in 1986, and the election early in the new year saw the party record its second lowest-ever percentage of the vote.

However, Spring was slowly asserting control over the party. His approach bore some fruit in 1989, with a recovery in the Labour vote. But the real break-through came in the early 1990s. The election of a former Labour senator, Mary Robinson, to the Presidency in 1990 was seen as a major boost for Labour and for Spring, who had promoted her candidacy. The party then succeeded in recording one of its best-ever election results in 1992. The vote was still slightly below its record 1922 figure, but the party won 33 seats, eleven more than its previous best performance. However, there were always fears that it would prove difficult to sustain this level of support, and at the most recent election in 1997 Labour lost almost half of its votes and seats. That defeat was followed by a disappointing result for the Labour-backed candidate in the 1997 presidential election, and Dick Spring resigned as party leader at the end of the year, with Ruarí Quinn taking over (Table 9.2).

ORGANIZATION AND PARTY PROFILE

The Labour Party's organizational structure is based on a system of branch membership, and the party currently has around 450 branches. Each branch is entitled to send delegates to party conferences, which are usually held on an annual basis and at two-year intervals at a maximum. Delegates can also be nominated by affiliated trade unions and by constituency and regional divisions of the party. The party constitution gives Conference 'ultimate control of the policies, organization and administrative affairs of the Party'. In practice, the conference can debate and approve party policy, but this is largely a ratificatory process. In addition, it elects delegates to the party's General Council, its Executive Committee and its specialist committees. Conference also elects the Party Chairperson, Deputy Chairperson and Financial Secretary.

The General Council and Executive Committee both came into being in 1991 (prior to that, an Administrative Council fulfilled both roles). The General Council meets at least three times a year, and is responsible for overseeing party activities between conferences. It also appoints the party's Secretary and Deputy Secretary, who are responsible for the party's administrative affairs. It is made up of all members of the Executive Council,

Table 9.2   Labour Party electoral performance in Ireland, 1948–1997

Year	Votes (%)	Seats	Year	Votes (%)	Seats
1948	8.7	14	1977	11.6	17
1951	11.4	16	1981	9.9	15
1954	12.1	19	1982a	9.1	15
1957	9.1	12	1982b	9.4	16
1961	11.6	16	1987	6.4	12
1965	15.4	22	1989	9.5	15
1969	17.0	18	1992	19.3	33
1973	13.7	19	1997	10.4	17

Source: Coakley and Gallagher (1993, pp. 265–6).

fifteen delegates elected by Conference, six delegates from the Parliamentary Party, and delegates from specialist committees. In addition, there is provision to co-opt additional members. The Executive Committee is responsible for the day-to-day running of the party. It consists of five party officers (the leader, deputy leader, chairperson, vice-chairperson and financial secretary) and a further seven delegates appointed by Conference. In addition, there are some non-voting members.

On the electoral side, the Parliamentary Labour Party consists of all Labour Dáil (lower house of Parliament) deputies, senators and MEPs. The parliamentary party and General Council elect the party leader and deputy leader from amongst the party's TDs. The party leader chooses spokespersons, who are usually members of the parliamentary party, and policy initiation and formulation is carried out by the spokespersons in consultation with the leader and the General Council. Candidates for election are nominated by agreement amongst all branches in the relevant constituency, subject to the approval of party headquarters.

Membership of the party currently stands at around 7,000. It was for a long time dominated by union officials, even though the formal link between the party and the unions had been severed in 1930. The 1960s saw a growth in the number of Labour members from professional backgrounds. Labour also allows for corporate membership of trade unions. In 1961 there were twelve affiliated unions; these did not include the three largest unions, but these affiliated by 1970, when there were 160,000 members affiliated to the Labour Party through the unions. In 1987, there were a total of seventeen unions affiliated to Labour, accounting for 175,000 members, and in 1997 there were ten. However, the unions have been a declining influence in the party. They do not have any formal role in selecting candidates, nor do they exercise a block vote at Conference (Table 9.3).

Labour's support has been concentrated in constituencies in Leinster and Munster, and it has rarely achieved any kind of presence in the Connacht–Ulster region. Its support in most constituencies has been built around the main town centres. However, Labour's support in the main urban centre in Ireland, Dublin, has been very volatile. Its vote has fallen as low as 3.6 per cent there (in 1933), and on three occasions the party has failed to win any seats at all in the capital. Recently, its support in Dublin has been more stable. It has twice polled over a quarter of the votes in Dublin, and in 1992 it even succeeded in surpassing Fine Gael to become the second largest party in the capital.

Generally, Labour's support has tended to come from skilled and unskilled working-class voters. But although most Labour voters are working class, most working-class voters are not Labour supporters. Instead, Fianna Fáil has consistently attracted more support from this section of the population, and even Fine Gael has on occasion surpassed Labour's working-class

Table 9.3 Number of Labour Party branches (a) and individual members (b) in Ireland, 1961–95

Year	(a)	(b)	Year	(a)	(b)	Year	(a)	(b)
1961	400	na	1974	499	4,961	1985	486	6,200
1964	248	na	1975	497	4,100	1986	486	6,300
1965	289	na	1976	538	4,800	1987	486	6,750
1966	357	na	1977	582	4,500	1988	490	7,760
1967	457	na	1978	490	4,500	1989	467	6,720
1968	477	na	1979	502	5,100	1990	480	7,500
1969	501	na	1980	510	5,600	1991	483	7,400
1970	479	na	1981	508	5,375	1992	500	10,000
1971	450	na	1982	470	5,230	1993	500	10,000
1972	436	na	1983	504	5,377	1994	450	7,000
1973	480	na	1984	497	5,860	1995	450	7,000

Note: na = not available.
Sources: Mair (1987, pp. 104, 105); *Irish Political Studies*, 1986–96, data sections.

vote. Middle-class support for Labour has occasionally boomed, as in 1992, but it has never outpolled Fianna Fáil or Fine Gael among these voters. Finally, Labour has never polled well among the farming community. However, Irish society is currently undergoing a major transformation. The country is becoming more urbanized and industrialized and agriculture is declining, changes which could benefit Labour.

Labour is clearly the dominant left-wing party in Ireland. Indeed, for long passages of time it has been the only party of any note. Only two significant challenges to its position have occurred. In 1943, five Labour TDs left the party to form the National Labour Party. This was a right-wing split, caused by a trade union dispute. National Labour contested two elections, in 1944 and 1948, before merging back into the Labour Party in 1950. The major contemporary challenge from the left emerged in the 1980s. The Workers' Party grew out of extreme nationalist origins, then developed as a kind of neo-communist party, before achieving a parliamentary breakthrough in 1981. It grew steadily through the 1980s, and in 1989 it succeeded in out-polling Labour in Dublin. In 1992 the party was reformed as Democratic Left (DL). Although policy differences have gradually declined as DL evolved towards a democratic socialist position, electoral competition and personal antipathies created a strained relationship with Labour. But the inclusion of DL in a coalition government with Labour and Fine Gael in 1994 led to better relations and even talk of a possible merger. In addition, some other left-wing parties and independent candidates have occasionally won Dáil seats, but they have never made a significant addition to the overall left-wing vote or parliamentary presence (Table 9.4).

The Irish Labour Party

Table 9.4 Parliamentary representation of other left-wing parties in the
Republic of Ireland, 1927–97

	Election	Votes (%)	seats
Irish Workers' League	1927	1.1	1
National Labour Party	1944	2.7	4
	1948	2.8	5
National Progressive Democrats	1961	1.0	2
Socialist Labour Party	1981	0.4	1
Democratic Socialist Party	1981	0.4	1
	1982*	0.4	1
	1982	0.4	0
	1987	0.4	1
	1989	0.6	1
Workers' Party	1973	1.1	0
	1977	1.7	0
	1981	1.7	1
	1982*	2.2	3
	1982	3.3	2
	1987	3.8	4
	1989	5.0	7
	1992	0.7	0
	1997	0.4	0
Democratic Left	1992	2.8	4*
	1997	2.5	4
Socialist Party	1997	0.7	1

* Democratic Left subsequently won two more seats in by-elections.
Source: Sinnott (1995, pp. 302–5).

GOVERNMENT ACHIEVEMENTS AND CURRENT POLICIES

Because of its marginal position in Irish politics, Labour's only participation
in government has been as a junior partner in coalitions (Table 9.5). Its first
taste of governmental power came in 1948, when a multi-party coalition led
by Fine Gael ended a spell of sixteen years uninterrupted Fianna Fáil rule.
Labour held two cabinet posts, the ministries of Local Government and of
Social Welfare (the National Labour Party held the ministry of Posts and
Telegraphs). The coalition was held together more by opposition to Fianna
Fáil than by any coherent common programme. The Labour Party did
succeed in instigating a major public housing drive, but was silent on the
main issue of the day, a proposal for a state-supported health scheme for

Table 9.5   Labour Party participation in government in Ireland, 1948–97

	Coalition partners	Taoiseach (Prime Minister)	Tánaiste (deputy Prime Minister)	Labour Party cabinet seats
1948–51	FG,[1] CnaT, CnaP, NLP	Costello (FG)	Norton (LP)	2/13*
1954–7	FG, CnaT, Inds	Costello (FG)	Norton (LP)	4/13
1973–7	FG	Cosgrave (FG)	Corish (LP)	5/15
1981–2	FG	Fitzgerald (FG)	O'Leary (LP)	4/15
1982–7	FG	Fitzgerald (FG)	Spring (LP)	4/15
1992–4	FF	Reynolds (FF)	Spring (LP)	6/15
1994–7	FG, DL	Bruton (FG)	Spring (LP)	7/15

[1] See pp. xiv ff for party acronyms.
Inds = Independents.
* National Labour Party also held one cabinet seat.
Source: Coakley and Gallagher (1993, p. 272).

mothers, which was bitterly opposed by the Catholic Church, the issue that eventually brought down the coalition.

Labour returned to power in 1954, again as the junior partner in a coalition. On this occasion, they were given responsibility for four cabinet posts: Social Welfare, Posts and Telegraphs, Industry and Commerce and Justice. However, the coalition was disastrous for Labour. A harsh austerity budget was introduced in 1956 to deal with a worsening economic situation, and faced with growing unemployment, stagnation of growth and increasingly critical trade unions, Labour made very little impact, and the experience persuaded the party to shun coalitions throughout the following decade.

Their failure to achieve an electoral break-through finally drew them back into coalition in 1973, again with Fine Gael. Labour took the posts of Social Welfare, Posts and Telegraphs, Industry and Commerce, Local Government and Labour. Its record in office was mixed. It again achieved an improvement in the provision of housing, and could also point to increased social welfare expenditure and new labour legislation. Against that, the most noticeable failure was in relation to health, where a Labour-backed scheme to legalize contraception in Ireland was defeated in remarkable circumstances when the Fine Gael Taoiseach and another Fine Gael minister both voted against the bill. However, in the context of economic turmoil due to the oil crisis and political turmoil due to the worsening situation in Northern Ireland, the government was reasonably successful.

The short-lived minority coalition of 1981–2 had little time to achieve anything, and the dreadful state of the economy would have made it difficult for Labour to have pushed their agenda. This was apparent when Labour and Fine Gael returned to power later in 1982, Labour held four cabinet posts: Health and Social Welfare, Labour, Environment and Energy. The Irish economy during the period of the 1982–6 coalition was suffering from serious problems as a result of excessive public exchequer borrowing. This meant that Labour had to confine itself to cushioning the worst blows arising from government cutbacks. As the coalition wore on, the strains grew increasingly pronounced, and ultimately Labour pulled out in protest at yet another budget designed to control public expenditure.

By the time Labour returned to power, in 1992, circumstances had changed. Economically, the worst of the crisis in public finances had been passed, and the economy was starting to grow. Politically, Labour had just won a spectacular victory, more than doubling their vote and seats. This left Spring as the effective 'kingmaker' in subsequent coalition talks, and after preliminary talks with Fine Gael broke down, Labour negotiated an arrangement with Fianna Fáil. This placed a strong emphasis on job creation, on limiting privatization of industries, and on a number of social reforms. Labour took six ministries, including for the first time ever Foreign Affairs. The other posts were the new ministry of Enterprise and Employment, Education, Health, Arts and Culture, and Equality and Law Reform.

All the signs were that this Fianna Fáil–Labour coalition would prove stable and effective. However, two years into its term of office, it collapsed when Fianna Fáil attempted to push through a controversial appointment for Attorney General. Efforts to achieve a reconciliation failed, but for the first time in Irish history the consequence was not an election. Instead, Labour succeeded in putting together an alternative coalition deal, this time with Fine Gael and Democratic Left, which took office in December 1994. There were some significant changes in Labour's cabinet portfolios as a result. They kept Foreign Affairs, Education, Arts and Culture and Equality and Law Reform. The new posts were Environment, and for the first time ever, Finance. However, despite going in to the 1997 election at a time when the Irish economy was expanding rapidly, Labour suffered as a result of public opposition to their earlier coalition arrangement with Fianna Fáil.

Labour's experience in government underlines the fact that it is a conservative, reformist party which has never had to go through any Bad Godesberg-style ideological conversion. Labour's overall approach to the economy has stressed planning and government intervention. However, it has not advocated widespread nationalisation, and its basic principles include explicit support for an open, mixed economy. The emphasis has been on helping the working class through improved welfare provisions, labour laws and state investment. On industrial relations, its strong trade union origins have made the party a firm advocate of social partnership, and it has supported a series of pay agreements between unions, employers and government.

On social policy, Labour for a long time reflected the conservatism of Irish society and the male-dominated world of the trade unions. It was not until the shift to the left in the 1960s that the party began to adopt a more liberal stance. Even then, efforts in the 1960s to introduce contraception and divorce met with some resistance within the party. It was not until later decades that Labour became more responsive to such concerns, and in this regard the party was really following the shift that had already taken place in public attitudes.

Labour had very few international links until the late 1960s. It supported Irish neutrality during the Second World War, and remains strongly in favour of neutrality. Labour initially opposed Irish membership of the European Community, and led the campaign for a 'No' vote in Ireland's referendum on membership in 1972. However, the referendum revealed overwhelming popular support for membership, and Labour rapidly dropped its opposition. It supported ratification of the Maastricht Treaty when it was put to a referendum in 1992. On Northern Ireland, Labour has traditionally been a constitutional nationalist party, though a less assertive one than Fianna Fáil. In recent years, in common with most Irish parties, its Northern Irish policy has become increasingly reconciliatory.

Select Bibliography

Chubb, B. (1992) *The Government and Politics of Ireland*, 3rd edn, Harlow: Longman.

Coakley, J. and Gallagher, M. (eds) (1993) *Politics in the Republic of Ireland*, 2nd edn, Limerick and Dublin: PSAI Press and Folens.

Collins, S. (1993) *Spring and the Labour Story*, Dublin: The O'Brien Press.

Gallagher, M. (1982) *The Irish Labour Party in Transition, 1957–82*, Manchester: Manchester University Press.

Gallagher, M. (1985) *Political Parties in the Republic of Ireland*, Manchester: Manchester University Press.

Holmes, M. (1996) 'Irish political parties and the EU', in Gaffney, J. (ed.), *Political Parties and the European Union*, London: Routledge.

Horgan, J. (1986) *Labour: the Price of Power*, Dublin: Gill & Macmillan.

Mair, P. (1987) *The Changing Irish Party System: Organization, Ideology and Electoral Competition*, London: Pinter.

Sinnott, R. (1995) *Irish Voters Decide: Voting Behaviour in Elections and Referendums Since 1918*, Manchester and New York, Manchester University Press.

Contact Information

Address of Headquarters:
17 Ely Place,
Dublin 2,   Tel: 353 1 661 26 15
Ireland.   Fax: 353 1 661 26 40

Web page on the Internet: www.labour.ie

10 The Italian Democrats of the Left*
Stefano Guzzini

HISTORY

Foreword

With just two major parties, a social-democratic *Democratici di Sinistra* (Democrats of the Left – DS) and a smaller (Euro) communist *Partito di Rifondazione Comunista* (Party of the Communist Refoundation – PRC), the political landscape of the Italian left looks more familiar to the outsider today than ever before. True, there had been two parties before. Yet, unique in western Europe, the *Partito Comunista Italiano* (Italian Communist Party – PCI) often appealed to twice as many voters as the *Partito Socialista Italiano* (Italian Socialist Party – PSI). Moreover, neither was initially a member of the Socialist International. Here Italy was represented by a splinter group of the PSI, the *Partito Social-Democratico Italiano* (Italian Social Democratic Party – PSDI) which lacked some of the major attributes of social-democratic parties in Western Europe (e.g. privileged link to trade unions, mass organizations).

When the party landscape was rearranged by the heavy hand of Italian magistrates investigating on *Tangentopoli* ('bribesville'), the PSI and PSDI collapsed under the weight of their leaders' accumulated guilt of corruption and illegal party finance. Hence, neither the PSI or the PSDI were the precursors of the DS, nor (the majority of) the PCI the forerunner of the PRC. Instead, the two new parties emerged from a schism within the PCI in 1991.

After only seven years of existence, DS can therefore not be understood without its roots within the PCI. A succinct history of the Italian left will be followed by an analysis of the reasons which pushed the PCI to turn into the DS. These reasons are necessary to understand the organizational and ideological bases of the DS's very identity within the 1998 governmental coalition.

A Short History of the Italian Left

In the 1880s, socialist ideas became prominent among the landless labourers of the Po Valley and the working class in the newly industrialized areas of the

Italian North-West. 1882 saw the first socialist Member of Parliament (from Ravenna). In 1892 several small parties merged in what was to become the PSI in 1895.

Similar to other socialist parties in Western Europe at the time, the PSI was, despite periodical persecution, increasing its share of votes. In particular in its heartland, the Po Valley, a socio–political sub-culture developed which was centred around the 'houses of the people' and a network of associations and co-operatives. Before the First World War, the PSI became the largest Italian party in Parliament, a success repeated after the war, when it won 32.4 per cent of the vote in the 1919 elections.

In 1921 the party's executive decided to join the Third International. This decision was overturned during the party congress of Livorno. The minority group left and founded the PCI whose most famous inter-war representative, and party leader from 1922–4, was Antonio Gramsci, imprisoned in 1924 where he died in 1937. The PCI was mainly a party of cadres with as yet little hold over large parts of the territory. Both socialists and communists were persecuted under fascism, and joined together in a 'pact of unity of action' in the mid-1930s, a pact renewed during the war.

It was only its crucial role in the Resistance movement that gave the PCI a greater status and allowed it to rise to an importance comparable with the PSI. In 1944, its party secretary Palmiro Togliatti, vice-president of the Comintern, returned from Moscow and proclaimed a new strategy of the PCI at the *svolta di Salerno* (the 'turn taken at Salerno'). The PCI would use its recent grass-roots experience and territorial presence to change from a party of cadres into a mass party. In 1946, the PSI scored for the last time more than the PCI (20 per cent to 18.9 per cent).

Both parties were member of the first post-war Italian governments led by Christian Democrats (*Democrazia Cristiana* – DC), most prominently by Alcide de Gasperi. But the division of Europe was to make this coalition government short-lived. A minority of the PSI which sought more independence from the communists, and which received massive US support split, and in January 1947 founded the *Partito Socialista dei Lavoratori Italiani* (Socialist Party of the Italian Workers – PSLI – in 1952 to become the PSDI). The PSLI took a third of the PSI membership and 40 per cent of its delegates with it. In May 1947, as a condition for obtaining Marshall Aid, both the communist and socialist members of the government were ousted. The PCI and the PSI made an electoral alliance for the decisive 1948 elections in which they suffered an important defeat, getting together only 31 per cent of the vote. The DC had its highest vote ever (48.5 per cent) and formed a coalition government, including the PSLI which was openly in favour of the Marshall Plan.

The elections of 1948 were historically significant because they paved the way for uninterrupted DC rule until 1994. It divided Italy in two camps.

whose trenches were joined by the Vatican when it declared in 1949 to excommunicate anyone who joined the PCI or voted for it. Moreover, with these elections the PCI took the upper hand on the left for the rest of the post-war period. Despite these adverse trends, the PSI stuck to its strategy of alliance (*frontismo*), starting to take its distance from the PCI only when it was reduced to 12.8 per cent in the elections of 1953. The two parties thereafter pursued different paths.

The PSI's electoral inferiority, but also the by then weaker organization at the grass-roots level as compared to the PCI, made its leadership increasingly look for an alliance with the centre where the DC was in need of junior coalition partners. The PSI therefore changed its international reference. In 1956, the socialist leader Pietro Nenni condemned the Soviet intervention in Hungary and by the end of the decade the PSI had accepted NATO membership. In 1962 it gave external support to the DC-run government, before eventually joining the first centre–left government in Italian history in 1963. It tried to strengthen its position in the coalition through a merger with the much smaller PSDI in 1966 which proved unsuccessful and disintegrated again in 1969. By the early 1970s the formerly greatest party of the left had plunged under 10 per cent, was ideologically more divided than ever and disoriented. In 1974, it withdrew from government.

Togliatti's strategy to keep the PCI fairly close to the Cominform line barely survived his death in 1964. During his tenure, the PCI proposed its own path to socialism – but only after it had become official policy of the USSR, that is, when Khrushchev accepted Tito's national way to socialism. Similarly, Togliatti's PCI did not condemn the Soviet intervention in Hungary in 1956. By the end of the 1960s, the PCI under Luigi Longo took more distance from the USSR when it condemned the Soviet crushing of the 'Prague Spring' in 1968 – although still not enough for part of its intellectual left who asked also for more internal democracy and were expelled from the party in 1969 (*il Manifesto*).

Supporter of a 'Third Path' between Soviet communism and capitalism, the PCI followed with great interest the experiments of the 'Prague Spring' and later of Allende's Chile. After Pinochet's coup in 1973, the new party secretary Enrico Berlinguer argued in a series of articles for a change of strategy. Instead of looking for a left-wing majority whose policies would be blocked at all levels, the PCI should seek an alliance with the DC, the so-called *compromesso storico* (historical compromise). Another inspiration for this strategy might have been the *große Koalition* of the SPD and the CDU/CSU in Germany between 1966 and 1969 which successfully paved the way for the first post-war SPD-led government in 1969 (see Chapter 6).

The PCI was ideologically and electorally ready for such a gamble, moving towards a national consensus. It had accepted the European Union – indeed, one of the Union's architects, Alfredo Spinelli, was elected on a PCI ticket.

In 1974, the PCI accepted NATO. Moreover, whereas the DC vote was steadily, if slowly, decreasing, the PCI triumphed with 34.4 per cent of the vote in the national elections of 1976 – falling just short of the DC vote. Hence, the PCI started to collaborate with a DC opened up to the left by its secretary Aldo Moro. The PCI first abstained on the formation of the Andreotti government, and then in 1978 went a step further by voting in favour of another Andreotti government. But it cut a bad deal. International pressure on the Italian government – for instance, at the 1976 Group of Seven (G-7) meeting where West German Chancellor Helmut Schmidt, on behalf of the group, declared that a government with the PCI would constitute a break with NATO – prevented the PCI gaining any executive posts. This produced an impossible situation as the PCI was held responsible for a situation it did not directly control. The PCI withdrew its government support in 1979 and suffered a heavy electoral defeat in the following elections. The historical compromise was abandoned in 1980.

ORGANIZATION AND PARTY PROFILE

The Crisis of the PCI and the Origins of the PDS

The causes which led the PCI to abandon its communist identity in 1991 can be found in the increasing mismatch between, on the one hand, its organizational structure, as well as its political strategy and programme, and on the other, the socio–economic transformations which swept over Italy in the previous decades. The PCI was at pains to balance its class base and regional concentration and its aim to become a party with possible governmental responsibilities. In the end, class identity and ideological support had to go, as well as party name and symbol.

The Falling Rate of PCI Membership
In general, the PCI was able, until the 1980s at least, to recruit many more members than any other party in Italy. Even in its worst years, as for instance in 1957, it recruited nearly 100,000 new members – that is, over 5 per cent of recruitment rate in relation to its total membership. At the same time, the PCI lost a relatively high number of members per year. In other words, the party has been an obligatory point of passage for many: if one adds yearly recruits to the initial membership in 1947, more than 7.6 million people have of some time been members of the party (This figure is, however, subject to caution, because some members are counted several times, having left and, after some years of non-membership, joined again.)

The post-war membership rate of the PCI has been on a historical down trend since the peak years in 1953–4, only interrupted by a temporary rise between 1971 and 1976. In a first period from 1947 until 1954, the party profited most from its newly acquired legitimacy and territorial presence during the Resistance years. Although, by the PCI's own admission (Baccetti, 1997, p. 123, n. 2), the figures were inflated by 10 per cent (roughly 200,000) until 1956, these are years when the PCI counted around 2 million members. The decline accelerated with the loss of many members after 1956, when the party leadership's position on the Hungarian Revolution led to the resignation of important party members. The drop was most dramatic within the youth movement. The party recovered only after 1968 when increased politicization of society attracted more members into (or back into) the party. The 1968 student movement itself stayed outside, the PCI had many troubles understanding and co-opting the student revolt and other new social movements, and lost members during these years to more radical left-wing parties (*Democrazia Proletaria*) or to the independent left which had split from the PCI (*il Manifesto*). Nonetheless It reached its second peak around the 1976 elections. With the crisis of the 'historical compromise', however, membership declined again until the very end of the PCI (Table 10.1).

The Inescapable Regional Concentration of the Party
In order to become a party with coherent electoral support in all the regions, the PCI had to conquer those regions where it was traditionally weak, that is,

Table 10.1   PCI and FGCI membership, 1947–90

Year	PCI	FGCI[*]
1944	501,960	—
1945	1,770,896	—
1946	2,068,272	—
1947	2,252,760	—
1956	2,035,353	358,126
1957	1,827,767	245,199
1958	1,818,606	241,747
1968	1,502,862	125,438
1976	1,814,262	142,200
1977	1,814,154	127,143
1978	1,790,450	113,509
1988	1,462,281	49,493
1989	1,424,035	54,195
1990	1,319,905	—

[*] FGCI (The Federation of Young Communists) was founded in 1949.
Sources: Baccetti (1997, pp. 120–2); Lazar (1992).

the North-East and the South. This aim was never reached. Indeed, at the end of the 1950s, the PCI had lost its grip on the industrial triangle (Milan–Turin–Genoa) in the North-West, a traditional stronghold.

Party membership remained concentrated in the Centre–North, the so-called 'red zone' with its core in the Po Valley. The membership gains of the early 1970s seemed to represent new hope. The North-West recovered some of its importance, and the PCI increased its membership (and its votes) in

Table 10.2   Regional distribution of PCI membership and vote (%), 1976 and 1990

	1976	1990
Valle d'Aosta	0.2	0.1
Piemonte	5.6	4.5
Liguria	4.5	3.9
Lombardia	12.0	10.8
North-West	22.3	19.3
(% of electorate)	(28.0)	(1987: 26.0)
Veneto	4.8	4.5
Trentino–Alto Adige	0.3	0.2
Friuli–Venezia Giulia	1.4	1.3
North-East	6.5	6.0
(% of electorate)	(7.9)	(1987: 7.7)
Emilia–Romagna	24.7	25.7
Toscana	14.2	15.1
Umbria	2.6	3.1
Marche	3.1	3.4
'Red Zone'	44.6	47.3
(% of electorate)	(26.1)	(1987: 30.0)
Lazio	5.3	5.1
Abruzzo	1.9	2.0
Molise	0.3	0.4
Campania	4.9	5.0
Puglia	4.3	3.7
Basilicata	0.8	0.9
Calabria	2.2	2.6
Centre–South	19.7	19.7
(% of electorate)	(29.2)	(1987: 28.1)
Sicily	3.9	4.7
Sardinia	2.2	2.4
Islands	6.1	7.1
(% of electorate)	(8.8)	(1987: 8.2)
Abroad	0.8	0.6
Total	100	100

Source: Baccetti (1997, pp. 128, 161).

the South. Only the North-East or 'white zone', traditional bastion of the DC, changed little. With the end of this trend in 1976, however, the concentration on its core regions was again exacerbated. In the 1980s, this part of Italy provided nearly half of the entire membership of the party.

As for its electorate, it was much less concentrated in regional terms. The 'red zone' was the only macro-region where, except for some pockets, the PCI got at least 40 per cent of the local vote. But given the higher population in the two other macro-regions, the absolute number of voters was fairly equally distributed on the territory. This striking discrepancy of membership and electorate reflected the PCI's hybrid identity which was both regional in socio–cultural terms, and national in electoral terms (Table 10.2).

The Ambivalent Opening to Other Social Categories

The PCI was initially a workers' party led by intellectuals. This remained so after the war. Yet, the socio–professional background of its base, leadership and electorate did change. One reason was the rapid industrialization of post-war Italy, the *miracolo* (miracle) which reduced the number of persons living from agriculture and, more recently, the number of manufacturing workers, both major electoral supporters of the PCI. But it was also due to the PCI's attempt to become something of an inter-class party, and hence a real challenger to the DC and its allies.

This inter-class strategy was only partly successful. The composition of its electoral support did show an increasing attraction of those professional categories where it used to be weak (see Table 10.3). In its membership, however, the party had a vast preponderance of people with lower incomes, which has increased over the years (except for the leadership of the party, however).

In other words, similar to the data on regional concentration, there was a diverging trend between the socio–economic composition of its (outside) electorate and its (internal) membership. The partly successful change of the identity of the PCI away from its traditional worker image was mainly driven from the outside by electoral changes and aspirations. The change towards the PDS was to adjust this mismatch to some extent.

Table 10.3 shows the difference between the percentage of socio–economic group/voters and the percentage of those who declared to vote for the PCI. A positive sign thus indicates an electoral over-representation of this group within the PCI as compared to the general electorate.

The Competition from PSI

The origins of the PCI's crisis and final decision to remove its communist identity are also to be found in the fierce competition that the PSI mounted in the 1980s. After the electoral defeat of 1976, Bettino Craxi was elected secretary of the PSI leading a coalition of the party's right and of its left

Table 10.3   Change in the socio-economic composition of PCI electorate,
1968–87

Socio–economic groups	1968	1978–9	1987
Business(wo)men, managers	−4.4	−3.7	−2.7
Trade and crafts(wo)men	−4.7	−5.6	−2.6
Employed, teachers, technicians	−11.4	−2.5	−2.5
Workers	+17.5	+14.5	+8.5
Farmers	−3.1	−2.8	−3.0

Source: Mannheimer (1990), quoted in Baccetti (1997, p. 130).

(Claudio Signorile), in a common front against the old secretary F. De Martino. Within a few years, he installed an unrivalled personal leadership over the party, ousting its left and massively recruiting new members, entirely loyal to him, into the direction. At the 42nd Party Congress in Palermo in 1981, 61 per cent of new members were elected into the party leadership. From the 43rd Congress in Verona in 1984 onwards, Craxi was re-elected by simple acclamation. At this Congress, speeches by simple delegates (and not members of the party leadership) had declined to an all-low of 20 per cent. His autocratic rule had little parallel in any other party of post-war Italy and served a new strategy. In 1980, the PSI entered again a coalition government with the DC. Craxi tried to attract the 'new middle classes' and more generally those disappointed by DC rule. Yet for the PSI to appear as the only credible alternative to the DC, it needed to attack the PCI as unreliable or unworthy for leading the country. At the beginning of the 1980s, Craxi ended the former policy of left alliances in municipalities and regions and moved to coalitions within the ruling *pentapartito* (DC, PSI, PSDI, PLI, PRI). With the steady decline of the DC, his image as a forceful leader of the second largest coalition party finally paved his way for becoming the second non-DC prime minister in post-war Italian history.

The PSI started to recover some of its former share of votes and succeeded in appearing as the 'modern' left as compared to the 'dinosaurs' in the PCI. Craxi's strategy put the PCI in a very difficult position. Electorally, the PSI was cashing in exactly where the PCI needed to develop its own votes: in the south and among the new middle classes. Ideologically, the PCI found itself isolated as a Eurocommunist party, when the tide of the time had moved to the right and Craxi was selling as modern left-wing policy the local version of Reaganomics (cutting some taxes – and increasing spending and debt). Politically, Craxi appeared as a credible leader exactly when the PCI was in a leadership crisis after the sudden death of Berlinguer in 1984. Alessandro

Natta, Berlinguer's successor, was not a politician able to face Craxi in a political campaign increasingly dominated by the public television (whose journalists were, in turn, increasingly co-opted by the PSI).

Change was needed in the PCI if it was not to lose its position as the main alternative to the DC. The PCI was perfectly aware of the similarity between Craxi's and Mitterrand's strategy which consisted in first isolating the formerly dominant communist party before proposing a union which would establish the socialist hegemony over the left. In this situation, it did not help much that the PCI had finally cut all international reference to the USSR after the martial law imposed in Poland in 1981. (To the great dismay of Moscow, it had already refused covert financing from the USSR in the late 1970s.) In the same year, Berlinguer declared this rupture with a sentence which sounded austere to the outsider, but could not be more mortal to the classical communist ideology: 'the propulsive drive of the October revolution has been exhausted.'

The electoral results of 1987, with a rising PSI and dropping PCI vote, worked as a catalyst. The party perceived this defeat not as yet another temporary obstacle to the inevitable strengthening of its position, but as an indicator of a party out of tune with the aspirations of society. The base started to discuss openly about changes. For the first time, the changes were not guided from the top. In a general mood of identity crisis, Achille Occhetto was elected vice-secretary. In 1988, he succeeded Natta as party secretary.

From the PCI to the PDS and PRC, 1987–91

Achille Occhetto decided to change course, although, similar to Gorbachov, he might not have foreseen the outcome. In the early days he tried to get closer to the PSI by renewing the old strategy of alliances. Craxi was expectedly uninterested, and by early 1989, Occhetto realized that something more radical was needed.

The first remarkable onslaught on the traditional PCI happened at the 18th Congress in March 1989. The party documents voted at this Congress testified to the ideological changes that had happened in the aftermath of the 1987 defeat. It declared a willingness to move beyond the various traditions of the labour movements, approved the central place of the market economy, moved democracy from a means to an end of politics, and stressed the protection of rights, whose bearers were not the working class, but the citizen. In other words, the PCI declared dead the tradition of the (socialist) October Revolution to claim the tradition of the (social–liberal) French Revolution in its bi-centenary.

By that time already, Occhetto recalls that the change of the name and the symbol had become something of an obsession for him (Baccetti, 1997, p. 51).

The double external shock of the brutal reaction against the student revolts at Tienanmen and of the fall of the Berlin wall provided the necessary pretext. In November, during a speech to party veterans at the Bolognina, Occhetto announced his intention to create a new political formation. This speech, not discussed with anybody else, produced uproar and polarization within the party. The party leadership invited an extraordinary congress.

The extraordinary nineteenth Congress in Bologna decided to found a new party, as proposed by Occhetto, but left the party internally divided and somewhat disoriented. Occhetto's motion gathered two-thirds of delegates, 30 per cent went to the motion led by Pietro Ingrao, the leader of the 'no', the remaining 3 per cent to the motion of the more orthodox Armando Cossuta. Occhetto's win depended upon the massive support by the Po Valley delegation which represented a third of the entire congress. Massive support was to play a central part: the Emilia–Romagna voted with 79.1 per cent in favour of Occhetto. Since it provided a third of the delegates, this vote corresponded to 40 per cent of the Occhetto voters.

Occhetto unsuccessfully tried to gather party outsiders into the new political formation, a strategy similar to Mitterrand's move from the SFIO to the PS. Not much materialized, except for a new name (PDS) and symbol (an oak tree taking its roots in communist symbols) chosen in November 1991. (Before that, the new formation was simply known as *la Cosa* (the thing) and its supporters as the *Cosisti* ('thingers') (see below). Hence, when the party arrived at its twentieth Congress in Rimini, nothing had changed except that the internal divisions had become trenches. This Congress, held in January–February 1991, was at the same time the first of the PDS. 27 per cent of the delegates still voted against the change. Many of them were to leave the PDS and form the PRC.

The PDS as Organization: Continuity and Change

Whereas there are two main changes which seem to indicate a clear shift beyond the PCI – the statutes and the socio–economic composition of its parliamentarians – in many organizational respects the PDS is the direct heir of the PCI.

Breaks with the Past
The PCI had kept a very tight system of internal co-optation to recruit its leadership. Always afraid of losing left unity, it forbade party factions and open articulation of diverging positions. This was the famous *centralismo democratico* (democratic centralism). The statutes adopted at the initial Congress in 1991 allowed PDS members to organize political platforms, propose candidatures for the congress delegations and, more generally,

factions. It fell short of a federalization, however, which had been proposed in earlier internal reform papers. Also, it stipulated that each gender should be represented by 40 per cent.

The second change involves the socio–economic composition of parliamentarians, which has seen a conspicuous decline of workers and former trade unionists at the expense of new and old middle classes. As with the loosening link to the trade unions, the party is moving away from a more traditionalist labourist type.

Exacerbation of Earlier Trends: Members, Finances and Collateral Organizations
For obvious reasons, both the passage from the PCI to the PDS, and the political turmoil in which the Italian system plunged after 1992, were often not very helpful to the new party.

Its membership declined further, moving from an initial 989,708 in 1991 to around 690,000 in 1996. The regional concentration of members increased in proportion, where the 'red zone' now covered 52.2 per cent of the members. Its membership is rising in the Centre–South, but falling in the two Northern regions, partly because of the efficient presence of the PRC in the industrial triangle. The two new parties diverge most markedly in the number of women members: 28 per cent in the PDS (which is similar to the PCI), faces a poor 11.8 per cent in the PRC. The distribution of the PDS electorate has been constant to the times of the PCI, with a slight gain perhaps of the Centre–South.

The PCI's financial position had been already strained since the late 1970s when it decided to cut the link to Moscow. The public financing of parties, introduced about that time, eased the pressure. But the PCI increasingly recruited members whose main task was to raise money from companies usually in return for some advantages. In other words, the PCI was belatedly following the same trail as all the other established parties. The PDS inherited 300 bn LIT debt in 1991 (approx. $160 mn). Thereafter, its inflow continued to drop – also because a referendum in April 1993 abolished public party financing. This financial crisis had an immediate effect on party staffing. In 1988 roughly 2,560 people were on the party's payroll. By 1994, the PDS paid a mere 670.

In general the move to the PDS enshrined the organizational hierarchy as it had developed over the last decades. The basic unit is no longer the cell at the work place but the territorial section which is both more open to other social actors and an important point at which to organize local politics. These sections feed into regional federations and then up to the central organs. For the PDS, these include the National Congress which elects the National Council which, in turn, elects the National Direction and the Secretary. The last two are the executive bodies of the party.

The relationship to collateral organizations, which had been an integral part of the PCI, had begun to change in the 1980s, a trend confirmed within the PDS. Most importantly, there were, of course, the trade-unions. Although officially all trade-unions were pluralist, the *Confederazione Generale Italiana degli Lavoratori* (Italian General Confederation of Labour, CGIL), the single largest, responded mainly to the PCI. Its leaders were chosen in agreement with the party. This happened through the factions within the union, where the communist faction dominated the socialist and a 'third' (independent left, Republican) one. In the wave of the changes introduced by Occhetto, Bruno Trentin, then leader of the CGIL, declared the end of the communist faction in 1990, quickly followed by the end of the others. This meant an end to the direct influence of the PCI/PDS on the CGIL. It had two consequences. For the trade union, it only exacerbated internal divisions instead of improving the possibility for more flexible cross-coalitions. For the PDS, it meant losing a conspicuous element of trade unionists, many of them joining the PRC (whose leader Fausto Bertinotti is trade unionist himself). Indeed, today the CGIL is often rather critical of government policies signed by the PDS.

In a similar vein, other important links to civil society loosened. ARCI, a cultural association close to the party, increasingly distanced itself from direct party control (although it still identifies itself with the left), a movement symbolized by the first non-party head voted in 1989. Similarly, the Youth Organization of the party, now called *Sinistra Giovanile* (SG), failed to build a bridge between civil society and the party. After a first attempt to pool different single-issue groups and to open their claims into the party, the SG had to come down on a double-track strategy, being both youth organization and a mouthpiece to civil society, without really bridging the gap.

GOVERNMENT ACHIEVEMENTS AND CURRENT POLICIES

The 1992 elections brought the PDS to an all-time low of 16.1 per cent (if compared to the PCI's 26.6 per cent in 1987), with 5.6 per cent going to the PRC. But, most importantly, the party had not been overtaken by the still strong PSI. The collapse of the PSI cleared the way for the PDS, not so much in terms of votes, however, which tellingly went to the right during the 1994 elections, but by opening the ideological space of a close competitor. By 1994, the PDS received 20.4 per cent of the votes (PRC: 6.0), and 21.1 (PRC: 8.6) in 1996, at which point it became the largest party in Italy and the backbone of a new centre–left coalition government.

With the end of the DC in 1993, and with the weak results of its successor, the *Partito Popolare Italiano* (PPI) in the elections in 1994, the political terrain of the centre, where elections are won in Italy, was open. With his 'red scare' propaganda, Silvio Berlusconi had manoeuvred the left out of the centre. But after ruling unsuccessfully for a year with the Northern League and the post-fascist National Alliance that electoral space appeared again.

When the 1994 elections made clear that the left would not be able to win a majority of votes in Italy, the PDS had no other choice but to return to older patterns, namely to collaborate with the centre in order to have a say in Italian politics. Whereas traditionally this worked through parliamentary commissions or passive support of DC governments now, in a rather risky bid, the PDS went for a double strategy of consolidating its role on the left, while aggregating a centre–left coalition force which could win the next elections.

Crucial for this strategy was both the programmatic renewal which would make the PDS acceptable to the centre, and finding a person who could be tolerable to both the centre–left and the left. The first was simply the pursuit of Occhetto's platform of the first PDS congress, enshrined by a programmatic paper of early 1995, and then accepted by the 'thematic congress' of July 1995: less state, better services and welfare state guarantees and reforms. By then the reference to the working class had all but vanished: it was not mentioned a single time in the document. The need for reforms was explicitly subordinated to the need to keep up with European and international standards (Gilbert, 1996; p. 108). The second arrived in the person of Romano Prodi, from the left wing of the Christian Democrats, who had a long-standing career as a civil servant managing the biggest public industrial holding in Italy, the IRI.

Prodi's electoral and programmatic alliance, l'*Ulivo* (the olive tree) gathered the PDS, the PPI and several small centre groups. The programmatic platform of the *Ulivo* was not much different from the reformed PDS platform. It proposes welfare state reform and constitutional reforms, much modelled on Germany's parliamentarian 'Chancellor Democracy': the reorganization of the executive with a strong Prime Minister supervising its own bureaucracy, the federalization of the regions into *Länder* with some fiscal autonomy, and the change of the Senate into a regional chamber.

The *Ulivo* has yet to realize any of the constitutional reforms, and is still searching a welfare reform formula. The Prodi government has embarked on a policy much similar to its predecessors C. Ciampi (who is Finance Minister) and L. Dini (who became Foreign Minister): financial rigour and the aim to reach the Maastricht criteria for EMU. On the long path from its early refusal of the Marshall Plan to the Prodi government, the PCI and PDS have become the fervent supporter of the European Union.

Only launched in 1991, the PDS has recently decided to merge into a larger left-wing party structure. The meeting of representatives of Italian centre-left parties in Florence between 12 and 14 February 1998 aimed to discuss the formation of a large 'social democratic front' with its allies of the *Ulivo*. A new party was founded on this occasion: it is called 'Democrats of the Left' (*Democratici di Sinistra*). Although the party emblem is still the PDS's oak tree, the PDS's reference to its communist heritage (i.e. the red flag with the hammer-and-sickle constituting the roots of the tree) was replaced by the social democratic rose with the blue stars of the EU member states around its stem. This seems to indicate a new recentring of the PDS. The leader of this new party is PDS's leader Massimo d'Alema. At the time of the Florence meeting, the PDS was hoping to gather together within DS members of the PSI, the left wing of the Republican Party, unitary communists, and the left wing of the former Christian Democracy. At the end of 1998, it is still not clear whether DS is really a new party or simply a temporary federation of different parties. For the time being, DS relies very strongly on the PDS membership and leadership, which seems to imply that, so far, the gathering of all centre left forces in Italy has not yet been achieved.

Note

* I am indebted to Martin Bull for helpful suggestions concerning this topic.

Select Bibliography

Baccetti, C. (1997) *Il PDS. Verso un nuovo modello di partito?*, Bologna: Il Mulino.

Barbagli, M., Corbetta, P. and Sechi, S. (1979) *Dentro il PCI*, Bologna: Il Mulino.

Bull, M. (1997) 'From PDS to Cosa 2: The Second Congress of the Democratic Party of the Left', *EUI Working Papers*, SPS 97/3, Florence: European University Institute.

Bull, M. and Daniels, P. (1994) 'Voluntary Euthanasia: From the Italian Communist Party to the Democratic Party of the Left', in Bull, M. and Heywood, P. (eds), *West European Communist Parties after the Revolutions of 1989*, London: Macmillan.

Bull, M. and Rhodes, M. (eds) (1997) 'Special Issue on Crisis and Transition in Italian Politics', *West European Politics*, 20(1).

Flores, M. and Gallerano, N. (1992) *Sul PCI. Un'interpretazione storica*, Bologna: Il Mulino.

Gilbert, M. (1996) 'The Oak Tree and the Olive Tree', in Caciagli, M. and Kertzer, D. (eds), *Italian Politics: The Stalled Transition (Italian Politics: A Review, vol. 11)*, Boulder, CO: Westview.

Guzzini, S. (1995) 'The "Long Night of the First Republic": Years of Clientelistic Implosion in Italy', *Review of International Political Economy*, 2(1).

Ignazi, P. (1992) *Dal PCI al PDS*, Bologna: Il Mulino.

Landolfi, A. (1990) *Storia del PSI*, Milan: Sugarco Edizioni.

Lange, P. and Vannicelli, M. (eds) (1981) *The Communist Parties of Italy, France and Spain: Postwar Change and Continuity*, London: George Allen & Unwin.

Lazar, M. (1992) *Maisons rouges. Les partis communistes français et italien de la Libération à nos jours*, Paris: Aubier.

Mannheimer, R. (1990) 'Vecchi e nuovi caratteri del voto comunista', in Caciagli, M. and Spreafico, A. (eds), *Vent'anni di elezioni in Italia*, Padua: Liviana.

Sapelli, G. (1997) 'Continuità e trasformazione della sinistra italiana dopo l'89', *Europa/Europe*, VI(1).

Contact Information

Party Address
Direzione Generale
Via delle Botthege Oscure, 4   Tel.: 39 67 111
00186 Roma   Fax: 39 67 92085

Web page on the Internet: http://www.democraticidisinistra.it

11 The Luxembourg Socialist Workers' Party*

John Fitzmaurice

HISTORY

Recent History of the Grand Duchy

After the Second World War, Luxembourg accepted that, because of inter-dependence, neutrality was no protection and entered into full and active participation in various international bodies such as the Council of Europe, WEU, NATO, the European Coal and Steel Community (ECSC) and later the European Communities, with the inevitable *de jure* and *de facto* limitations on its sovereignty. However, this was seen as the most effective and indeed only way of safeguarding its independence and capacity to defend its national interests. All major political parties accept this view. Almost as a small-state paradox, this has enabled Luxembourg not only to survive, but to prosper as an active participant in the integration process. It has in fact punched well above its weight in European affairs – providing, for example, two European Commission presidents (Gaston Thorn and Jacques Santer) and the EU presidency during the Gulf War.

The apparent sublimation of Luxembourg national interests and identity in Europe should not blind one to the fact that it does have, and indeed it defends, many very specific interests within the Union, though it has chosen to promote these interests through taking part in European integration. In some ways, of course, the success of European integration is its most vital interest. Among its most important specific interests are: banking secrecy; opposition to a capital withholding tax; the steel industry; nuclear safety (a French nuclear power station has been sited just next door); wine production; the siting of European institutions (several in the Grand Duchy), and strict EMU convergence criteria are all Luxembourg concerns.

The Political System

As in most European party systems, the characteristics of an individual party, such as the Luxembourg Socialist Workers Party (*Lëtzebuerger Sozialistesch Aarbechterpartei/Parti Ouvrier Socialiste Luxembourgeois* – LSAP/POSL) can

148

be understood in only relation to the party system as a whole and the political environment within which it operates, which influences it and to which it has itself contributed. The Grand Duchy is a hereditary constitutional monarchy and a parliamentary democracy. The Grand Duke is head of state, but executive power is in the hands of a Cabinet, headed by the prime minister, formally appointed by the Grand Duke after negotiations between the political parties after each election, and responsible to the popularly elected Chamber of Deputies. Responsible Cabinet government was introduced in 1868.

The Chamber of Deputies has 60 members elected in practice for a fixed five-year term, with elections normally coinciding with European elections in June of every fifth year. Elections are conducted under a unique system: PR using the Hagenbach–Bishoff divisor method and allowing voters the possibility of '*panachage*' between lists. The country is divided into four districts, each electing between seven and twenty-one deputies. There is no second distribution, nor any additional top-up seats. Voters have as many votes as there are seats and may split their ticket, voting for candidates on different party lists. Indeed, they can allocate up to two votes per candidate. Votes for a list are counted as one vote per candidate on that list. The total votes for each list is arrived at by totalling the votes for all the candidates on each list and this forms the basis of the distribution of seats between the parties. The average district magnitude is 16.02 and the effective threshold is 4.8 per cent. One effect of the '*panachage*' system may be to personalize politics to a greater degree and encourage the nomination of at least some candidates on each list who have a broad appeal outside their own party. The Council of State, with twenty-one members appointed by the Crown, acts as an advisory second Chamber, but can neither delay nor veto legislation. French was traditionally the official language and used in politics and administration. In 1984, Letzebuergisch was given equal status as an official language, alongside French and German.

The Party

The first independent socialist was elected to the Chamber in 1896. The limited nature of the franchise made progress difficult until after the First World War. The Party, then called the Luxembourg Social Democratic Party was founded in 1902 and at first worked with the Liberals in the *Bloc de Gauche*. After the communists split off in 1921, the party sought to restore its weakened position by strengthening its links with the trade unions and renamed itself the *Parti Ouvrier*. It first entered government in 1937 and took part in laying the foundations of the welfare state in Luxembourg just after the Second World War. It then faced severe competition from the *Parti*

Communiste Luxembourgeois (PCL), especially in the south and in the unions. After the war, there was an important debate in the party about its future strategy and development. Modernizers sought to extend its base and its image beyond the industrialized south. The party then took the compromise name of *Parti Socialiste Ouvrier Luxembourgeois* (LSAP/POSL) in 1924, combining both tendencies in the name. The rightist split, which led to the formation of small and quickly marginalized *Parti Social-Démocrate* (PSD) in 1971, was also linked to this debate. The leadership of Henri Cravatte was criticized both by the unions and the younger new left within the party for making too many concessions to the PCS (see below) in the 1964–8 coalition. The issue of municipal alliances with the PCL, forbidden by the leadership, that is usually cited as the immediate cause of the split, was only the spark that ignited the powder.

After the split, the party moved somewhat to the left, even debating Luxembourg's position in NATO, and then began to move back into the centre. In 1974, the renewed POSL made significant gains and went into government with the modernizing and reformist PD/DP. This unusual coalition worked well and undertook important social and educational reforms, as well as enacting a social restructuring plan for the Luxembourg steel industry that became a model. It was well supported by POSL activists. Had it retained its majority in the Chamber in 1979, it would have continued, but the POSL lost heavily for reasons that are even now not very clear. Possibly it had not yet fully recovered from the split and its internal left–right divisions and lost its profile in the coalition. It may too have made the tactical error of offering no front-line personality of its own, especially during the campaign, allowing Liberal Prime Minister Gaston Thorn to as it were represent the achievements of the coalition as a whole. After a period in opposition, the LSAP/POSL returned to its more usual partner and formed a new coalition with the PCS in 1984, which was reformed after both the 1989 and 1994 elections.

The Party System

The LSAP/POSL, like all Luxembourg political parties has been obliged to 'interiorize' the limitations on its freedom of action inevitably imposed on all parties in a very small and highly interdependent state like the Grand Duchy. Policy objectives must be realistic and moderate, having regard to the very limited capacity of the country to alter its external environment. Parties must therefore accept and indeed exploit interdependence and international co-operation; The option of an '*alleingang*' (literally, 'going it alone') that may exist for larger countries simply does not exist for Luxembourg. As a result, co-operation across domestic party lines is at a premium, in defence of national interests. All these considerations are central to an understanding of Luxembourg's political life and the role of the LSAP/POSL within it.

The party system has largely followed the usual Benelux pattern, with three major political 'families' dominating political life: a centre–right Christian Democratic Party (*Parti Chrétien Social/ Christlich-soziale Volkspartei* – PCS/CSV); a centrist, and at least historically mildly anti-clerical Liberal Party (*Parti Démocratique/Democratesch Partei* – PD/DP) and the social democratic Luxembourg Socialist Workers Party (*Parti Ouvrier Socialiste Luxembourgeois/Letzeburger Socialistesch Arbechterpartei* – LSAP/POSL). The PD/DP is more centrist than its Belgian or Dutch counterparts, lying between the PCS and the LSAP/PSOL. This has made all three coalition combinations real options in modern times (PCS/POSL, PCS/PD or PD/POSL). In 1921, a small communist party (PCL) split off from the LSAP/POSL and was represented in Parliament from 1934 to 1994. At its height, the PCL topped 20 per cent of the vote in the southern, industrial district, winning six seats in the Chamber as late as 1968. In the 1970s, there was a split from the right of the LSAP/POSL to form the *Parti Social-Démocrate* (PSD). It is now defunct and some of its members ended up in the PCS. More recently, after some initial difficulties, the Greens have established themselves as a permanent feature of the Luxembourg political landscape. From time to time, new single-issue parties have emerged, such as the Pensions Action Committee or the *Parti des Enrôlés de Force* (Party of the Forcibly Conscripted), acting as a pressure group for those conscripted involuntarily into the German *Wehrmacht*. Coalitions have more usually been between the PCS and the LSAP/PSOL, less often between the PCS and PD (three since 1945) and once between the PD and the LSAP/PSOL (1974–9). The PCS is usually the largest party, but the LSAP has achieved this once since 1945. The DP has been consistently in third place since the 1920s, except in 1979 when it achieved second place. There are three clearly identified areas in terms of electoral sociology: the rural north (North and East districts) where the PCS predominates; the capital city (Central district) where the PD is strong and the industrial south (Southern district) where the LSAP and earlier the PCL are strong.

ORGANIZATION AND PARTY PROFILE

The POSL has had between 5,000 and 6,000 members in recent times: its membership in 1997 was 5,800. Like all Luxembourg parties, it receives no public financing, but the group in the Chamber does receive financial assistance for maintaining its staff. It has a very small staff of two or three secretaries. It has 67 local sections, which must have at least ten members each. Above the sections are the four regional party organizations, based on the four constituencies into which the country is divided. The Congress meets annually, but only elects the seventeen members of the National Executive that are directly elected by the Congress in every second year. The National Executive has in all twenty-nine members. In addition to the seventeen elected by the Congress, two come from each of the four Constituency Organizations, one from the Young Socialists and three from the Women's Organization. Since a 1997 reform, the whole Congress elects the Party President, two Vice-Presidents, the General Secretary and the Treasurer. Since the split, the Statutes were revised in 1972 to decentralize power in the party, creating several different power centres. Thus, the President of the Party may not be a Minister or Chair of the party's group in the Chamber of Deputies. There is an intermediate tier in the General Council, a kind of mini-Congress that acts as an appeal body against decisions of the Executive and nominates the LSAP/POSL ministers when the party is in office. Any decision to enter or leave government, obviously key political decisions, must be put to a special Congress convened for that purpose. The party is strong in municipal government and its local government-elected officials represent another power centre in the party, alongside the Party President, Vice Prime Minister and the LASP/POSL ministerial team and the Chair of the group in the Chamber. The party no longer retains any organic link with the Trade Union Federation (OGBL), though there are of course close political links. Like all parties in Luxembourg, it finds it difficult to maintain an active profile while in government. It has created policy working groups to keep the party alive and provide a specific input into the policy process. The electoral system in the Grand Duchy, with preferential voting and *panachage* has discouraged strong party organization and encouraged individualism and local electoral fiefdoms of 'notables'. The leading personalities are the Party President for the past ten years, Ben Fayot MEP (President 1985–97) and the Vice-Prime Minister and Foreign Minister Jacques Poos.

Table 11.1   LSAP/POSL election results 1959–94 (%)

Year	%
1959	33.1
1964	35.9
1968	31.0
1974	27.0
1979	22.5
1984	31.8
1989	26.2
1994	25.4

Source: Compiled from official statistics.

The party is now a mainstream moderate social democratic party. It has extended its electoral base and image well beyond the dwindling industrial working class in the southern steel area and into the new white-collar and middle-class electorates. It remains weakest in the rural areas.

The LSAP's best result since the Second World War was 35.9 per cent of the vote in 1964 and its lowest result was 22.5 per cent in 1979 (Table 11.1).

GOVERNMENT ACHIEVEMENTS AND POLICIES

The PSOL, as we saw above, is a moderate mainstream European social democratic party. It is pragmatic and its differences both with its present coalition partners, the PCS, and its former partners, the DP, are more matters of nuance. It is closer to the DP on some 'life-style', educational and ethical issues, where it retains differences with the confessional PCS. It supports a social market economy and welfare state, without too rigid state intervention. It is strongly pro-European, though it has been obliged to defend some seemingly unsocialist national interests, such as banking secrecy and opposition to withholding tax on savings and fiscal harmonization, where it insists on retention of unanimity. In the 1980s, the party faced competition from two green parties and reacted by taking up green issues. In the 1970s there was also an internal debate about NATO, but the left line was eventually defeated. The POSL is an active member of the Party of European Socialists and the Socialist International. During the 1980s, it took part in the Scandilux grouping of socialist parties from the smaller NATO countries.

Note

* This chapter is based on an extensive interview accorded to the author on 23 October 1996 by Mr Ben Fayot MEP, President of the POSL/LSAP 1985–97 and materials provided by the Secretariat of the party. There is little source material on the POSL in English.

Select Bibliography

Fayot, B (1985) *Sozialismus in Luxemburg*, 2 vols, Esch sur Alzette: Edipress.
Jacobs, F. (1989) '*Luxembourg*', in Jacobs, F. (ed.), *West European Political Parties*, London: Longman.

Contact Information

Affiliated Bodies
Jeunesses Socialistes Luxembourgeoises
Femmes Socialistes Luxembourgeoises
Fédération des Conseillers Communaux Socialistes

Party Addresses
Lëtzebuerger Sozialistesch Aarbechterpartei
16, rue de Crécy   Tel: 352 455 991
L-1247 Luxembourg   Fax: 352 473 021

President of the LSAP Parliamentary Group
34, rue du Marché aux Herbes   Tel: 352 225 914
L-1728 Luxembourg   Fax: 352 473 021

Deputy Prime Minister and Minister of Foreign Affairs
5, rue Notre Dame   Tel: 352 478 2306
L-2911 Luxembourg   Fax: 352 223 144

Web page on the Internet: http://www.lsap.lu

12 The Dutch Labour Party
Kees van Kersbergen

HISTORY

The social democratic party of the Netherlands, the *Partij van de Arbeid* (PvdA), was founded in 1946. Although an attempt to 'break through' the traditional party cleavages of pre-war society and to establish a broad people's party, the PvdA is in fact the successor and heir of the Marxist *Sociaal-Democratische Arbeiderspartij* (SDAP) which was founded in 1894. The SDAP, in turn, was a split-off from the *Sociaal-Democratische Bond* (SDB) which under the charismatic leadership of F. Domela Nieuwenhuis, the first socialist member of parliament (1888), had become anti-parliamentary and anarchist. In the early 1890s conflicts had intensified between advocates of a revolutionary strategy and those who viewed parliamentary action as useful in itself or at least for purposes of propaganda. In fact, the decision at the SDB's convention in 1893 to no longer take part in elections was the direct cause of the schism and led to the foundation of the SDAP the following year.

The SDAP was a socialist party with a political ideology initially rooted in Marxism. It viewed parliamentarism and the struggle for universal suffrage as complementary to rather than incompatible with the revolutionary class struggle. Its founders represented what were to become the main constituents of the party: working-class leaders, propagandists and teachers; political representatives of the union movement; and left-wing intellectuals. The model for organization was the German social democratic party which provided not only the ideology (the 1891 Erfurt programme) but also financial aid (Perry *et al.*, 1994, pp. 25, 32). In 1897, the party had its first two representatives in Parliament, among whom was one of the party's most important leaders, P.J. Troelstra. In the wake of the railway strike of 1903 and Troelstra's wavering position with regard to a political strike against the government's repressive reaction, the struggle over the leadership of the party eventually took the form of a clash between those who defended the purity of Marxism and those who advanced the SDAP's reformist practice. The Marxist faction in the party established its own newspaper in order to fight the increasing revisionism of the socialist faction led by Troelstra. The ideological struggle ended by the removal of the orthodox Marxists in 1909 who then founded their own party which was to become the Dutch communist party (*Communistische Partij in Nederland* – CPN) in 1918.

The SDAP focused on two main issues: the extension of universal suffrage and the so-called 'social question' – urging, for instance, a shortening of the working day. In 1917, the socialists and liberals managed to obtain the support of the religious parties for universal (male) suffrage and proportional representation in exchange for an equal right to public financing of religious schools. This grand political bargain, called 'the Pacification', partly established and partly codified the rules of the political game in the Netherlands as a game of accommodation (Lijphart, 1968). It also reinforced the already existing pattern of segregated social organization known as 'pillarization', which is characterized by a highly organized network of affiliated social, economic and cultural organizations. The social democratic 'pillar' was called the 'red family'. Paradoxically, the SDAP had its 'greatest' revolutionary moment in the wake of 'the Pacification'. Troelstra, misinterpreting the revolution in Germany and the revolutionary inclination of the Dutch working class, announced in November 1918 (in Parliament!) that the working class and social democracy would seize power. The government did not resign, police and army were mobilized and positioned strategically in major cities, and essentially nothing happened, except that the debate within the party over legal and illegitimate means of politics was intensified.

By 1919 the SDAP had become the second largest group in Parliament but – unlike elsewhere in Europe – was not powerful enough or, for that matter, eager to assume a position in government (except at the local level). Dutch social democracy nevertheless developed slowly but gradually into a reformist and highly pragmatic party. In fact, the SDAP was one of the first socialist parties to abandon Marxist revolutionary theory entirely and adopt a quasi-corporatism of a mixed but planned economy. This was already the case – although perhaps latent – in the 1920s but became manifest both in the 1935 *Plan van de Arbeid* and in the party manifesto of 1937. Moreover, the electoral strategy of the party changed to incorporate the middle class. In other words, the SDAP had developed into a broad people's party before the Second World War. By that time the SDAP had also already fully adopted the pattern of social and political organization typical of 'pillarization'. The 'red family', too, consisted of a complex network of social and cultural organizations affiliated with the SDAP.

Immediately after the liberation in 1945 a new political movement was launched, which had as its main objective the 'break-through' of the pillarized political system. The main driving force behind the new Dutch People's Movement (*Nederlandse Volksbeweging*, NVB) consisted of the élite of the SDAP that sought to transform itself through the NVB into a broader people's party. In addition, the drive for renewal was backed by left-wing liberals and catholic groups united around an unequivocal longing for unity of the Dutch people. The cement of this blend of miscellaneous political currents was found in a new set of ideological concepts, labelled 'personalist socialism', which was an odd mixture of socialist, liberal, and catholic–corporatist conceptions, generally inspired by the doctrines of socialism, humanism and Christianity. This became the gist of the political ideology of the PvdA.

The new party rapidly developed into a governmental party that held power (in varying coalitions with the Christian Democrats) until 1958. The party leader Willem Drees became Prime Minister in several governments and his name is inextricably bound with a centrepiece of the welfare state, the universal old-age pension scheme. The party's political ideology was strongly characterized by a statist conception of social and economic planning. The then director of the scientific bureau, Joop den Uyl, was the main author of the influential *De weg naar vrijheid* (The Road to Freedom) of 1951 in which planning was the crucial concept and 'freedom' meant freedom from want. The political ideology of a planned economy and society remained dominant until roughly the mid-1960s. By that time a younger generation, known as 'New Left' (*Nieuw Links*), was taking over and considerably influenced the party's views, particularly with regard to postmaterialist values and democratization. *Nieuw Links* also pushed for a more critical perspective on foreign policy (Vietnam, NATO, American policies in general).

By the late 1960s the party had adopted a new polarization strategy that aimed at fragmenting the powerful Christian Democratic centre and at speeding the 'depillarization' process of Dutch society and politics. At the same time the PvdA sought new forms of co-operation with other left parties and in 1973 a parliamentary basis was found for the Den Uyl government, the first government in which social democrats prevailed numerically and politically.

In 1977, the party adopted a new party manifesto, which was somewhere midway between a codification of its ideology of the early 1970s, an electoral declaration for the near future and a rhetorical adoption of the radicalization of the era and its new issues of feminism and the environment. The catchword of the ideology during the Den Uyl era was unmistakably 'equality', which already had been one of the key ideological concepts of the government, but was to characterize the party's ideology at least until 1990. Formally, the 1977 manifesto is still in force. However, it is now considered as entirely obsolete as a result of which the PvdA started to reformulate its ideological principles after the mid-1990s. The debate has centred around the extent to which the new principles should be explicitly directed against neo-liberalism as the dominant ideology, to what extent traditional values such as solidarity, equality and justice need to be redefined or even abandoned, to what extent the traditional welfare state needs to be ideologically defended, to what extent ecological issues need to be incorporated more thoroughly into political doctrine and whether a new party manifesto summing up the party's basic principles is politically useful at all (Becker *et al.*, 1996).

ORGANIZATION AND PARTY PROFILE

As with all Dutch political parties, the PvdA's organizational structure reflects the organization of the political system. The party consists of local branches (*afdelingen*) operating at the level of the municipalities, regional bodies (*gewesten*) that function at the provincial level and a national congress. The local branches delegate representatives to the national congress. The congress is the highest decision-making institution within the party and it elects the national committee (*partijbestuur*). Daily affairs are run by selected members of the national committee who constitute the national executive (*dagelijks bestuur*). Until recently, the regional bodies also elected a party council (*partijraad*). However, under the leadership of former chairman Felix Rottenberg, the party was reorganized: the party council has been abolished and the political power of the regional bodies as well as the political influence of the local branches, were restricted. In general terms, therefore, intra-party decision-making power within the party has become more centralized.

Party finances are made up from approximately 60 per cent membership fees, about 15 per cent state subsidies and 25 per cent from other sources such as fundraising among members (such private donations are tax-deductible). State subvention depends on the electoral strength of parties. Membership fees are levied according to income on a progressive scale with a maximum of 2 per cent of gross annual income. Financial aid by private business is virtually absent in the Netherlands; although formally legal, such donations are considered morally improper. The more important reason, however, is that business and the trade unions already have easy access to the political system via the corporatist institutions of interest intermediation and do not need party-political aid (Koole, 1994, p. 289).

Since 1945 membership of the PvdA has fluctuated considerably. The party mobilized from 105,000 to 147,000 members between 1946 and 1970. Total membership declined in the first half of the 1970s, but rose again after the Den Uyl government (1973–7). Membership has recently declined rapidly and continues to do so, from over 100,000 members in 1987 to 64,000 in 1995. The degree of organization – i.e. the ratio of total membership to the electorate – has declined from 3.2 in 1946 to about 0.6 in 1994 (see Table 12.1).

In sociological terms the members of the PvdA differ considerably from the party's electorate (data were available for the mid-1980s, Hillebrand, 1992). Approximately 50 per cent of the voters and about 25 per cent of the members have a basic level of education. Just about 5 per cent of the voters, but over 19 per cent of members, have a university degree. Wage-earners in the private sector are under-represented among the members as compared to the voters, while the number of people employed in education

Table 12.1   Pvd A membership, 1946–95

Year	Members	Year	Members
1946	114,558	1975	100,524
1950	105,609	1980	112,929
1955	124,641	1985	100,979
1960	142,853	1990	91,784
1965	140,389	1995	64,523
1970	98,671		

Source: Voerman, G., De ledentallen van politieke partijen, 1945–1995, *Jaarboek Documentatiecentrum Nederlandse Politieke Partijen 1995* (Groningen, DNPP/RU-Groningen, 1996).

among the members is over-represented. On average, PvdA voters tend to be younger than the members of the party. Men are over-represented among party members, while the electorate is not distinctive according to gender. The majority of both members and voters is not religious, although there are slightly more religious (especially catholic) voters than religious members. The PvdA is a people's party to the extent that voters are attracted from all classes in society. Nevertheless, the party has long been class-distinctive as it disproportionally attracted voters from the working class. However, it seems that increasingly PvdA voters see themselves as middle class (see Table 12.2).

The PvdA is no longer the undisputed political representative of the 'red family'. Although to some extent political affinity characterizes the relationship between the party and the union federation (Federation of Dutch Trades Unions, FN), there are no formal ties. In fact, particularly since the

Table 12.2   Class composition of the PvdA vote, 1971–94 %

Class (self image)	1971–89	1994
Upper class	0.8	1.8
Upper middle class	5.8	12.2
Middle class	34.5	48.5
Upper working class	10.9	7.4
Working class	47.8	30.1

Note: Data for 1994 are computed on a sample of PvdA voters of only 348 respondents.
Sources: Data are taken from the Dutch Parliamentary Election Studies. See Horstman, R. and van Deth, J., *Dutch Parliamentary Election Studies Data Source Book* (Amsterdam: Steimetz Archive); Anker, H. and Oppenhuis, E., *Dutch Parliamentary Election Study 1994* (Amsterdam: Steimetz Archives/SKON).

disintegration of the social-democratic pillar, the PvdA has a history of redefining its approach towards and relations with other organizations. In the late 1960s the party, influenced by the *Nieuw Links* faction, severed its formal ties with traditional organizations and aimed to strengthen ties with new social movements. The party was to become an 'action party' with stronger emphasis on direct political action outside Parliament. This had a profound impact on organization in the 1970s and early 1980s. After the elections of 1986, when the PvdA had won extra seats but had been unable to participate in government, the strategy changed into one of a broad orientation towards social and cultural organizations, including the labour unions, the women's movement, environmental groups and churches.

The PvdA does have a number of organizations that are directly linked to the party, such as the Centre for Local Government (co-ordination of local representatives), the Training Institute (training delegates), the Alfred Mozer Foundation (in charge of contacts with sister parties in Central and Eastern Europe), the Evert Vermeer Foundation (development aid, North–South relations), the Wiardi Beckman Foundation (scientific bureau), the Young Socialists (youth organization), the Anne Vondeling Foundation (promotion of the party's role in European affairs) and the recent 'Dazzling Prospect' Foundation, which develops and presents planning scenarios for various policy areas.

The party is principally oriented towards participating in government. In the Netherlands, governments are necessarily coalitions. Until recently the PvdA excluded co-operation with the conservative (free market) liberals and primarily sought co-operation with the centre (Christian Democrats). However, since 1994 the party is leading a government coalition between social democrats, conservative liberals and radical democrats, labelled the 'purple coalition'. This coalition is unique to the extent that, for the first time since 1918, the Netherlands is governed by a coalition without Christian Democrats.

In a sense, the new political course has been facilitated by the ideological transformation of the party since 1977, a change that accelerated after 1986. Since then, the party has become much more moderate, less statist as it gradually introduced a cautious free market orientation and, most importantly, much less conservative in its defence of the traditional, transfer-oriented welfare state. The latter change has been the most painful to the extent that it has brought the party into several crises, both as a membership organization and as an electoral machine. The party had its lowest electoral result since 1946 in 1994 – 24 per cent of the vote or 37 of the 150 seats in the Second Chamber (*Tweede Kamer*). It did, however, return the party back to power in 1989 and smoothed the path towards the 'purple coalition'.

GOVERNMENT ACHIEVEMENTS AND CURRENT POLICIES

The 'break-through' movement of the mid-1940s turned out to be only a partial success. It was a failure in the sense that the pre-war political and social system of pillarization was restored in very much its traditional form. The three main achievements of the 'break-through', however, involved the foundation of a modernized social democratic party, the PvdA; the modernization of the Catholic party, according it a moderate reformist disposition; and the construction of a government coalition between these two parties which established the foundation of a qualitative change in ideas and practices of macroeconomic policy-making in the Netherlands.

The main achievements of the PvdA's governmental period until 1958 were the reconstruction of the Dutch economy and society after the Nazi occupation; the introduction of a strict policy to control wages and prices (the guided wage policy); and the foundation of the welfare state, partly by way of compensation for low wages. This policy was to stimulate exports, profits and full employment by keeping wages down. The guided wage policy in a sense became a victim of its own success, as it generated near-full employment by the mid-1950s. The favourable economic conditions of the late 1950s created a tight labour market and employers had already started to pay higher wages than those that were strictly permitted by law, the main reason for the collapse of the coalition between catholicism and social democracy was that the latter consistently refused to give up wage policy as the last bastion of social democratic interventionism, while the former had started giving in on the demands of the employers and their representatives within the party to ease political control over wages and prices. The PvdA lost the battle and remained in opposition from 1958 until 1973, with the exception of the years 1965–6.

The prosperity of the Dutch economy in the 1960s and the initially gradual, but in the end quite sudden structural changes of society in the form of depillarization and deconfessionalization constitute the structural background for the ideological offensive of social democracy in the early 1970s. These processes, too, explain why the Catholic party was forced to adopt more radical views on social policy in order not to lose its labour wing and the votes of Catholic workers altogether to the PvdA. It also clarifies why some factions within the Catholic party were in favour of a return of the 'Roman–Red' coalition that had governed the Netherlands in the 1950s.

In 1973, a coalition between the PvdA and some Christian Democratic factions was constructed. The Den Uyl government had a fragile parliamentary base as it was merely 'tolerated' by the Catholic party. Nevertheless, the government was capable of expanding or perfecting the welfare state. However, the more radical changes it was seeking to implement, such as income redistribution, public-housing policy and profit-sharing, were time and again blocked by the majority voting alliances of conservative liberals and the Christian Democratic parties. These alliances finally sealed the downfall of the government in 1977.

Growing tensions between the Catholics and the PvdA and successful experiments with cross-confessional co-operation at the local level prepared the way for the first joint Christian Democratic list for the election of 1977. The social democrats won an additional ten seats in parliament, but the new Christian Democratic alliance managed to stabilize its electoral strength. A combination of social democratic strategic errors and christian democratic power play led to the exclusion of the PvdA from the government. The christian democrats entered a coalition with the conservative liberals. With the exception of the intermezzo of 1981–2, the PvdA remained in opposition until 1989. The ideological cleavage between the PvdA and its main competitors remained considerable and primarily concerned the view on how to reform the welfare state (austerity), although it also involved defence policy, particularly the deployment of American nuclear missiles on Dutch territory.

At the elections of 1986 the PvdA managed to win 33.3 per cent or 52 seats, mainly as a result of a successful mobilization of popular discontent with the conservative government's austerity policies (Table 12.3). However, the electoral victory became a defeat in victory as the party was unable to enter a government coalition and the party remained in opposition. Between 1986 and 1989 the party reoriented its conservative welfare statism by emphasizing the need for fiscal responsibility, changed its leadership by appointing Wim Kok as Den Uyl's successor and by replacing the chairman and modified its style in opposition. Electorally the strategy was not

Table 12.3 PvdA share of the votes at parliamentary elections, 1946–94 (%)

Year	Share (%)	Year	Share (%)
1946	28.3	1971	24.6
1948	25.6	1972	27.3
1952	29.0	1977	33.8
1956	32.7	1981	28.3
1959	30.4	1982	30.4
1963	28.0	1986	33.3
1967	23.6	1989	31.9
		1994	24.0
		1998	29.0

Sources: Volkens, A. *et al.*, *Data Handbook on Election Results and Seats in the National Parliaments of 26 Contemporary Democracies, 1945–1990* (Berlin: WZB); Holsteyn, J. and Niemöller, B. (eds), *De Nederlandse Kiezer 1994* (Leiden: DSWO Press).

successful as the party won 31.9 per cent of the vote. However, this time the party managed to close a deal with the christian democrats and entered the government with its leader as the Minister of Finance (1989–94).

The government's goal to reduce the budget deficit substantially could not be achieved without cutting back on social spending. In 1991 the PvdA decided to approach the problem of the disability scheme which had got out of hand. Originally meant to support no more than 200,000 people, the scheme was paying over 900,000 benefits in 1990. The proposal to reform the scheme was highly controversial and politically risky. The PvdA was internally divided over the proposed measures, one faction adhering to the traditional welfare state and another more willing to seek new solutions, including market options (e.g. private insurance). Party leader Wim Kok almost fell over the disability issue, and the party's representatives in Parliament remained ambiguous towards the reform. The costs were high for the party as the PvdA experienced a haemorrhage of its membership. Not surprisingly, the governmental period was electorally costly, too. The social democrats were held responsible for what the union members among the voters in particular interpreted as an attack on established rights. The party did not recover in time and at the elections of 1994 it was punished with a historic defeat, winning only 24 per cent of the vote or 37 seats.

In spite of this defeat and thanks to an even bigger electoral loss by the christian democrats, the PvdA became the largest party in Parliament and therefore secured the initiative in forming a new government. As already observed, the Kok government was a coalition of conservative liberals, radical democrats and social democrats and excluded the christian democrats. The influence of the new PvdA was clearly discernable in the government's policy profile, which emphasized employment growth and the maximalization of labour market participation. The social democrats have promoted active labour market policies at the expense of passive transfer spending. The conservative liberals as well as a considerable number of social democrats are favouring market solutions and privatization in social security and marketization in other areas such as health care. The combination of these two political actors and the exchange this has fostered indicates a new political consensus which is based on a re-definition of the relation between state, market and family in the pursuit of welfare according to a social–liberal formula. This formula mixes traditional social democratic ideas such as justice and equality with neo-liberal elements such as the market and individualization. The PvdA's original ideological position of statist social and economic planning, as well as the party's emphasis on radical income equality, have disappeared. The 'purple coalition' has been very successful, both in promoting economic and job growth and in reforming the welfare state. The party's new ideologial position and its participation in the 'purple coalition' have also turned out to be electorally rewarding. At the general elections in

May 1998 29 per cent of the voters supported the PvdA. The party won an additional 8 seats and now has a total of 45. The 1998 election marked the first electoral victory of Wim Kok. The PvdA is the leading party of a renewed purple coalition and Wim Kok remains Prime Minister.

In social and economic terms, the PvdA now very much looks like a social democratic party that still stresses social justice and solidarity as its main values, but has lost its faith in the state as an omnipotent political agent and accepts the market as an efficient allocator of scarce resources, even if this means accepting a slightly higher degree of inequality. Equality is increasingly defined in equal opportunities on the labour market.

The PvdA has always been in favour of European integration and supports the enlargement of the European Union. The party also lends its support to monetary union. The PvdA favours subsidiarity as it is hesitant to support the transfer of additional political authority to Brussels. It also is sceptical with respect to the democratic quality of European decision-making and favours making up the democratic deficit by strengthening parliamentary control. The party also stresses the need for social policy innovation, especially with respect to unemployment. Its official position with respect to the Treaty of Amsterdam is that it represents a small step towards further integration and that further democratization is imperative.

Select Bibliography

Andeweg, R.B. and Irwin, G.A. (1993) *Dutch Government and Politics*, London: Macmillan.

Becker, F. *et al.* (1996) *Inzake Beginselen. Het Zeventiende Jaarboek voor Het Democratisch Socialisme*, Amsterdam: Arbeiderspers/Wiardi Beckman Stichting.

Hillebrand, R. (1992) *De antichambre van het parlement. Kandidaatstelling in Nederlandse politieke partijen*, Leiden: DSWO Press.

Koole, R.A. (1992) *De opkomst van de moderne kaderpartij. Veranderende partijorganisatie in Nederland 1960–1990*, Utrecht: Het Spectrum.

Koole, R.A. (1994) 'The Vulnerability of the Modern Cadre Party in the Netherlands', in Katz, R.S. and Mair, P. (eds), *How Parties Organize. Change and Adaptation in Party Organizations in Western Democracies*, London: Sage.

Lijphart, A. (1968) *The Politics of Accommodation: Pluralism and Democracy in the Netherlands*, Berkeley: University of California Press.

Orlow, D. (1995) 'The Paradoxes of Success. Dutch Social Democracy and its Historiography', in *Bijdragen en mededelingen betreffende de geschiedenis der Nederlanden*, 110 (1).

Perry, J. *et al.* (1994) *Honderd Jaar Sociaal-Democratie in Nederland, 1894–1994*, Amsterdam: Bert Bakker.

Van Kersbergen, K. (1994) 'Socialisme, Sociaal-Democratie en Het Den Uyl-Socialisme. De Nederlandse Sociaal-Democratie en Het Denken Over de Verzorgingsstaat', in Bussemaker, J. *et al.*, *Verzorgingsstaat Tussen Individualisme en Solidariteit*, Amsterdam: Wiardi Beckman Stichting.

Wolinetz, S.B. (1993) 'Reconstructing Dutch Social Democracy', *West European Politics*, 16 (1).

Wolinetz, S.B. (1996) 'Internal Politics and Rates of Change in the *Partij van de Arbeid*', *1957–1994. Jaarboek Documentatiecentrum Nederlandse Politieke Partijen 1995.*

Contact Information

All the institutions mentioned in the text as linked to the party (except the Anne Vondeling Foundation) are located at the party office

Party Addresses
Nicolaas Witsenkade 30
PO Box 1310   Tel: 31 20 551 2155
1000 BH Amsterdam   Fax: 31 20 551 2330

PvdA parliamentary group
Binnenhof 1a
2513 AA The Hague   Tel: 31 70 318 2211

PvdA Eurodelegation European Parliament
Belliardstraat 97–113   Tel: 32 2 284 2966
B-1047 Brussels   Fax: 32 2 284 2668

Web page on the Internet – the PvdA has a beautiful website, although the information available in English is limited: http://www.pvda.nl

13 The Portuguese Socialist Party

José Magone

HISTORY

The Portuguese Socialist Party (*Partido Socialista* – PS) was refounded in a congress at Bad Munstereiffel between 16 and 19 April 1973. From the start the new party was supported by the Socialist International, in particular by the German Social Democratic Party. The history of the PS can be divided into three main parts: the pre-1974 period, the revolutionary 1974–5 period and the post-revolutionary period.

The Pre-1974 Period: Factionalism and Personalism

The first period until 1974 was characterized by factionalism and charismatic leadership. The Socialist Party was originally founded in 1875 by José Fontana and Antero de Quental. The Portuguese Section of the Workers' International remained small throughout the late constitutional monarchy and the First Republic (1910–26). In the latter period other parties such as the Portuguese Republican Party (*Partido Republicano Portugues* – PRP) and later on the Portuguese Communist Party (*Partido Comunista Portugues* – PCP) were also able to occupy the left side of the political spectrum. The party was dissolved in 1932 due to the growing repression of opposition groups by the authoritarian regime (1926–74). Several more or less successful attempts were later made to refound the Socialist Party. In the post-war period Portuguese socialists remained in close contact with the international network of socialist parties in other west European democracies. This internationalization of the party facilitated the foundation of the PS in 1973. After 1945, the most important leader was Mário Soares, a lawyer and historian, who was arrested several times and deported to the Sao Tomé islands in 1968 by the regime. He was forced into exile to Paris in 1970.

The Revolutionary Period, 1974–5

The Socialist leadership was taken by surprise when the military *coup d'état* against the authoritarian regime took place on 25 April 1974. Mário Soares returned as soon as possible from the Federal Republic of Germany and became one of the main leaders among the civilian politicians. By the time he arrived, the *coup d'état* had turned into a participatory revolution. From the beginning the PS stressed the wish to co-operate on an equal footing with all political forces. In the early phase of the Revolution, socialists and communists worked together in government to stabilize the political situation. Moreover, the political field was dominated by the Movement of Armed Forces (*Movimento de Forcas Armadas* – MFA) which had undertaken the *coup d'état* and were committed to playing the central role in shaping the new political system. In autumn 1974, the relationship between the Socialist and Communist Party deteriorated considerably, due to the Communist Party's attempt to colonize the state apparatus, the media and other areas. In the second party conference of the PS on 15–16 December Mário Soares fiercely criticized this strategy of the Communist Party and urged party members to oppose the further expansion of Communist dominance. Meanwhile the party had become a mass party of over 100,000 members and as such gained more legitimacy to confront the Communist Party.

Two factions emerged during the party conference which challenged Mário Soares' leadership. The Socialist People's Party (*Movimento Socialista Popular* – MSP) and the Autonomous Political Socialist Group (*Grupo Autonomo Politico Socialista* – GAPS) wanted the inclusion of more workers in the leading positions of the party. The motion put forward by these factions was defeated and the MSP of Manuel Serra decided to leave the party and found the People's Socialist Front (*Frente Socialista Popular* – FSP).

In January 1975 the PS was successful in blocking legislation put forward by the military concerning trade unions which tended to a communist model of streamlining the movement into one big trade union confederation (*Unicidade*). However, the radicalization of the revolution led to a sub-ordination of the parties to the political goals pursued by the military. In spite of this unfavourable environment for competitive party politics, elections to the Constituent Assembly took place on 25 April 1975. The party won a relative majority with 34.71 per cent. Along with other moderate forces such as the People's Democratic Party (*Partido Popular Democratico* – PPD) and the Democratic Social Centre (*Centro Democrático e Social* – CDS), it began a campaign against the communist-led faction of the Movement of Armed Forces under the leadership of Prime Minister Vasco Goncalves and the Communist Party. Mário Soares could also count on the support of the Socialist International which set up a 'Committee of Solidarity with Democracy in Portugal' (Eisfeld, 1983, 1984). This alliance led to the victory of the moderate forces on 25 November 1975, after an extreme left-wing military coup attempt was prevented by colonel Ramalho Eanes.

The Democratic Period since 1975

One of the most important transformations of the PS in the democratic period was the 'social democratization' of its ideology. The process of de-marxification was completed in the Sixth Party Conference in 1986 with the adoption of a new programme. Such distancing from its former ideological foundations could already be observed in the Fourth (1981) and Fifth Party Conference (1983).

The party was able to secure a relative majority of 34.87 per cent in the first legislative elections of 1976. Under the leadership of Mário Soares, it made up the first constitutional government. The revolutionary legacy was a major impediment to the formulation and implementation of short-term socialist policies, which were designed to stabilize the very unstable political and economic situation along liberal lines. This led to opposition inside the party and in Parliament. In December 1977, the PS failed to win a motion of confidence. A coalition government with the conservative Democratic and Social Centre was opposed inside the party. In December 1978, a faction inside the party under former agriculture minister Lopes Cardoso decided to leave the party; the Left Union of Socialist Democracy (*Uniao da Esquerda Socialista Revolucionaria* – UEDS) was opposed to the policies of prime minister Mário Soares. The break-up of the coalition in mid-1978 led to a more active role for president Ramalho Eanes, who decided to nominate an independent prime minister to replace Mário Soares. Consequently, at the Third Party Conference in March 1979, Soares opposed the decision of the party secretariat to support the re-election of Ramalho Eanes. His defeat inside the party led to his resignation from his position as Secretary-General. This situation of acute factionalization was overcome only in the Fourth Party Congress in 1981, when Soares won the majority of party delegates against the ex-Secretariat and the Socialist parliamentary group under the leadership of Salgado Zenha. Between 1981 and 1983, Mário Soares again led the party to success. The victory in the elections of 1983 led to the formation of a coalition government between the PS and the second largest party, the Social-Democratic Party (*Partido Socialdemocrata* – PSD). The so-called *Bloco Central* government abruptly ended in 1985, when the PSD ministers left the coalition. In the October elections, the PSD won a relative majority and the PS suffered huge losses. Between 1985 and 1995 the PS remained in opposition without any increase in its vote. The main reason for this situation was the dominance of the charismatic PSD Prime Minister, Anibal Cavaco Silva, who was able to win an absolute majority in 1987 and 1991.

The election of Mário Soares as president in early 1986 led to a crisis of leadership inside the party. This was due to the lack of strong personalities to unite the party and the negative balance sheet of the party in government.

The crisis was resolved only with the emergence of Antonio Guterres as Secretary-General in 1992. Within three years, seconded by Antonio Vitorino and Almeida Santos, he was able to increase the electoral support for the PS from 29.30 per cent to 43 per cent and gain victory in the elections of 1 October 1995.

ORGANIZATION AND PARTY PROFILE

Nature of the Party: A Cartel Party

The very short history of the Socialist party did not allow it to develop as a mass party. Instead, the party was always a party of cadres which has shifted since 1976 to becoming more of a 'cartel party' – that is, highly dependent on state subsidies.

A Centralized Party Structure

The party is run by the national commission and the Secretary-General. Both are elected by the national party conference, the highest body of the party. The national commission is the legislative body of the party. Parallel to that, the 40 elected members and *ex officio* members of the political commission carry through the policies approved by the party conference. Although the party is highly centralized, it has branches in all districts as well as major cities and villages. The lowest unit of the party are the local branches with five–fifty members. They are part of a larger confederation at regional level. The regional confederations send delegates to the national party conference, the number of members determining the eventual number of delegates each branch is allowed to send.

Membership

In terms of membership, the existing figures are very unreliable because the list of members is not up to date, including members who are not paying fees or who even died some time ago. The membership as been subject to major shifts since 1974, as Table 13.1 clearly shows.

Members come mainly from large and middle-sized urban centres. They are white-collar workers and members of the traditional (small shopkeepers) and new middle classes; there are fewer members from the agricultural sector. This sociological outlook has remained very stable throughout the years, however, in the 1995 elections the PS was able to improve its electoral support by gaining voters from other social groups who had tended to vote for the more conservative parties.

Table 13.1   Membership of the PS, Portugal, 1974–92

Year	Total membership
1974	35,971
1975	77,625
1976	91,562
1983	34,109
1986	46,655
1989	62,117
1991	69,351
1992	70,000

Source: *Expresso* (4 July 1992, pp. 20–1).

The Electorate: Increase in Volatility

The PS electorate was very stable until 1985, with between 88 and 95 per cent voting for the party in consecutive elections. The emergence of the Democratic Renewal Party (*Partido Renovador Democratico* – PRD) in the elections of October 1985 changed everything. The new party was able to attract over 17 per cent of the vote, mainly former PS voters. Between 1985 and 1991 the party was unable to recover completely from this loss in votes, however, in the elections of 1995 the party was able to win a strong relative majority at the expense of the PSD. In terms of composition of the electorate, PS voters come from the white-collar working class and the new mobile urban middle classes of the large urban centres of Lisbon, Porto and Setubal. The PS is also strong among the small farmers in the southern regions of Portugal. Geographically, the PS is stronger in the regions of the western coast and in the south, although since the 1995 elections it has been able to gain stronger electoral support in the north. The nature of the party (between catch-all and cartel party) makes it very vulnerable to changes in the preferences of the electorate. For the moment, the PS is the strongest party in the Assembly of the Republic. Its vote is evenly distributed across the territory. Since 1975, the main transformation of the PS electorate has been the growing decline of the traditional middle classes of shopkeepers, artisans and other similar professions and the growth of the volatile new middle classes of professionals.

Relations with the Trade Unions

During the revolutionary process the Communist Party and the MFA tried to push through the principle of trade union unity (*Unicidade*) by forcing the opposition to accept as the sole representative trade union confederation the communist-led *Intersindical*. This met extreme opposition from the Socialist Party. After the Revolution, the PS and the PSD tried to prevent further communist dominance over the trade union movement. Socialist and social-democratic trade unionists formed a movement against the communist-led leadership called 'Open Letter' (*Carta Aberta*) within *Intersindical*. The 'Open Letter' was formed in 1976, and regarded itself as a faction in the Second Extraordinary Congress of *Intersindical* in January 1977. Nevertheless, the faction was very soon absorbed into the structures of *Intersindical*. In spring 1978 the socialists and social democrats founded an alternative trade union, the *Uniao Geral dos Trabalhadores* (General Union of Workers – UGT), with representatives from both main parties – PS and PSD – in equal numbers in leading positions. Logistics for the establishment of the alternative trade union movement was provided by the Friedrich Ebert and the Friedrich Naumann Foundations, close to the German SPD and the FDP, respectively. It was formed mainly against the communist-dominated *Confederacao Geral dos Trabalhadores Portugueses – Intersindical* (General Confederation of the Portuguese Workers – CGTP-In), but in the second half of the 1980s became less radical and attempted to establish a joint platform with the CGTP-In. The UGT has been quite supportive of the newly created Economic and Social Committee (*Comissao Economico e Social* – CES), a consultative institution of the government in economic and social matters. During the Cavaco Silva governments of 1985 and 1995, the CES opposed its liberalization policies and uncompromising policy-style in the Permanent Council of Social Concertation (*Conselho Permanente de Concertacao Social* – CPCS) (Magone, 1997, pp. 119–22; Optenhogel and Stoleroff, 1985, p. 187; Eisfeld, 1984, p. 176)

The return to power of the Socialist Party led to a co-operative attitude by the UGT in the Agreement on Strategic Concertation 1996/1999 approved on 20 December 1996. This was achieved without the support of the CGTP-In. In spite of its origins, the UGT was able to establish a more autonomous position in relation to the PS and PSD.

Relations with Other Parties of the Left

The PS' relations with other parties of the Left have evolved over time. During the early phase of the revolutionary period the PS maintained a co-operative attitude towards what was perceived as being the largest and best organized party on the left, the Communist Party. By the end of the revolution, the PS had become anti-communist in its ideological orientation. It avoided any cooperation with the PCP at national level, yet at local level a limited co-operation between the two parties was preserved. In the second half of the 1980s, the relationship between socialists and communists became less conflictual. Mário Soares and Jorge Sampaio advocated a more compromising stance to the PCP. Nevertheless, since Antonio Guterres became

Secretary-General in 1992 the party position has been to avoid any coalition with the PCP. At local level, the relationship between the two parties is more conciliatory – in fact, the coalition in Lisbon between the PS, the communist coalition (CDU), the Trotskyist Revolutionary Socialist Party (PSR) and the Maoist People's Democratic Union (UDP) was renewed in 1993. With the other parties on the left such as the UDP, PSR and the PRD the relationship has been sporadic. The PS has been an important vehicle for independent left candidates in the European Parliament – for example, the former Communist José Barros Moura in the 1994–9 legislature or José Canavarro from the PRD in the previous one. Before the 1995 elections, it established a platform of the left called the *Estados Gerais* (General Estates) which aimed at mobilizing the population for a socialist majority (Table 13.2). This strategy was supported by many independent personalities sympathetic to the left.

Table 13.2   Left vote over time in Portuguese legislative elections, 1975–95 (%)

	PS^1	PCP*	PRD	UDP	PSR	MRPP	Other parties	Left	Right
1975	37.87	12.53		0.79			7.30	58.49	41.51
1976	34.87	14.35		1.67		0.66	2.31	53.86	46.14
1979	27.33	18.80		2.18	0.62	0.89	0.99	50.81	49.19
1980	26.65	16.75		1.38	1.00	0.59	1.44	47.81	52.19
1983	36.12	18.07		0.48	0.23	0.37	1.09	56.36	43.64
1985	20.77	15.49	17.92	1.27	0.61	0.34	0.55	56.95	43.05
1987	22.24	12.14	4.91	0.89	0.58	0.37	0.33	41.46	58.54
1991	29.30	8.80	0.61	0.11	1.12	0.85	1.68	42.47	57.43
1995	43.76	8.65	–	0.57	0.64	0.70	0.25	54.57	45.43

Notes: 1 See pp. xiv ff for party acronyms.
* PCP collaborated with other left-wing parties in an alliance called the Front of the United Political Left (FEPU) from 1975 to 1979, the United People's Alliance (APU) from 1979 to 1987 and Democratic Unity Coalition (CDU) after 1987.

Sources: based on data provided by *Eleicoes em Abril* (1975), Rosário and Migueis (1991), official tables with the results of the elections to the Assembly of the Republic on 6 October 1991, *Diário da República-I Serie-A,nr.249–29–10–1991*, *Diario da República-I Serie-A nr.249–29–10–1991*; and elections to the Assembly of the Republic on 1 October 1995, *Diario da Republica-I Serie-A nr.246–24–10–1995*.

GOVERNMENT ACHIEVEMENTS AND CURRENT POLICIES

Main Government Achievements

The Socialist party was present in all provisional governments but one during the Revolution. Policy-making during this period was controlled by the MFA officers. Nevertheless, in terms of supporting a transition to a democratic political system, socialist leaders played an important role in preventing a further radicalization of the Revolution. The PS was active in four out of thirteen constitutional governments. After the first legislative elections on 25 April 1976, the PS formed a minority government which lasted until December 1977. The policy agenda was designed to achieve the consolidation of the economy after its collapse during the Revolution. Soares was in an awkward position, because he had to face an ideologically highly fragmented Parliament. Moreover, some factions inside the party wanted Soares to pursue policies of redistribution, which the economic situation did not allow. More importantly, Soares was confronted with a lack of political experience and a scarcity of human and material resources to fulfil his programme. Growing contradictions inside the party and between government and opposition led to his resignation after a motion of confidence failed to gain support in Parliament. The need to implement a severe austerity policy imposed by the International Monetary Fund (IMF) in 1978 led to a coalition government with the conservative CDS. The coalition did not last long due to problems between the coalition partners regarding land reform in the agricultural sector, and after six months the coalition was terminated by the junior coalition partner. Following this second constitutional government, Soares resigned again. President Ramalho Eanes nominated an independent figure to form a new government, a move contested by Soares (Rother,1985).

The second major government experience occured between April 1983 and October 1985. After the general elections of 25 April 1983, Soares decided to enter a coalition with the PSD, so that a second IMF austerity plan could be implemented in 1983/84. The programme of the *Bloco Central* (Central Bloc), as it was subsequently called, included a list of 100 measures to be implemented in the first 100 days. These were only partially fulfilled, moreover, growing problems inside the coalition led to its early break-up. The deputy prime minister Carlos Mota Pinto died in February 1985, and the new leader of the PSD, Anibal Cavaco Silva, elected in May 1985 in the Twelfth party conference of the PSD of Figueira da Foz, decided to withdraw his ministers from the coalition. In the October elections of 1985 the PS lost a substantial amount of votes to the PRD as well as the PSD.

The PS was in office again in October 1995 (Table 13.3). For the first time, the party was able to achieve a comfortable plurality of 43 per cent of the votes. Governmental policies are linked with EU objectives, the main priority of the government being to meet the criteria of the Maastricht Treaty set up in 1993, so that it could qualify for membership of EMU from the outset. Throughout the election, education and regionalization were also emphasized as priorities. The implementation of the EU structural funds to achieve qualitative, sustainable development has become one of the essential long-term aims of the socialist government. An agreement on strategic

Table 13.3   PS in constitutional governments in Portugal, 1976–95

	Date in	*Date out*	*Government composition*
Soares I	23.7.1976	9.12.1977	PS
Soares II	23.1.1978	28.7.1978	PS–CDS
Soares III	9.6.1983	3.11.1985	PS–PSD
Guterres	1.11.1995		PS

Source: Author's compilation.

concertation (*Acordo de concertacao estrategica*) in December 1996 was signed by all social partners with the exception of the communist CGTP-In; the agreement focused mainly on aspects of employment and education, and advocated the continuation of reform in the administrative sector.

The Party Programme

The most recent party programme was approved in 1986 and the last electoral campaign began in 1994. A so-called symbolic 'contract of legislature' (*contrato de legislatura*) was established with the electorate which was formulated after several discussion meetings involving over 30,000 people between the summer of 1994 and the spring of 1995.The main slogan was 'For a New Majority' (*Por Uma Nova Maioria*), it asked the electorate to give the PS a stable majority so that it could replace the PSD in power. Guterres tried to display a more humane approach to politics by emphasizing the centrality of solidarity in his elected programme. His slogan 'With Heart and Reason' (*Com Coracao e Razao*) attempted to convey a moderate image of the PS, in order to attract voters from the PSD and CDS for the socialist project. This strategy drew inspiration from previous party programmes and emphasied of the cultural and educational needs of the Portuguese people.

Select Bibliography

Aguiar, J. (1994) 'Partidos, Eleicoes, Dinamica Politica', *Analize Social*, 29(125–126).

Cruz, M. Braga da (1995) *Instituicoes Politicas e Processos Sociais*, Lisboa: Bertrand.

Eisfeld, R. (1983) '*A Revolucao dos Cravos*' e a Politica Externa: O Fracasso do Pluralismo Socialista em Portugal a Seguir a 1974, *Revista Critica de Ciencias Sociais*, 11.

Eisfeld, R. (1984) *Sozialistischer Pluralismus in Europa. Ansatze und Scheitern am Beispiel Portugal*, Cologne: Verlag Wissenschaft und Politik.

Gallagher, T. (1990) 'The Portuguese Socialist Party: the Pitfalls of Being First'. in Gallagher and Williams, A. (eds), *Southern European Socialism*, Manchester: Manchester University Press.

Magone, J. (1997) *European Portugal. The Difficult Road to Sustainable Democracy*, London: Macmillan/St Martin's Press.

Optenhogel, U. and Stoleroff, A. (1985) 'The Logics of Politically Competing Trade', in de Sousa Ferreira, E. and Opello, W.C. (eds), *Conflict and Change in Portugal 1974–1984*, Lisboa: Teorema.

Partido Socialista (1975) *Declaracao de Principios, Programa e Estatutos do Partido Socialista*, Aprovado no Congresso do PS em Dezembro de 1974, Lisboa: Partido Socialista.

Partido Socialista (1986) 'Declaracao de Principios e Programa, Aprovado no VI Congresso Nacional, Lisboa 1986, Lisboa: Partido Socialista.

Robinson, R. (1951) 'The Evolution of the Portuguese Socialist Party, 1973–1986 in International Perspective', *Portuguese Studies Review*, 1(2).

Rosario, E. do and Migueis, J. (1991), 'Assembleia da Republica – Resultados Eleitorais (1976–1991)', *Eleicoes. Revista de Assuntos Eleitorais*, 2.

Rother, B. (1985) *Der verhinderte Ubergang zum Sozialismus. Die sozialistische Partei Portugals im Zentrum der Macht (1974–1978), Frankfurt-am-Man: Materialis.*

Contact Information

Addresses of Party Headquarters

Partido Socialista
Largo do Rato nr 2   Tel: 3511 383 03 78
1250 Lisboa   Fax: 3511 383 38 45

Fundacao José Fontana   Tel: 3511 301 38 08
Avenida das Descobertas 17
1400 Lisboa–Portugal

Fundacao Antero de Quental   Tel: 3511 301 35 34
Avenida das Descobertas 17   Tel: 3511 301 89 68
1400 Lisboa–Portugal   Fax: 3511 301 59 59

Web page on the Internet: www.partido-socialista.pt

14 The Spanish Socialist Workers' Party

Paul Kennedy

HISTORY

Early Development, 1879–1921

The Spanish Socialist Workers' Party (PSOE) was founded on 2 May 1879 by a group of printers and other workers in a small restaurant which still stands, called the *Casa Labra*, in the calle Tetuán, just off the Puerta del Sol in the centre of Madrid. The most prominent of the party's founders was Pablo Iglesias (1850–1925), an austere Galician under whose leadership the party was notable for its derivative, reductionist understanding of Marxist theory. Wary of the competition within the political arena provided by the rival anarchist and republican movements, Iglesias concentrated on painstakingly developing the party's organization. Strategy was based on an adherence to legalistic, reformist practice which belied the leadership's frequent recourse to revolutionary rhetoric.

Jealously guarding his party's independence, Iglesias in effect condemned the PSOE to a position of political irrelevance by refusing to countenance any electoral alliance with political rivals. It was only when this stance was abandoned and a more pragmatic approach was adopted that Iglesias became the PSOE's first parliamentary representative in 1910 by means of a 'conjunction' with the republicans.

In August 1917 the socialists placed themselves at the head of a national general strike sparked by a fall in living standards occasioned by rampant inflation. The failure of the strike and its brutal repression by the security forces convinced the socialist leadership of the need to pursue a legalist course rather than risk a direct confrontation with the state. Those within the party opposed to this stance were further alienated by the party leadership's reaction to the Russian Revolution and its rejection of Lenin's Third International; in 1921 a pro-Bolshevik faction abandoned the party to form the Spanish Communist Party (*Partido Comunista Español* – PCE).

Growth and Political Prominence, 1921–39

Following Primo de Rivera's (1870–1930) *coup d'état* in September 1923, the socialist movement's collaboration with the dictatorship in the field of labour

176

relations enabled it to escape the repression visited upon its Anarchist and Communist rivals. When popular support for the regime waned in the context of the international economic crisis of the late 1920s, the socialists distanced themselves from Primo and placed themselves at the head of the broad anti-monarchist coalition which declared the Second Republic in April 1931. By now the best organized and most popular political party in the country, the PSOE contributed three ministers to the government of the Republic: Francisco Largo Caballero (1869–1946), Indalecio Prieto (1883–1962) and Fernando de los Rios (1879–1949). However, the great hopes placed in the Republic by progressive Spaniards were frustrated as the government's attempts to implement an ambitious programme of social and political reforms were undermined by the land-based reactionary élites, whose representatives won elections held in 1933.

Frustrated by the paucity of the Republic's achievements and fearful that the participation of the Confederation of Autonomous Right-Wing Groups (*Confederación Española de Derechas Autónomas* – CEDA) in government presaged a lurch towards fascism, a section of the PSOE associated with Largo Caballero adopted an ostensibly revolutionary position. This radicalization was further promoted by the entry of large numbers of landless peasants into the affiliated land-workers' association (*Federación Nacional de Trabajadores de la Tierra* – FNTT). The government's bloody suppression of the revolutionary rising of October 1934 exacerbated the split which was developing within the PSOE between the supporters of Largo Caballero, who were by now openly advocating a bolshevization of the party, and those of the moderate Prieto. Prieto was instrumental in constructing the progressive Popular Front Alliance which defeated its conservative adversaries at elections held in February 1936, although opposition from Largo Caballero prevented him from accepting the post of Prime Minister in the new government.

The Popular Front government's attempts to proceed with the progressive package of reforms implemented between 1931 and 1933 was aborted by the outbreak of Civil War in July 1936. Despite the fact that the PSOE provided the republic with two Prime Ministers, Largo Caballero and Juan Negrín (1892–1956), the party increasingly found itself eclipsed by the Communist Party in the prosecution of the Republican war effort. Franco's victory over the Republic in 1939 left the PSOE broken, divided and facing an uncertain future.

The Wilderness Years, 1939–74

In the wake of the Civil War, the party's structures proved to be poorly suited to the style of clandestine political activity mastered by the more effective communists. In the eight-year period 1945–53, which culminated in the torture and murder of the prominent PSOE leader, Tomás Centeno, six entire executive committees were imprisoned by the Francoist authorities.

By the 1960s, the Toulouse-based leadership found itself increasingly out of touch with a Spain which was undergoing rapid and profound socio–economic change. In 1974 activists within Spain succeeded in consolidating their ascendancy over the exiled leadership when the 32-year old lawyer, Felipe González (1942–) was voted leader at the party's 26th Congress held in Suresnes, France.

The scale of the task facing the new party leadership was awesome: the transformation of the fortunes of a party which had effectively become marginal to political developments within Spain. Crucial to the legitimacy of the new leadership was the support provided by prominent European socialist and social democratic leaders, including François Mitterrand and Willy Brandt, who were instrumental in ensuring that the party was re-cognized by the Socialist International. Moreover, financial aid from abroad, particularly from Brandt's SPD (see chapter 6), funded the creation of a modest party apparatus whose role was vital in the next stage of the PSOE's development.

From Clandestinity to Power, 1975–82

The death of General Franco (1892–1975) marked the start of a volatile and unpredictable period in Spanish history. Still illegal, the PSOE held its first Congress within Spain for forty years in December 1976. Concerned not to be outflanked on the left by the larger and better-organized Communist Party, the party presented a radical, non-compromising image, emphasizing its Marxist heritage and advocating a clean break, or *ruptura*, with the political system which had survived the death of the dictator. Events moved quickly, however, and the party's legalization in February 1977 and its surprisingly strong showing at the general election held in June 1977, when it came second to Adolfo Suárez's (1932–) Democratic Centre Union (*Unión de Centro Democrático* – UCD), established both the party's hegemony on the left and its key role in the nascent democratic system. The PSOE's failure to build significantly on this success at the general election held in March 1979 convinced the leadership that the party's Marxist label was hindering further electoral progress. At the party's 28th Congress held two months after the election, González backed a proposal that the PSOE drop its Marxist self-definition. When the motion was defeated, González stunned the party by resigning the leadership in protest. By the time that an Extraordinary Congress was held in September 1979 to decide on the issue, organizational changes masterminded by the deputy leader, Alfonso Guerra (1940–), allied to the left's inability to put forward an alternate candidate for party leader, ensured that González was overwhelmingly re-elected as party leader.

During the three years which followed the PSOE's own 'Bad Godesberg', González re-positioned his party further towards the centre of the political spectrum and prepared to take over the reins of power from a UCD government which, by the turn of the decade, appeared to be at an advanced stage of disintegration. The contrast between the critical condition of the government and the highly organized and tightly disciplined PSOE was not lost on the electorate, whose ten million votes – the highest total ever achieved at a Spanish election – swept the PSOE into power at the polls held on 28 October 1982.

PSOE in Office, 1982–96

High on the new government's agenda was the improvement of an economy which was in crisis. Conscious of the difficulties encountered by their French counterparts in prosecuting an expansionist course, the Spanish socialists implemented from the very start a tough economic policy. The goal of policy was to secure the country's membership of the European Community before the end of the government's first term. Integration was viewed as providing a framework for the country's 'modernization', a constant theme throughout the socialists' entire period in office.

By 1986 the government's stewardship of the economy had been favourable in several areas, although the patience of the trade unions was already wearing thin as government industrial policies led to mass redundancies. Spain became a member of the European Community on 1 January 1986 and the government's risky *volte-face* on NATO membership paid off when Spaniards voted to remain in the Alliance in a referendum held in March. In the general election held three months after the government's referendum triumph, the socialists maintained their overall majority.

From 1986 to 1990 Spain enjoyed a quite exceptional period of economic growth which outstripped that of all other European countries, and the PSOE remained the largest party at the general election held in October 1989. However, the subsequent period proved far more problematic for the government. A seemingly never-ending stream of corruption scandals involving figures connected with the PSOE, a break-down in the party's much-vaunted unity and discipline and the Spanish economy's plunge into its worst recession in decades all combined to undermine the party's credibility. Significant achievements in the field of welfare provision during the 1990s nevertheless did much to retain the support of many voters and undoubtedly played a part in the PSOE winning the general election held in June 1993. Dependent on the support of the Catalan nationalist party, Convergence and Union (*Convergència i Unió* – CiU) to remain in power, González was forced to call fresh elections for March 1996 when the Catalans withdrew their backing. Defeated by the right-wing Popular Party (*Partido Popular* – PP) by the surprisingly narrow margin of 1.4 per cent of the vote, the PSOE left power with a solid base on which to prepare for a return to office. The revival of the party's fortunes is in the hands of Joaquín Almunia (1948–), who became party leader following Felipe González's surprise resignation at the PSOE's 34th Congress held in June 1997.

ORGANIZATION AND PARTY PROFILE

Political Tradition

Although the leaders of the early PSOE viewed themselves as being orthodox Marxists, their understanding of Marx was primitive and derivative. The theoretical contributions of early party figures to the international movement were negligible and the party frequently and uncritically looked to French political theoreticians. The early party was therefore incapable of applying Marxist theory to Spanish socio–economic and political conditions. Despite the vehemence of its revolutionary rhetoric, the PSOE under Iglesias was anxious not to endanger the painstaking growth of the party organization by actually engaging in revolutionary activities. The Restoration regime's bloody suppression of the Socialist-led general strike in 1917 confirmed the leadership's commitment to legalist reformism.

In the period leading up to the outbreak of Civil War, the confrontation between followers of the radical Largo Caballero and those of the moderate Indalecio Prieto was highly damaging and served as an object lesson for future generations of Socialists determined to maintain party unity.

Following the death of Franco, the party once again emphasized its Marxist credentials as a means of competing on the left with a Spanish Communist Party which, at the time, appeared to be stronger than the Socialists. With hegemony over the Communists assured at the 1977 general election, the party found it politic to play down its Marxist heritage in the search for further votes. The PSOE therefore went from being a party whose statutes in 1979 defined it as being Marxist to being a moderate party of government just three years later.

Relations with the Trade Unions

Nine years after the party was founded, its leaders took the initiative in creating a socialist trade union, the General Workers' Union (*Unión General de Trabajadores* – UGT). For many years there was considerable overlap between the membership and leadership of the two branches of the movement, despite the fact that party and trade union were formally independent organizations.

The UGT played a key role in the organizational survival of Spanish social-ism during the dictatorships of Primo de Rivera and General Franco, and during the transition from dictatorship to democracy following Franco's death, the PSOE and the UGT presented a united front. PSOE–UGT relations were tested far more after the socialist electoral triumph in 1982. Prepared to accept Felipe González's argument that a radical overhaul of the economy was necessary if Spain were to enter the European Community, the UGT signed a number of agreements on wage restraint and redundancies with the govern-ment during its first term. However, rising unemployment and government cuts in pensions strained relations throughout 1985, and the government's change of tack on NATO membership further exacerbated divisions over policy.

By 1987, the UGT leader, Nicolás Redondo (1927–), who was also a PSOE Member of Parliament, resigned his seat in protest at the government's refusal to make significant improvements in social provision at a time when the Spanish economy was thriving. In December 1988 a nadir was reached in relations between the UGT and the government when the Socialist Union, together with the Communist-led trade union federation, the Workers' Commissions (*Comisiones Obreras* – CC.OO.), co-ordinated a highly effect-ive one-day general strike which obtained massive support.

In 1990, the UGT broke off its formal links with the party which had created it over a century before. Two further general strikes in May 1992 and January 1994 called to protest at government cuts in unemployment benefit and labour market reforms failed to repeat the success of the 1988 stoppage and the influence of the trade unions in Spain continued to decline.

Party Structure and Organization

The PSOE possesses a federal structure in which regional parties based on the seventeen autonomous communities are in turn made up of local branches (*agrupaciones locales*) and provincial branches (*agrupaciones pro-vinciales*). The actual autonomy enjoyed by the regional parties (the Basque PSE–PSOE, the Catalan PSC–PSOE, the Galician PSG–PSOE, Madrid's FSM–PSOE, etc.), each of which has its own general secretary, is in practice limited by the national leadership's tendency to intervene in the appointment of regional party leaders.

The political activity of the basic unit of the party, the *agrupación local*, is co-ordinated and directed by its local committee (*comité local*) which is elected at the local assembly (*asamblea local*), the body charged with mon-itoring the activities of the local committee. Another function of local assemblies is the election of the provincial congress (*congreso provincial*), which itself elects the provincial executive committee (*comisión ejecutiva provincial*), overseen by the provincial committee (*comité provincial*). A similar system operates at the level of the autonomous community, whilst at national level, the major party entities are the Federal Congress (*Congreso Federal*), the sovereign body of the party which meets every two–three years; the Federal Executive Committee (*Comisión Ejecutiva Federal*), which is charged with the implementation of policy, meeting several times a year; and the Federal Committee (*Comité Federal*), which is the highest authority in the party between Congresses. The basic organizational pattern is therefore reproduced at all levels: an assembly, an executive and a body charged with overseeing the executive.

Membership

Membership of the still-illegal PSOE was around 2,000 at the beginning of the 1970s, reaching the 100,000 mark by the end of the decade (see Table 14.1). By 1982, when the party commanded almost half of the national vote, party membership was still relatively small at around 116,000. Once in power, however, the PSOE enjoyed a steady rise in membership, which totalled

Table 14.1   PSOE membership, 1888–1997

Year	Membership	Year	Membership
1888[1]		1926	8,561
1890[1]		1927	8,083
1892[1]		1928	9,001
1894[1]		1929	10,528
1899[1]		1930	18,287
1902	4,288	1931	25,999
1905	6,155	1932	75,133
1908	6,000	1933	81,177
1912	13,000	1936	59,846
1915	14,332	1976	9,141
1918	30,630	1979	101,082
1919	42,113	1981	97,320
1920	52,897	1984	153,076
1921	45,477	1988	213,028
1923	9,089	1990	262,854
1924	8,215	1994	349,626
		1997	373,030

[1] Accurate membership figures are difficult to establish, due to the clandestine character of the party and overlap between PSOE and UGT membership.

Sources: Adapted from Tezanos, J.F., *Historia ilustrada del socialismo español* (Madrid: Editorial Sistema, 1993, pp. 72, 78, 142, 198) and PSOE Web site.

370,000 by 1997. The ratio between members and voters nevertheless remained amongst the lowest of all Western European socialist parties.

With regard to the party's internal social composition, educated middle-class members predominate at the top levels of the party hierarchy, particularly liberal professionals, lawyers, doctors, economists and teachers (see Table 14.2). Members of this group were the main beneficiaries of the

Table 14.2 Sociological characteristics of PSOE members, 1980–93 (%)

	1980	1983	1986	1989	1993
Sex					
Men	91.0	88.8	86.8	82.8	77.0
Women	9.0	11.2	13.2	17.8	23.0
Age					
<30	15.0	19.3	18.1	16.8	14.0
31–40	24.0	25.8	28.1	26.2	26.0
41–50	19.0	16.9	20.1	22.2	23.0
51–60	20.0	15.1	13.7	14.5	15.0
>60	23.0	22.8	20.1	20.2	22.0
Profession					
Self-employed	(20.0)	(22.6)	(18.9)	(22.9)	(16.0)
Farmers	4.0	5.5	3.5	3.9	2.9
Self-employed entrepreneurs in industry and services	15.0	15.1	13.4	13.0	11.6
Independent professionals	1.0	2.0	2.0	2.0	1.5
Waged	(79.0)	(69.9)	(78.2)	(80.5)	(84.0)
Managers	1.0	1.3	1.7	2.2	2.1
Professional, waged and technical	4.0	2.4	4.4	5.2	4.2
Teachers	4.0	3.4	3.4	3.5	7.0
Public officials	–	6.8	9.1	11.9	9.7
Office workers and sales	16.0	13.8	8.8	11.2	11.7
Land-workers	14.0	9.8	10.2	10.7	4.1
Workers in industry and services	36.0	28.1	35.9	30.0	39.7
Foremen and overseers	4.0	2.7	3.0	3.1	4.6
Other	1.0	1.5	2.2	2.8	0.9
Religion					
With religious ideas	(39.0)	(45.4)	(50.4)	(53.7)	(56.0)
Practising Catholics	–	–	4.7	12.6	14.1
Non-practising Catholics	27.7	34.7	33.9	38.3	38.8
Other faiths	9.8	7.7	6.3	2.4	2.8

Source: Tezanos, J.F. *Historia ilustrada del socialismo español* (Madrid: Editorial Sistema, 1993, p. 194).

leadership's allocation of public posts, patronage constituting a key element in the maintenance of party discipline throughout the party's lengthy period in office. Conversely, manual workers, pensioners and housewives are more in evidence at the lower levels of the party.

Sociology of the Electorate and Electoral Performance

The PSOE's adoption of a more 'catch-all' electoral strategy bore fruit at the October 1982 general election when the party proved itself to be largely representative of the electorate as a whole by capturing almost half of the vote (see Table 14.3). Throughout the 1980s, the bulk of support came from workers, whether employed or unemployed, pensioners and housewives, whilst younger urban dwellers were also attracted to the party's progressive image (see Table 14.4). The PSOE also relied on the votes of employees in a public sector which expanded rapidly under the socialists.

In geographical terms, the PSOE triumphed in regions well beyond its traditional strongholds, Madrid, Asturias, the Basque Country and Andalusia. By 1996 support for the PSOE had waned to such an extent that the party emerged victorious only in Andalusia, Castile–La Mancha and Asturias. This electoral reliance on the country's most economically backward regions was mirrored by a dependence on the least dynamic social groups, particularly the elderly, who benefited significantly from socialist welfare reforms (Table 14.4). However, whilst the loss of the youth vote to the PP was worrying, it was hardly surprising given the consistently high levels of youth unemployment under the socialists.

Table 14.3   Share of the vote (%) and seats won by
the PSOE at general elections, 1977–96

Year	% share of vote	Number of seats
1977	29.3	118
1979	30.5	121
1982	48.4	202
1986	44.6	184
1989	39.9	175
1993	38.7	159
1996	37.5	141

Source: Compiled from official statistics.

Table 14.4 Sociological characteristics of PSOE voters, 1977–93 (%)

	1977	1979	1982	1986	1989	1993
Sex						
Men	57.8	50.8	49.3	48.4	45.9	48.2
Women	42.2	49.2	50.7	51.6	54.1	51.8
Age						
18–21	13.4	9.4	8.9	9.6	6.9	6.9
22–25	6.2	7.9	10.0	9.4	9.0	7.3
26–35	19.5	23.6	22.3	19.6	19.8	20.1
36–55	37.2	36.4	33.9	34.3	36.6	30.7
> 55	28.0	22.6	24.7	27.0	27.6	35.1
Profession						
Housewives and inactive	50.9	50.2	61.8	61.5	56.8	50.8
Skilled workers in industry and services	20.1	18.3	13.2	13.0	16.4	20.2
Unskilled workers in industry and services	4.7	6.0	4.6	8.0	8.6	6.9
White-collar workers, sales, technical and professional	11.9	12.3	8.6	3.1	8.5	13.3
Land-workers	3.4	4.0	1.3	8.7	2.7	4.6
Small farmers	3.9	2.1	1.7	1.8	2.1	1.8
Self-employed and independent workers	5.7	6.4	6.0	3.4	4.2	1.8
Waged business	0.9	0.8	0.3	0.6	0.7	0.5
Religion						
Practising Catholics	40.9	36.1	36.1	35.4	38.3	33.6
Non-practising Catholics	48.5	55.1	47.5	55.4	54.7	54.3
Other religions	0.4	0.8	1.1	0.7	1.1	0.8
No religion	2.5	6.6	13.1	8.5	5.6	6.9

Source: Tezanos, J.F., *Historia ilustrada del socialismo español* (Madrid: Editorial Sistema, 1993, p. 195).

GOVERNMENT ACHIEVEMENTS AND CURRENT POLICIES

The main tasks facing the socialists when they entered government in 1982 centred on the consolidation of a democratic system whose fragility had been exposed only the year before in a failed *coup d'état*; the introduction of a basic welfare state; and the implementation of an economic policy which would serve as the basis for the country's modernization, as well as opening the door to Spain's membership of the European Community.

During the PSOE's first term in office, economic policy took centre stage as the government engaged in a wide-ranging liberalization of the economy and massive restructuring of industry. By 1986, the economy had improved sufficiently for the country to be accepted into the European Community and over the next five years, the Spanish economy was the fastest growing in Europe.

Pressurized by the trade unions and rocked by the scale of the general strike called in December 1988 to protest at Felipe González's failure to introduce a significant package of social reforms, the government set to work on some quite historic achievements. Health care was extended to the entire population and pension rights were universalized. Government spending on education increased five-fold during the decade 1982–92, permitting the creation of 1.4 million new school places, the school leaving age was raised to 16 and the number of university students doubled. Between 1983 and 1995 the amount spent by the state on unemployment benefits more than doubled in terms of percentage of GDP. By 1995, total public sector spending accounted for about 50 per cent of GDP, around half of which was accounted for by outlays on the welfare state, in line with the EU average.

Despite these achievements, by the time the socialists left office in 1996, Spain still had the third lowest *per capita* welfare spending in the Union after Greece and Portugal, and it is important to note that only half of Spain's jobless qualify for unemployment pay.

Another area which the socialist government was able to claim as a significant achievement of its period in office was the improvement of Spain's infrastructure. The basic premise behind the government's willingness to commit vast sums of public money was its conviction that public investment in infrastructure was vital if the country was to make good the gap with the Union's leading member-states. Between 1986 and 1991 public investment in roads, railways, ports and airports, oil and gas pipelines, communications and hydraulic projects almost tripled. The government's use of the highly successful Olympic Games in 1992 as a springboard for the transformation of Barcelona into one of Europe's great cities must also be considered a major achievement. Public funding accounted for 70 per cent of the $6 billion investment in urban development, sports installations and infrastructural works considered an integral part of the Olympic project.

In the field of civil liberties, the government set up an Institute for Women's Affairs (*Instituto de la Mujer*) in 1983, which was given generous state funding and charged with the promotion of women's rights. Two years later an Abortion Act became law. The PSOE also took the significant step in 1988 of ensuring that at least 25 per cent of party posts would be held by women, with women accounting for a similar proportion in the party's lists at general, autonomous and local elections.

Undoubtedly, the chief *leitmotif* of the socialist government during its period in office was the concept of 'modernization' and the virtually synonymous

'Europeanization'. The PSOE has long been one of the keenest supporters of European integration which, more than any other single factor, provided the socialists with a framework for economic policy. The Single European Act and the Maastricht Treaty obtained the enthusiastic approval of Felipe González's governments and the socialists remain firm advocates of the benefits of a single currency. In effect, the PSOE was able to make skilful use of European integration as a catalyst for a rapid socio-economic and political process aimed at consolidating Spanish democracy and 'catching up' with Europe. As the economy boomed in the late 1980s, the PSOE was able to make much political capital from its identification with ever-closer European integration. However, this scenario was dramatically altered after Maastricht when, in the context of the Spanish economy's worst recession for thirty years, Spain's participation in the single currency project was placed in considerable doubt.

In addition to the economic difficulties suffered by the country in the 1990s, a seemingly endless stream of PSOE-related corruption cases involving highly placed figures such as the Governor of the Central Bank and the Director of the Civil Guard (*Guardia Civil*) did much to undermine support for the socialists. Allegations that the government had been behind the creation of hit-squads engaged in the killing of alleged Basque terrorists and the revelation in 1995 that the Spanish secret service had bugged the telephone conversations of prominent Spaniards – including the King – contributed to a widespread expectation that the PSOE was likely to suffer a massive defeat at the 1996 general election. When, after thirteen years in power, the PSOE was narrowly defeated by a PP whose relief at finally gaining power was almost matched by its disappointment at the exiguous margin of victory, observers were reminded that the PSOE still remained a formidable political vehicle with staunch support throughout Spanish society.

The PSOE left office with its main aims successfully met: the fragility of Spanish democracy was no longer an issue; greater economic efficiency had been achieved; a basic welfare state had been consolidated; and Spain had become a key member of the European Union. In short, Spain was much like other advanced European states – no mean achievement in just thirteen years.

During its first year out of office, the PSOE provided a surprisingly ineffectual opposition. Aware that he now constituted 'both a problem and a solution' for the party, and admitting that he felt like a 'political dinosaur' at the Socialist International Congress in September 1996, Felipe González unexpectedly stepped down as leader after twenty-three years in charge at the party's 34th Congress in June 1997.

González was replaced as General Secretary by Joaquín Almunia. In primaries held in April 1998 to select the party's candidate for Prime Minister at the next general election Almunia was unexpectedly defeated by José Borrell. It remains to be seen whether Borrell can move on from the

González era and provide the leadership which will enable the party to secure a swift return to power.

Select Bibliography

Gillespie, R. (1989) *The Spanish Socialist Party: A History of Factionalism*, Oxford: Clarendon Press.

Gillespie, R. (1990) 'The Break-up of the "Socialist Family": Party–Union Relations in Spain, 1982–89', *West European Politics*, 13 (1).

Graham, H. (1991) *Socialism and War. The Spanish Socialist Party in Power and Crisis, 1936–1939*, Cambridge: Cambridge University Press.

Guerra, A. and Tezanos, J.F. (eds), *La década del cambio. Diez años de gobierno socialista*, Madrid: Editorial Sistema

Heywood, P. (1990) *Marxism and the Failure of Organised Socialism in Spain*, Cambridge: Cambridge University Press.

Heywood, P. (1992) 'The Socialist Party in Power, 1982–92: The Price of Progress', *ACIS* (Journal of the Association for Contemporary Iberian Studies), 5 (2).

Juliá, S. (1997) *Los socialistas en la política española, 1879–1982*, Madrid: Taurus.

Kennedy, P. (1996) 'Europe or Bust? Integration and its Influence on the Economic Policy of the PSOE', *International Journal of Iberian Studies*, 9(2).

Kennedy, P. (1997) 'The PSOE: Modernization and the Welfare State in Spain', in Sassoon, D. (ed.), *Looking Left: European Socialism After the Cold War*, London: I.B. Tauris.

Maravall, J. M. (1992) 'From Opposition to Government: The Politics and Policies of the PSOE', in Maravall, J.M. *et al.*, *Socialist Parties in Europe*, Barcelona: ICPS.

Tezanos, J.F. (1993) *Historia ilustrada del socialismo español*, Madrid: Editorial Sistema.

Contact Information

Party Address
Partido Socialista Obrero Español
c/ Ferraz 68-70   Tel: 582 04 44
28008 Madrid   Fax: 582 04 22

Affiliated Centre for Research
Fundación Pablo Iglesias
c/ Monte Esquinza, 30 – 2o. y. 3a. Dcha   Tel: 310–43–13
28010 Madrid   Fax: 319–45–85

The PSOE publishes a monthly journal, *El Socialista*

Web page on the Internet: http://www.psoe.es
e-mail: psoe@psoe.es

15 The Swedish Social Democratic Party

Nicholas Aylott

HISTORY

Introduction

The Swedish Social Democratic Party is often referred to in English by its acronym, SAP, from its name in Swedish, *Socialdemokratiska Arbetarepartiet*. SAP can justifiably lay claim to being Europe's most successful political party. By 1998 it had been in government for a remarkable 61 years since universal suffrage was established in Sweden in 1921, all but ten without the need of a coalition partner (excluding the national government that governed during the Second World War, see Table 15.1). Twice, in 1940 and 1968, it won a majority, not just a plurality, of votes cast. As recently as 1994 it was capable of winning an impressive 45.3 per cent. However, maintaining its political hegemony will be an immense challenge for the party.

Table 15.1   Swedish governments, 1945–98

	Prime ministers	Parties
1945	**Per Albin Hansson, Tage Erlander**[1]	Social Democrats
1951	**Tage Erlander**	Social Democrats, Agrarian League*
1957	**Tage Erlander, Olof Palme**	Social Democrats
1976	Thorbjörn Fälldin	Centre, Liberals, Moderates
1978	Ola Ullsten	Liberals
1979	Thorbjörn Fälldin	Centre, Liberals, Moderates
1981	Thorbjörn Fälldin	Centre, Liberals
1982	**Olof Palme, Ingvar Carlsson**	Social Democrats
1991	Carl Bildt	Moderates, Centre, Christian Democrats, Liberals
1994	**Ingvar Carlsson, Göran Persson**	Social Democrats

Notes: * The Agrarian League became the Centre Party in 1957.
[1] Prime ministers in bold print are Social Democrats.

Source: Author's compilation.

Background

SAP's founding congress took place in 1889 in Stockholm. The meeting comprised 50 delegates from fourteen parts of the country, representing 69 trade unions and political and social organizations. Three local administrative units were set up, based around socialist strength in the capital and two other cities, Gothenburg and Malmö, and a seven-member administrative committee was established. This committee was given limited powers, however. The party congress was to be the highest decision-making body, the committee's brief being only to implement congress decisions and to represent the formative party externally between congresses. A general desire, held particularly amongst radical elements from southern Sweden, to limit the power of the centre was chiefly responsible for this structure; SAP thus contradicted the hierarchical organization of other contemporary social democratic parties, most notably that in Germany (see Chapter 6). Meanwhile, the Trade Union Confederation (*Landsorganisationen*, LO) was established in 1898 at a gathering of twenty-four trade associations and around thirty-five other workers' organizations. Collaboration between social democratic and trade union activists in forming local organizations was extensive, particularly in the south and west, and delegates voted 175 to 83 at LO's founding congress to establish compulsory, automatic membership of the party for members of affiliated trade unions. Two of the five members of LO's executive were nominated by SAP.

It was soon recognized in SAP's upper echelons that the attempt to guard against authoritarianism and encourage members' participation in the party had somewhat impaired its cohesion, and in 1894 the party congress voted to institute a National Executive, in which the Stockholm members acted as an Executive Committee. In 1900 the National Executive was expanded to 23 members, and the post of party secretary, with national administrative and co-ordinating responsibilities, was instituted. Most contentiously, the three-district structure was abandoned, with local organization being reallocated to around 80 Social Democratic branches, or 'labour communes', which were to be directly subordinate to the National Executive. While many of these labour communes had been established autonomously by local activists, after the turn of the century their rapid proliferation was largely the work of agitators, appointed by the central party authorities, who travelled the country, organizing meetings, co-ordinating strikes and setting up the framework for social democratic associations. These efforts dominated the party's expenditure in its early years, and by 1911 SAP's leadership claimed the existence of 427 affiliated labour communes. It is clear, then, that soon after its foundation, and belying its initial structure, SAP had become a genuinely cohesive party (see Gidlund, 1992, pp. 101–6).

The SD's relationship with the trade unions was very close. By the outbreak of the First World War, perhaps 80 per cent of the party's membership was through trade unionists' collective affiliation. But SAP's formal establishment pre-dated LO's; so did its development into a cohesive, centralized organization. (LO embraced its characteristic 'vertical' trade unionism, giving it a dominant relationship with its constituent unions, only in 1912.) Unlike, for example, the British Labour Party (see Chapter 7), SAP had had its own existence and identity, separable from the trade unions' sectional interests. The strong trade union movement was thus an advantage to the party rather than a millstone.

The 'Swedish Model'

Ideologically, SAP has been most renowned for its role in shaping the 'Swedish model'. The model's most identifiably Social Democratic element was a plan designed by Gösta Rehn and Rudolf Meidner, two LO economists, which was first presented at the trade unions' congress in 1951. They succeeded in persuading SAP to eschew conventional incomes agreements and support instead a system of 'wage solidarity', in which LO, with SAP's full support, pressed for a levelling of wage differentials throughout the economy. This was not simply to promote social justice; it also had an economic function. By putting downward pressure on wages paid by the most efficient firms, it was hoped to contain demand-pull inflation; and by putting upward pressure on wages in the lowest-paying sectors, it was hoped to squeeze greater efficiency from less competitive firms. Naturally, this also put some workers in weaker sectors out of work as their companies folded, but that was where the activist state came in.

First, it ran highly interventionist labour market and industrial policies. These were based on a Labour Market Board, managed in classic corporatist style, which sought to encourage workers to join the most productive parts of the economy. Generous subsidies for retraining and relocation – with penalties for non-co-operation, too – were the main means through which such economic restructuring was to be achieved. Second, the state was activist in its welfare policy. In contrast to those European states in which the provision of pensions, unemployment insurance, child care and even health and education were left to non-state actors, such as churches and trade unions, in Social Democratic Sweden these became the state's direct responsibility. Moreover, welfare was universal in character. It was designed not as a safety net for those who could not afford private insurance, but as a collective scheme in which the middle classes would have a stake, because benefits were income-related. The middle classes' propensity to revolt against necessarily high tax rates was thus mitigated.

Clearly, there was something distinctive about the Swedish brand of social democratic ideology. As early as 1889 SAP had abandoned revolution in favour of accommodation with more progressive elements among the bourgeois (that is, non-socialist) parties. Its reformism had two important characteristics. The first was the nationalist image that the Social Democrats arrogated to themselves. Embracing a parliamentary path to socialism meant the rejection of exclusively class-based politics. It was Per Albin Hansson, SAP's leader from 1928, who coined the term *folkhemmet*, the 'people's home', to describe his party's project; the language of class conflict was never as strident as in other European countries. The second important characteristic was the party's relative market-friendliness. Before the First World War, influential members were talking of how markets could be used rather than abolished (Tilton, 1991), and very little industry was nationalized when SAP took power. An agreement in 1938 between trade unions and employers on wage-bargaining, reached in the town of Saltsjöbaden, came to epitomize a 'class compromise'. Social Democrats tended to see free trade not just as unavoidable, but as positively desirable.

Although unity and discipline have been arguably the party's foremost strengths, SAP has experienced some internal differences since its formation in 1889, and since it first held government office in 1914. Defence has been a recurring question. Elements advocating unilateral disarmament have come to the fore at different times, and it was partly this issue that prompted a radical faction to leave the party in 1917, its members unable to accept Social Democratic leaders' insistence on strong national defence. (In 1921 this faction became the Communist Party of Sweden, and is now the Left Party.) A Social Democratic government resigned in 1936 after losing a parliamentary vote on defence policy. Disarmament again rose to the top of the internal agenda in the 1950s, when the party became divided over a suggestion by the commander-in-chief of the Swedish military that the country consider equipping its forces with nuclear weapons. Only as the Cold War became entrenched did the security debate subside within SAP. Relations with the trade unions have in general remained exceptionally close, but after the 1960s the unity of the country's labour movement begin to fracture. As the Swedish economy declined rapidly towards the end of the 1980s and early 1990s, relations reached their lowest point. As we shall see, this period also saw internal discord over questions that went beyond traditional socio–economic arguments.

ORGANIZATION AND PARTY PROFILE

Structure

The Social Democratic Party's congress is officially its highest organ. Congress comprises 350 delegates elected by the regional party organizations (the representation of each is weighted according to the size of its membership), plus the National Executive, a tenth of the party's MPs, and certain other representatives. Motions are submitted by individual members first to a SAP local branch, which either adopts it, rejects it or agrees to submit it to congress without having adopted it. The main congress does not meet annually, but rather a year before Sweden's regular parliamentary election. However, in 1993 it decided to respond to the extension of the parliamentary term from three to four years by instituting special mid-term congresses, focusing on both general policy and particular themes, as and when they were deemed necessary. Special congresses can be convened by the National Executive or after a ballot of the national membership, which can be undertaken on the initiative of 5 per cent of the party's members.

Congress has the power to elect the party leader, the thirty-five members of the National Executive (plus fifteen deputy members), the seven members of the Executive Committee (plus seven deputy members) and certain other bodies, as well as to decide on changes to the party's rules (which can be proposed by members, local branches or the Executive Committee). Individual Social Democrats can nominate delegates or stand themselves at local selection meetings. Regarding party lists for elections, before 1969 local branches sent delegates to selection meetings at constituency level, but since then local congresses based on regional organizations have appointed election committees (which, since 1975, include a representative of a regional LO committee). The election committee proposes a list of candidates to the regional congress, although candidates may be subject to a ballot of members throughout the region if demanded by at least a third of the delegates to its congress.

SAP would appear, then, to have a decentralized formal structure: the leadership is subservient to the ultimate power of congress and has no power over selection of candidates. However, in reality the leadership is rather more powerful than it appears. Congress has no power over party finances, and public subsidies to parties have made SAP, like others in Sweden, less dependent on maintaining the active participation of its members, and has thus enhanced elites' scope for shaping policy more independently of grassroots' views. This trend has been exacerbated by these subsidies being based on parties' electoral performance rather than the size of their membership. Although debates at congress are often lively, defeat for motions proposed by the leadership is rare, and the leadership has grown adept at engineering an imprecise outcome to a question if it senses the possibility of defeat. In any case, the power of congress has always had limits; in practice, the leadership has always had scope for deciding which resolutions to act upon, and in what way. The growth of media attention has also changed the role of congress, making it less a mechanism for democratic steering of the party by its membership and more a means of conveying the party's message to the wider electorate. This has obvious implications for the policy-making role of congress. The more intense and fractious the debate at congress, the more divided and less attractive the party is likely to appear to voters, so pressure to avoid significant challenges to the leadership has increased (see Pierre and Widfeldt, 1994).

This increasingly direct relationship between party and voter has also affected the situation of political parties' parliamentary groups. Social democratic members of the Swedish parliament, the Riksdag, are formally responsible to congress. But until 1972 this involved only the submission of an annual report, as the Riksdag group refused to disclose the minutes of its meetings to congress; even now, the control of congress amounts to little more than having its committees audit these minutes. The parliamentary group retains its own budget, and its financial autonomy from the main party is considered strong. As regards the parliamentary group's relations with the party leadership, there are signs that the party's MPs have become more independent-minded in recent years, a trend that can be traced back to their first experience of opposition for four decades, in 1976–82, and thereafter, when minority governments became the rule. But discipline has traditionally been strong within the SAP's Riksdag group. Despite heated private argument over recent government austerity measures, there were no rebellions among Social Democratic MPs.

SAP has a considerable organization outside parliament, and has a highly developed relationship with its local bodies. The number of local branches climbed to 2,836 in 1960, although the party decided to respond to a large-scale reorganization and amalgamation of municipalities during the 1960s and 1970s by drastically reducing the number of these branches and, at the same time, establishing a uniform pattern of local and regional organization throughout the country. However, the number of basic party units – which comprise local branches based in towns and villages, and workplace organizations – grew concomitantly. So-called 's-representatives' are the cornerstones of around 700 workplace organizations. These were originally designed to provide a political platform in union elections, but later assumed a wider, activist role.

Within the party, ideological factions are proscribed, although Social Democratic Youth, the Federation of Social Democratic Women and the Association of Christian Social Democrats (the 'Brotherhood Movement') are recognized as important institutional components, and are represented at the party congress. Various other organizations are associated with the party, and are seen as belonging to the broader labour movement. These include educational bodies (the Workers' Educational Association, the Correspondence School), publishing firms (the A Press, Tiden), co-operative clubs, the Workers' Temperance Society, the Folksam insurance company and housing and tenants' associations.

Membership

In 1960 SAP had members who came overwhelmingly from the industrial working class, whose education was mostly limited to the basic secondary level, and of whom nearly three-quarters were male. Social Democratic voters had a similar profile, except that women formed a small majority. Since then, however, both the party's membership and its electorate have changed, reflecting wider trends in Swedish and western societies generally. De- industrialization, the expansion of education and the growth of the middle class, whose members work in the service sector of the economy (in both the public and private sectors), have altered the composition of the party's constituency (as can be seen in Tables 15.2 and 15.3). Leading social democrats have acknowledged that their party is no longer solely one of the working class, and now has a broader, cross-class identity. This has brought problems. Internal conflict is more likely when a movement contains a broad range of economic interests, from (on the one hand) export-dependent steel workers to (on the other) local government child-care providers, fearful of international market pressures to reduce the cost of the state sector. Debate about European integration, for example, sometimes illustrates these

Table 15.2 SAP members' age, educational and socio–economic profiles,[a] 1960–94

	1960	*1970*	*1985*	*1994*[c]
Female	30	31	35	34
Male	70	69	65	66
18–30-year-olds[b]	11	4	21	11
31–60-year-olds	74	64	59	56
61–80-year-olds	15	32	20	33
Upper secondary education or higher	1	4	13	24
Less educated	99	96	87	76
Working class	80	79	65	49
Salaried employees	15	21	30	44
Self-employed	5	0	4	6
Farmer	0	0	1	1

Notes:
[a] Figures do not include members of youth organizations.
[b] In 1960 the youngest age category comprised 22–30-year-olds, and in 1970 20–30-year-olds.
[c] 1994 figures reflect the situation after the end of trade union members' collective membership of the party.

Source: Widfeldt (1997).

Table 15.3   SAP voters' age, educational and socio–economic profiles,
1960–94

	1960	1970	1985	1994
Female	53	50	52	46
Male	47	50	48	54
18–30-year-olds[a]	20	24	22	22
31–60-year-olds	65	56	53	54
61–80-year-olds	15	20	25	24
Upper secondary education or higher	2	3	15	29
Less educated	98	97	85	71
Working class	76	70	60	52
Salaried employees	18	25	35	43
Self-employed	4	4	4	4
Farmer	2	1	1	1

Note: [a] In 1960 the youngest age category comprised 22–30-year-olds, and in 1970
20–30-year-olds.

Source: Widfeldt (1997).

different priorities. The Metal Workers' Union tends to be more sympathetic
to integration, while the Municipal Workers' Union is among the most
Eurosceptical in the labour movement.

Yet the sheer size of the party has meant that SAP has always been an
eclectic movement. Moreover, the basis of its historic dominance of Swedish
politics has been its ability to forge cross-class alliances, most notably with
the Agrarians in the 1930s and 1950s (see Esping-Andersen, 1985). To be a
catch-all party is by no means a recipe for weakness and inevitable internal
conflict. Rather more worrying than its sociological diversity *per se* has been
the party's loss of support among particular categories of voters. The proportion of young people in its membership has declined in recent years; the
young have been especially tempted by the attractions of the Green Party,
the largely post-communist Left Party, and single-issue pressure groups.
SAP's voters also now comprise notably more men than women. Half the
new Social Democratic cabinet of 1994 was female, but this symbol of the
party's commitment to gender equality has been offset by perceptions at
grass-roots' level. Employment in the public sector in general, and in municipal services in particular, is dominated by women, and many have been
disillusioned, it seems, by the restrictions imposed on public spending by
Social Democratic governments since the late 1980s.

As regards finance, by 1905 membership subscriptions had become the
main source of social democratic funds, and even though their level was not
raised between 1920 and 1956 they still comprised 20–30 per cent of the

party's income at the end of that period. In 1965, however, state subsidies for political parties were introduced in Sweden, and by 1989 subscriptions had become only about 10 per cent of the party's income. Similarly, whereas trade union contributions accounted for 30 per cent of its funds in 1968, this figure had fallen to 18 per cent twenty years later (Pierre and Widfeldt, 1994, pp. 346–9). Indeed, public money has become the mainstay of all the main Swedish parties. There are four types of national subsidy, two going to the party's central administration and two to the parliamentary party. In 1993–4 SAP received a total of SKr65,400,000 ($8.3 mn) from these subsidies. In addition, local and county councils are also obliged to disburse public funds to the parties' branches at these levels. Because all Sweden's major parties obtain most of their resources from the public purse, this source is unlikely to dry up.

Public subsidy has also served to lessen SAP's financial dependence on the trade unions. The system of automatic collective membership of the party through belonging to an affiliated trade union greatly inflated the nominal total of party members. It exceeded 1 million between 1971 and 1989, and in 1983 reached 1.23 million – equivalent to around 15 per cent of the entire Swedish population. The party congress decision in 1987 to end corporate membership through the trade unions and make all membership individual by 1991 reinforced the distinction between the two wings of the labour movement. Since then, SAP's membership has numbered around 260,000 (Widfeldt, 1997, p. 91). But there remains significant overlap between individual membership of the two organizations, at both grass-roots' and élite levels; LO's chair usually still sits on SAP's Executive Committee.

GOVERNMENT ACHIEVEMENTS AND CURRENT POLICIES

SAP in the 1970s and 1980s

The century up to 1970 saw Sweden's economy grow faster than any country's bar Japan, leaving it the fourth-richest in the world – with a luxuriant welfare state to go with it. Full employment was achieved more or less consistently. At the same time, Sweden's foreign policy profile became another facet of its distinctly Social Democratic identity. Olof Palme, its most renowned Prime Minister, took Swedish neutrality into a more activist phase, drawing the ire of both Cold-War superpowers as he vociferously criticized their military adventures in Vietnam and Afghanistan. Yet Sweden today is a very different country from the one that became the object of the western left's admiration. It is an unhappy member of the European Union, which it joined at the start of 1995 after a referendum the previous November. Worse, it suffers from an unemployment rate of around

8 per cent – which would be some 4–5 per cent higher if those on government make-work and training schemes were included.

SAP has suffered some fairly bad luck since the 1970s. After a six-year period of non-socialist rule in 1976–82, the party found itself back in office and having to deal with the consequences of the previous coalition government's expensive propping up of failing industries. Four years later the party suffered a grievous blow with the death of Palme at the hands of a still unknown assassin. More recently the party was thrown temporarily into confusion after its prime minister, Ingvar Carlsson, announced his retirement. His popular deputy, Mona Sahlin, looked certain to become Sweden's first woman prime minister. But in October 1995 she was exposed as having used a government credit card for personal items, and then being tardy in repaying the money. It was less Sahlin's carelessness with her personal accounts, and more her lying about the initial accusations, that prompted a revolt against her candidacy; she resigned from the government the following month. There followed an embarrassing period for SAP in which none of its potential candidates for party leader seemed to want to stand. Eventually, after repeatedly denying any interest in the job, the finance minister, Göran Persson, accepted both it and the prime ministership.

The Social Democrats made their own policy errors. Over-investment in housing contributed to another misallocation of resources, which was exposed in property slumps in the mid-1970s and early 1990s. The deregulation of bank lending and foreign exchange transactions in the mid-1980s was badly timed, as it poured fuel onto a rapidly overheating economy – what a Social Democratic Finance Minister, Kjell-Olof Feldt, called later the 'great consumption party'. Monetary policy was much too lax during this period. Then the ill-advised attempt to combat inflation by pegging the Swedish krona to the ECU in May 1991, continued by a non-socialist government even at the cost of punishingly high interest rates, aggravated the deep recession the country went through in the early 1990s. GDP fell by 6 per cent between 1991 and 1993.

Perhaps more seriously, however, the labour movement over-reached itself politically in the 1970s in its attempts to move on from welfare-statism and construct economic, as well as political, democracy in Sweden. The establishment of a fourth supplementary-pension fund, which was allowed to buy shares in commercial enterprises, and the passing of various laws further improving employees' rights, were strongly opposed by the non-socialists. Even more provocative to Swedish capitalists was the attempt in the 1970s to create wage-earner funds. Also proposed by Gösta Rehn, their original design involved all enterprises of a certain size contributing shares annually to a fund, controlled by the trade unions, which would gradually increase its stake in the firm. The employers and non-socialist parties were bitterly against what they saw as creeping socialism. Indeed, the forces of the centre–right were united by the issue in a way unseen hitherto in Swedish politics. After a long campaign, a watered-down version of wage-earner funds was enacted in 1983. But Swedish employers considered that the labour movement had breached the terms of the country's 'class compromise'. Centralized, peak-level wage-bargaining, so crucial to keeping wages in check, began to lose its discipline.

Even during its 'golden age', however, there were weaknesses in the Swedish model. Above all, from around 1970 the Swedish economy seemed to lose its capacity for growth. Between 1952 and 1973 growth had averaged 3.9 per cent; between 1973 and 1990 it was just 1.6 per cent, markedly lower than the average in the rest of the OECD. Meanwhile, the people's home was becoming increasingly expensive to maintain. Between 1950 and 1972 public spending rose from 25 per cent of GDP to 70 per cent, and from 1970 to the early 1980s it rose 20 per cent faster than GDP in relative terms (Lindbeck, 1994, p. 5). This was partly due to ever more generous welfare provision, but also to spectacular growth in public sector employment, particularly in local government. In 1960 the public sector employed around one in five Swedish employees; by 1990 it was more than one in three.

Sweden as a whole suffered from a gathering crisis of competitiveness. The easiest way to stave off this crisis was devaluation; the 12 per cent depreciation of the krona announced by a new Social Democratic government in 1982 was just one example. With corporatist discipline intact, Swedish workers might have been persuaded to make up the competitive disadvantage by accepting this cut in their real wages. But wage restraint had been broken. With sub-peak-level wage-bargaining becoming more prevalent, the means of preventing individual unions breaking ranks and seeking wage rises became increasingly ineffective. Devaluation sparked high inflation in Sweden throughout the 1980s, as the cost of imports rose and workers demanded higher pay in compensation. It was a crisis that further devaluation and an inflationary, over-heated economy in the late 1980s could only postpone, and eventually make worse.

Bitter recrimination, a 'war of the roses', broke out between SAP's leadership and the trade unions in 1989–90. An emergency austerity package presented by the Social Democratic government seemed to have won LO leaders' support – until it emerged that as well as imposing a freeze on rents, dividends, local taxes, prices and wages, the 'stop package' also proposed, remarkably, the temporary banning of strikes, with fines for transgressors. Without LO's support for the package, in February 1990 Carlsson resigned as prime minister; Feldt retired from politics the following day. Within a fortnight, however, Carlsson had formed a new government with the passive support of the Communist Left and Centre parties. The ban on strikes and the wage freeze were dropped, but in the election of September 1991 SAP recorded 37.7 per cent of the vote, its worst score since 1928. The Moderate

Table 15.4   Recent Swedish national elections

	R	R	R	R	E	R
	1985	*1988*	*1991*	*1994*	*1995*	1998
Left Party	5.4	5.8	4.5	6.2	12.9	12.0
Social Democrats	44.7	43.2	37.6	45.3	28.1	36.4
Greens	1.5	5.5	3.4	5.0	17.2	4.5
Centre Party	9.8	11.3	8.5	7.7	7.2	5.1
Liberals	14.2	12.2	9.1	7.2	4.8	4.7
Christian Democrats	2.6	2.9	7.2	4.1	3.9	11.8
Moderates	21.3	18.3	21.9	22.4	23.1	22.9
New Democracy	–	–	6.7	1.2	*	*

Notes: R=election to the Riksdag, E= election to the European Parliament.
* New Democracy's score in these elections was less than 1 per cent.

Source: Compiled from official statistics.

leader, Carl Bildt, became prime minister, heading a four-party non-socialist coalition (Table 15. 4).

SAP in the 1990s

Carlsson led his party to victory in the 1994 election, but the social democrats' difficulties since have reinforced the hypothesis that, without the 'growth dividend' to keep all its interests happy, it faces a difficult future. Various issues have revealed considerable division within the party.

One fault line has been over environmental issues. Differences between the 'green' and 'grey' wings of the party found expression in argument about plans to build a bridge over the Öresund between southern Sweden and Denmark, which a Social Democratic government agreed to support in spring 1991. A persistent and more damaging row has occurred over nuclear power. A referendum in 1980 on Sweden's nuclear programme, held in the aftermath of the accident at Three Mile Island, found a plurality in favour of phasing it out gradually by 2010. SAP and LO, many of whose members were concerned at the consequences for employment of abandoning nuclear energy, backed this line, but it only just defeated another of the three options on offer to voters, that of closing the reactors forthwith. Polls suggested that only about two-thirds of the party's supporters backed its leadership's line, despite its mounting a strong campaign for a 'cautious decommissioning'. In February 1997 the Social Democratic government incurred strong criticism from both business and trade unions for announcing the closure of two reactors, one by mid-1998 and the other by 2001, before their useful life had been completed – the first such decision in the world.

Even more injurious to the party, however, is the continuing split over European integration, an issue that has been every bit as damaging to SAP as it has to its sister parties in Britain, Norway and Denmark. Polls suggested that Social Democratic voters were split down the middle in Sweden's referendum on joining the European Union (Holmberg, 1996, p. 227) and while most party élites were in favour of membership, opposition in the grass-roots was very strong, especially in the north of the country. Why has Europe been so controversial for the Social Democrats? Part of the reason may concern the sheer speed of its change of policy towards the European Community. Ostensibly, it had been neutrality that had kept Sweden from applying for membership during the Cold War. Despite various tentative enquiries, a consensus had formed in Sweden that EC membership would make the country's neutrality less convincing than it needed to be. But there had also been an implicit assumption in Social Democratic circles that Sweden had little to gain from integration. Not only was it richer than the EC, the latter was also characterized as 'conservative, capitalist and Catholic' – that is, incompatible with Swedish Social Demo-cracy's fiercely rationalist egalitarianism. Steeped in a Eurosceptic tradition, therefore, it was disorientating for Social Democrats to find their party leadership performing a dramatic *volte-face* in autumn 1990 and, as the government, announcing Sweden's intention to apply for membership.

The Union's plan for economic and monetary union is likely to pose further difficulties for the party. The issue seemed to have been neutralized, albeit temporarily, in June 1997, when the Social Democratic National Ex-ecutive announced that it would not support Sweden's joining the single currency in 1999. (This was, in effect, a declaration of government policy, and it was confirmed at the party congress the following September.) The uncertainty surrounding the timetable and sceptical Swedish public opinion were cited as the reasons. However, if the project does go ahead, strong support for and opposition to Sweden's subsequent participation can both be expected from within SAP.

Whether the ideological causes of contemporary internal division are attributed to 'traditionalist' Social Democrats opposing their leaders' harsh budgetary policies and failure to make a dent in unemployment, or to a post-materialist youth that objects to polluting industry and unresponsive big government, other parties have profited from the discord. The Left Party has been most successful in gathering the first type of emigrants from the SAP. Its 12.9 per cent in the 1995 European elections was a great success for the party, and the Greens' 17.2 per cent was still more impressive. The rise of these Eurosceptical parties has opened a second front for the Social Demo-crats to defend. Moreover, this attack has occurred just as a challenger from the right has become genuinely menacing. In March 1997 opinion polls showed, for the first time, not only the Moderates ahead of SAP, but Social Democratic voters defecting directly to their banner.

The nightmare scenario for many Swedish Social Democrats is that they might lose enough of their core support to be, like their equivalents in Denmark and Norway, able to muster at best only around a third of the vote, a '30 per cent party'. For the party's idealists, meanwhile, the acute economic crisis has been profoundly disappointing. For many years, Swedish identity became fused for many Social Democrats with their ideological allegiance. Palme's assassination was the first traumatic blow to the sanctity of the people's home. The question marks against the relevance of neutrality after the Cold War, and Sweden's grudging accession to the Union, have further confused the sense among Swedes in general, and Social Democrats in particular, of their place in the world. To see the winning combination of economic growth and comprehensive public welfare apparently lost has been even harder to bear.

SAP's biggest advantage is that, as throughout the century, the Swedish non-socialists remain divided. For example, Carlsson tempted one of the non-socialist coalition partners of 1991–4, the Centre Party, into a parliamentary alliance with the Social Democrats in April 1995, and Persson subsequently cemented the pact, partly through agreeing to decommission the nuclear reactors. But the golden age is probably over for SAP. Its 36.6 per cent in 1998 was the party's worst performance in a parliamentary election since the advent of universal suffrage, and it may settle down as, if not a 30 per cent party, then a 35–40 per cent one.

Select Bibliography

Bäck, M. and Möller, T. (1990) *Partier och organisationer*, 2nd edn, Stockholm: Publica.

Esping-Andersen, G. (1985) *Politics Against Markets: The Social Democratic Road to Power*, Princeton: Princeton University Press.

Gidlund, G. (1992) 'From Popular Movement to Political Party: Development of the Social Democratic Labor Party Organization', in Misgeld, K. Molin, K. and Åmark, K. (eds), *Creating Social Democracy: A Century of the Social Democratic Labor Party in Sweden*, Pennsylvania: Pennsylvania University Press.

Holmberg, S. (1996) 'Partierna gjorde så gott som de kunde', in Gilljam, M. and Holmberg, S. (eds), *Ett knappt ja till EU: Väljarna och folkomröstning 1994*, Stockholm: Norstedts Juridik.

Lane, J.-E. (1995) 'The Decline of the Swedish Model', *Governance*, 8.

Lindbeck, A. *et al.* (1994) *Turning Sweden Around*, Cambridge, MA: MIT Press.

Lindström, U. (1994) *Euro-Consent, Euro-Contract or Euro-Coercion? Scandinavian Social Democracy, the European Impasse and the Abolition of Things Political*, Oslo: Scandinavian University Press.

Pierre, J. and Widfeldt, A. (1994) 'Party Organizations in Sweden: Colossuses with Feet of Clay or Flexible Pillars of Government?', in Katz, R.S. and Mair, P. *How Parties Organize: Change and Adaptation in Party Organizations in Western Democracies*, London: Sage.

Sannerstedt, A. and Sjölin, M. (1992) 'Sweden: Changing Party Relations in a More Active Parliament', in Damgaard E. (ed.), *Parliamentary Change in the Nordic Countries*, Oslo: Scandinavian University Press.

Tilton, T. (1991) *The Political Theory of Swedish Social Democracy*, Oxford: Clarendon Press.

Widfeldt, A. (1997) *Linking Parties with People? Party Membership in Sweden 1960–1994*, Gothenburg: Department of Political Science, Göteborg University.

Contact Information

Central Headquarters
Socialdemokraterna
105–60 Stockholm

Visiting Address
Sveavägen 68
Stockholm   Tel: 46 08 700 26 00

Web Page on Internet: http://www.sap.se/

LO Headquarters:
105–53 Stockholm

Web page on the Internet: http://www.lo.se/

16 The Party of European Socialists
Simon Hix

HISTORY

The Party of European Socialists (PES) was founded in The Hague on 9 November 1992. Its roots can be traced back to the Socialist International (SI), of 1950, and even to the First International of 1864. More recently, the PES is the present incarnation of two organizations linked to the first institutions of the European Communities: the Socialist Group in the Assembly of the European Coal and Steel Community (ECSC), established in June 1953; and the Liaison Bureau of the Socialist Parties of the European Community, established in April 1957 between the SI parties in the Communities. In June 1957, the Liaison Bureau decided that only delegates from its member parties could sit in the Socialist Group in the European Parliament (EP). This set the precedent that the 'extra-parliamentary' party determines EP Group membership.

In 1968, Henk Vredeling and several Dutch PvdA members proposed a 'Progressive European Party' (PEP), while Sicco Mansholt (PvdA) and Lionelli Levi-Sandri (PSI), the socialist members of the EC Commission, called for a 'European Socialist Party' (ESP). In response, in October 1969, Lucien Radoux (Chairman of the Liaison Bureau) and Francis Vals (Chairman of the EP Group) outlined a joint plan for a federal political party. However, this plan was rejected by the national parties as too integrationist.

But, at the Hague Summit in December 1969, the EC Heads of Government agreed in principle to direct elections to the EP. This decision forced the national parties to reconsider their position. At the 8th Congress in 1971, Alfred Mozer (PvdA) was instructed to prepare a report on a new Socialist party organization. In the meantime, Britain, Denmark and Ireland joined the Community in January 1973, and the British Labour Party insisted that it would not participate in any 'supranational' party. The Confederation of the Socialist Parties of the EC (CSP) was subsequently launched on 5 April 1974, but the British party did not join until January 1976.

The CSP was the first EC 'party federation', followed in 1976 by the European People's Party–Christian Democrats (EPP) and the Federation of European Liberal, Democrat and Reform Parties (ELDR). Despite their names, these were not real 'parties'. The CSP had a President, an executive organ, rules of procedure, a secretariat and provisions for majority decision-making. However, the CSP was dependent on the national parties for its resources, most decisions were by a unanimity of the member parties, and its decisions were not binding. The differing attitudes of the member parties was also reflected in the various versions of its name: where the Dutch *Federatie* implied a more integrated organization than the German *Bund* or French *Union*; and the English *Confederation*, Italian *Confederazione* and Danish *Samenslutingen* suggested a looser structure.

In the EP elections, the CSP was more an umbrella organization of national parties than a real European party. In 1979, intractable disagreements in the preparation of a common manifesto meant the CSP was able to adopt only a short 'Appeal to the Electorate'. And, on the eve of the first elections, at a joint press conference with Willy Brandt (SP–D) and François Mitterrand (PS–F), James Callaghan (LP–GB) proclaimed that each national party must pursue its own strategy, independent of the CSP and the newly elected EP Socialist Group. By the 1984 elections the political climate had changed, the EP Socialist Group had proven to be relatively cohesive. The U-turn of the French Socialists over their 'independent socialist strategy' also persuaded many socialist parties that common European policies were essential for economic recovery. Consequently, the 1984 and 1989 Manifestos contained concrete proposals for European-level policies.

However, none of the EP elections were genuine European contests. Turnout fell between 1979 and 1989, the campaigns were fought on the performance of national parties and not on European issues. Consequently, in the next stage of EC institutional reform, the socialist parties emphasized the need for 'democratization' of the Community. In 1990, during the Intergovernmental Conferences preparing the Treaty on European Union (Maastricht Treaty), the socialist leaders outlined a plan. This included a Single Currency, equal powers for the EP, a Common Foreign and Security Policy (CFSP), EU citizenship, and implementation of the Social Charter.

In parallel, the CSP President, Guy Spitaels (SP–B), made a series of joint proposals with the Presidents of the EPP and ELDR for a new 'party article' in the Treaty. This led to the last-minute inclusion of a clause in the Maastricht Treaty, stating that:

> Parties at the European level are an important factor for integration within the Union. They contribute to forming a political awareness and to expressing the political will of the citizens of the Union. (Treaty on European Union, Article 138a)

Meanwhile, the CSP had already began the process of internal reform. At the 17th Congress in Berlin, in February 1990, Wim Kok (the leader of the PvdA) presented a report proposing increased policy co-ordination and involvement of parties from the European Free Trade Association (EFTA) states, in preparation for their countries' membership of the European

Union. Following this report, and inspired by the new Party Article, in February 1992 the Bureau set up a Working Group on internal reform, chaired by Ben Fayot (POSL) and Thijs Woltgens (PvdA). By October 1992, the Fayot–Woltgens Report was ready. However, a final sticking point was the name of the new organization. Backed by Björn Engholm (SPD Leader), Fayot and Woltgens proposed the name 'European Socialist Party'. But this was rejected by the British Labour Party. Fayot suggested the compromise 'Party of European Socialists', which was subsequently accepted. Rumour had it, however, that Fayot was unaware that the British Labour Party had been willing to back down at the last minute.

At the next Congress, in The Hague, in November 1992, the Party of European Socialists (PES) was launched. The new 'statutes' were moderately more integrationist than the old 'rules of procedure': with more majority voting, provisions for binding decisions, and a newly strengthened Party President. However, the PES was still a 'confederation' rather than a truly federal party. The Party Leaders' Conference was established as the main organ, guaranteeing the centrality of national parties in the structure. Also, most decisions still required unanimity, the PES remained financially dependent on the national parties, and organizationally dependent on the EP Group – which under the new statutes became the Group of the PES. Finally, under the principle of 'subsidiarity', each member party was allowed its own version of the name: 'Party of European Socialists' in English, French, Spanish and Greek; 'Party of European Social Democrats' in Danish, Dutch, Finnish, Norwegian and Swedish; 'European Social Democratic Party' in German; 'European Socialist Party' in Portuguese; and 'Party of European Socialism' in Italian.

In September 1993, the socialist leaders held a special 'conclave', at Arrábida in Portugal. This was the first off-the- record meeting of just the party leaders, without the various advisors, party officials and the media. This enabled a frank exchange of views on common socialist policies in the Union. At the meeting, the leaders agreed to set up the first working group of representatives from each of the leaders' personal offices, to prepare a common strategy on growth and employment in Europe (the 'Larsson Report').

In the 1994 EP Elections, the PES agreed a common Manifesto and logo that was used by the national parties to a greater extent than in any previous EP election. Finally, at the Second Congress of the PES, in Barcelona, in March 1995, the PES began preparing its position on the reform of the Maastricht Treaty, and these deliberations continued in the PES party leaders' summits in 1996 and the first half of 1997.

Overall, co-operation between socialist parties at the European level has come a long way since its beginnings in the 1950s. As the largest Group in the EP, and with the regular party leaders' summits prior to each European Council, the PES is an influential organization in the complex architecture of EU decision-making. However, unlike parties in the domestic arena, parties at the European level are not the dominant political organizations, linking voters' preferences to political decisions. European elections are still fought by national parties and on national issues. The executive authority of the Union (the Commission and the Council) is not accountable to cohesive party organizations in the EP. Ultimately, the development of the PES towards a real 'Euro-party' depends on the evolution of the Union towards genuine political union.

ORGANIZATION AND PARTY PROFILE

The PES has two interlinking organizations: the PES party federation and the Group of the PES in the EP (hereafter, 'PES Group'). The party federation is the 'extra-parliamentary' organization at the European level, comparable to the party Head Offices, executive committees and congresses in the domestic arena. Like these domestic bodies, the PES Party Federation brings together the members of the organization (the national parties), to decide on common policies (towards the Union), and links the member parties to the PES Group and the Socialists in the other EU institutions. The PES Group, in contrast, is the 'parliamentary faction' at the European level. Like domestic parliamentary factions, the PES Group co-ordinates the committee work and the voting behaviour of the PES Members of the European Parliament (MEPs).

The PES Party Federation

Members According to the party statutes, the PES party federation comprises
- *Full member parties* (from the EU member states and from states that have applied for EU membership and have received a positive opinion from the EU Commission)
- *Associate parties* (from the EFTA countries, who can attend the Bureau and speak at the Congress)
- *Observer parties* (from any other country deemed suitable by the Bureau and the Congress, who can attend but not vote in Bureau meetings)
- *The PES Group* (as a single body, with a status equal to the national full member parties)
- *The PES Group in the Committee of the Regions* (as a single body, with a status comparable to the national associate and observer parties)
- *Socialist associations and organizations* recognized by the PES.

Membership of the PES is thus corporate rather than individual: via the member parties of the PES (see Table 16.1) and the PES Group. A European citizen cannot join the PES directly. This was considered when the statutes were drafted, but rejected by a majority of the member parties.

Table 16.1 Member parties of the PES, 1957–95

Full Member Parties		
June	1957	Parti Socialiste (PS–B, Belgium/Wallonia and Brussels)[1]
		Socialistische Partij (SP, Belgium/Flanders)[1]
		Parti Socialiste (PS–F, France)[2]
		Socialdemokratische Partei Deutschlands (SPD, Germany)
		Partito Socialista Democratico Italiano (PSDI, Italy)[3]
		Parti Ouvrier Socialiste Luxembourgeois/Lètzeburger
		Socialistesch Arbechterpartei (LSAP/POSL, Luxembourg)
		Partij van de Arbied (PvdA, The Netherlands)
January	1966	Partito Socialista Italiano (PSI, Italy)
April	1973	Socialdemokratiet (SD, Denmark)
		The Labour Party (LP–I, Ireland)
January	1976	The Labour Party (LP–GB, Great Britain)[4]
		Social Democratic and Labour Party (SDLP, N. Ireland)[4]
January	1979	Partido Socialista (PS–P, Portugal)
		Partido Socialista Obrero Español (PSOE, Spain)
February	1989	Panellinio Socialistiko Kinima (PASOK, Greece)
February	1990	Sozialdemokratische Partei Österreichs (SPÖ, Austria)
November	1992	Soumen Sosialidemokraattinen Poulue (SSDP, Finland)
		Partito Democratico della Sinistra (PDS, Italy)
		Sveriges Socialdemokratiska Arbetareparti (SAP, Sweden)
November	1993	Det Norske Arbeiderparteri (DNA, Norway)
March	1995	Ethniki Demokratiki Enosi Kyprou (EDEK, Cyprus)
Associate Parties		
February	1990	Sozialdemokratische Partei de Schweiz/Parti Socialiste
		Suisse/Partito Socialista Svizzero (SPS/PSS, Switzerland)
		Althuduhusinu – Social Democratic Party (A, Iceland)
Observer Parties		
March	1980	Israel Labour Party (ILP, Israel)
		Malta Labour Party (MLP, Malta)
February	1990	Sosyaldemokrat Halkçi Parti (SHP, Turkey)
November	1992	United Workers' Party of Israel (MAPAM, Israel)
		Partito Socialista Sammarinese (PSS, San Marino)
March	1995	Ceskastrana Socialne Demokraticka (CSSD, Czech Republic)
		Magyar Szocialista Part (MSZP, Hungary)
		Socjademokracji Rzeczypospolitej Polskiej (SDRP, Poland)
		Strana Demokratickej Lavice (SDL, Slovakia)
		Socialnodemokraticka Strana Slovenska (SDSS, Slovakia)
		United List of Social Democrats (ULSD, Slovenia)

Notes:

1 Until November 1978, the Belgian PS and SP were united.
2 Until May 1969 the French member was the Section Française de l'Internationale Ouvrière (SFIO).
3 The Italian PSDI was expelled from the PES in June 1994, following their support of the Berlusconi government.
4 Although eligable for membership when the UK joined the Community in 1973, the British Labour Party and the Northern Irish SDLP did not participate in the work of the party until January 1976.

Source: Author's compilation.

President and Vice-Presidents In December 1994, Rudolf Scharping, Leader of the German SPD, took over from Willy Claes (SP) as the President of the PES – setting a precedent that the party leader at the European level would be a leader of one of the national parties (see Table 16.2). Underneath the President are eight Vice-Presidents, drawn from the senior ranks of the national parties. Each Vice-President is responsible for co-ordinating party policy on a particular area of EU policy-making (see Table 16.3).

Organs and decision-making According to the statutes, the supreme decision-making organ of the PES Party Federation is the bi-annual Congress, which sets down the political guidelines of the party (e.g. adopts the European Election Manifesto). The Congress comprises about 250 delegates from the member parties and the PES Group, and votes by a qualified majority.

However, in practice, the Party Leaders' Conference is the dominant political body of the PES. These meetings are held at least twice a year, usually immediately prior to and in the same venue as the European Council (of EU Heads of Government). These meetings are composed of the national party leaders, the PES Group leader, the EU Commissioners from the PES member parties, and the PES Vice-Presidents. They set the policy agenda of the PES through 'Leaders' Declarations' that are often subsequently ratified by the national parties as statements of 'European policy'. Since 1993, special Leaders' Conclaves have been held every second year, of just the national and EP party leaders, and without minutes, a Declaration or the attention of the press and the various 'hangers-on'. As a result, these Conclaves allow a more open exchange of views.

Between Congresses and Party Leaders' Conferences, executive functions are carried out by the Bureau. The Bureau consists of the President, two representatives from each member party (including the Vice-Presidents) and two representatives from the PES Group (including the Group Leader). In

Table 16.2   Leaders of the PES party federation and EP group, 1974–94

Presidents of the Party Federation	Leaders of the EP Group
Wilhelm Dröscher (SPD), 1974–9	Ernest Glinne (PS–B), 1979–84
Robert Pontillon (PS–F), 1979–80	Rudi Arndt (SPD), 1984–9
Joop Den Uyl (PvdA), 1980–7	Jean-Pierre Cot (PS–F), 1989–94
Vitor Constancio (PS–P), 1987–9	Pauline Green (LP–GB), 1994–
Guy Spitaels (PS–B), 1989–92	
Willy Claes (SP), 1992–4	
Rudolf Scharping (SPD), 1994–	

Source: Author's compilation.

Table 16.3 PES leadership, 1997

Party Federation	EP Group
President	**Leader**
Rudolf Scharping (SPD)	Pauline Green (LP–GB)
Vice-Presidents	EP President (1994–6 term)
Philippe Busquin (PS–B)	Klaus Hänsch (SPD)
Communications and information,	
relations with the Commission	EP Vice-Presidents (1994–6 term)
Heinz Fischer (SPÖ)	David Martin (LP–GB)
Central and Eastern Europe	Nicole Pery (PS–F)
Pierre Guidoni (PS–F)	Paraskevas Avgerinos (PASOK)
Common foreign and security policy	Josep Verde i Aldea (PSOE)
Raimon Obiols (PSOE)	Renzo Imbeni (PDS)
Mediterranean policy	
Achille Occhetto (PDS)	*Chairs of EP Committees*
Central and Eastern Europe	Roberto Speciale (PDS), *Regional*
John Prescott (LP–GB)	Detlev Samland (SPD), *Budgets*
Common Foreign and	Antonio Vitorino (PDS),
Security Policy,	*Civil Liberties*
Relations with trade unions	Stephan Hughes (LP–GB), *Social*
Monica Sahlin (SAP)	Ken Collins (LP–GB), *Environment*
Justice and home affairs	Bernard Kouchner (PS-F),*
Akis Tschatzopoulos (PASOK)	*Development*
Mediterranean policy	Fernando Moran Lopez (PSOE),
	Institutional Affairs
	Ben Fayot (POSL/LSAP), *Rules*
	Eddie Newman (LP–GB), *Petitions*
	EP Representative in the 1996–7 IGC
	Elisabeth Guigou (PS–F)
Secretary-General	*Secretary-General*
Jean-François Vallin (PS–F)	Joan Cornet Prat (PSOE)

Source: Author's compilation.

the Bureau and the Party Leaders' Conference, most decisions are made by 'the broadest possible consensus' (i.e. unanimity). However, on issues where the EU Council decides by a qualified-majority vote, the PES also decides by a qualified majority – by a system of weighted votes according to the results in the last EP elections, and requiring a 75 per cent majority.

The final organ of the Party Federation is the Secretariat, which prepares meetings and liaises with the member parties. In 1995, Jean-François Vallin (PS–F) became Secretary-General of the Party Federation. The Secretariat shares the offices and organizational resources of the PES Group

Secretariat, in the EP building in Brussels. In 1996 there were twelve members of staff in the party federation Secretariat.

The PES in the EU institutions   The PES Group in the EP plays a central role in the work of the PES Party Federation, providing valuable informational, financial and organizational resources (see below). However, the PES Party Federation has also developed links with socialists in the other EU institutions. The socialist Commissioners regularly attend Party Leaders' Conferences and Congresses, and initial steps have been taken towards the creation of a 'PES caucus' between the socialist Commissioners. The PES also holds occasional meetings of socialist government ministers, opposition spokespersons and PES Group *rapporteurs* before important meetings of the EU Council. Finally, the PES Group in the Committee of the Regions has been involved in the PES organs since its establishment in November 1994.

Relations with external organizations   The PES has one formal affiliate organization: the European Community Organization of Socialist Youth (ECOSY) which links the Youth organizations of the member parties. The PES is also the EU branch of the Socialist International. There are no formal links to the trade union movement or other civil-society organizations. However, representatives from the European Trade Union Confederation (ETUC) and non-governmental organizations (NGOs) are invited to Congresses and occasionally participate in PES working groups.

Finances   The Party Federation is funded half by subscriptions from the national parties (relative to their own membership size) and half by the PES Group. The total budget for the Party Federation in 1993 was Ecu17.4 mn (£12.5 mn).

The PES Group in the European Parliament

Members   The members of the PES Group are the MEPs from the member parties of the PES Party Federation – this is specified under the statutes of the Party Federation and the Group. The PES Group is the largest in the EP, closely followed by the European People's Party (the Christian Democrats). As Table 16.4 shows, as a proportion of all MEPs, the PES Group has increased since 1979. Within the PES, MEPs are organized into 'national delegations', which vote *en bloc* in Group meetings. The Group tries to act cohesively in EP votes, and has been fairly successful in this task relative to the other EP Groups. However, if a national delegation decides to vote against the PES Group line, and makes a formal statement to this effect at a Group meeting, there is little the Group can do to impose its wishes on the

Table 16.4   The Socialist Group/Group of the PES in the EP, 1979–94

National Delegation	Party	No. of MEPs				
		1979	1984	1989	1994	Jan. 97
Austria	SPÖ	–	–	–	–	8
Belgium	PS–B	4	4	5	3	3
	SP	3	3	3	3	3
Denmark	SD	4	4	4	3	3
Finland	SSDP	–	–	–	–	4
France	PS–F	21	20	22	15	15
Germany	SPD	35	33	31	40	40
Greece	PASOK	–	10	9	10	10
Ireland	LP–I	4	0	1	1	1
Italy	PSI	9	9	12	2	2
	PSDI	4	3	2	–	–
	PDS	–	–	–	16	16
Lux.	POSL	1	2	2	2	2
NL	PvdA	9	9	8	8	8
Portugal	PS–P	–	–	8	10	10
Spain	PSOE	–	–	27	22	22
Sweden	SAP	–	–	–	–	11
UK	LP–I	17	32	45	62	62
	SDLP	1	1	1	1	1
Total		112	130	180	198	221
Total No. of MEPs:		410	434	518	518	626
% in Socialist Group:		27	30	35	38	35

Source: Author's compilation.

MEPs from that country. MEPs are selected for European elections by their national parties, which is a strong incentive to take the national delegation line over the majority in the PES Group.

PES Group leadership   As Table 16.2 shows, in June 1994, Pauline Green (LP–GB) became the fourth Leader (also referred to as President) of the PES Group since direct elections to the EP in 1979. The Leader co-ordinates the activities of the Group and is the main spokesperson for the Group in EP debates and to the national and European press. The Leader is assisted in her duties by the Treasurer and the Vice-Presidents of the PES Group. As Table 16.3 shows, several leading members of the PES Group also hold important positions in the administration of the Parliament. In the 1994–6 term, the PES held the office of the EP President, and had five out of the fourteen Vice-Presidents of the Parliament. In the 1994–9 session, the PES

Group held nine of the twenty Chairs of the EP Committees. Finally, Elisabeth Guigou (PS–F) of the PES Group was one of the two MEPs representing the EP in the 1996–7 Intergovernmental Conference on the reform of the Maastricht Treaty.

Organs and decision-making   The executive organ of the PES Group is the Bureau (not to be confused with the Bureau of the Party Federation). The Bureau is elected by the members of the Group at the beginning and halfway through each term of Parliament. The Bureau comprises the Leader, the Group Vice-Presidents, the Treasurer and several other members, and is elected on a proportional basis according to the number of MEPs from each national party. The number of women in the Bureau has to be at least proportional to the number of women in the Group as a whole. In the 1994–6 term, when 58 per cent of the Bureau were women, this exceeded the required number. The Bureau organizes the agenda and makes recommendations to, the Group meetings. The Bureau makes its decisions by a simple majority.

The PES also has a Group of Co-ordinators. A 'Co-ordinator' is elected by the PES members of each EP Committee. The role of the Co-ordinator is to support the work of the PES members of the committee, be the spokesperson for the PES members of that Committee in relevant Group business, and liaise with the other Co-ordinators. The Group of Co-ordinators facilitates a coherent PES policy agenda across all the EP Committees.

The third main organ of the PES Group is the Group Secretariat. In June 1994, Joan Cornet Prat (PSOE) became the Secretary-General of the PES Group. Under the direction of the Secretary-General, the Secretariat administers the work of the Group and provides technical and political advice to the MEPs, the Committee Chairs and the Leaders. The main office of the PES Group Secretariat is in the EP building in Brussels. The forty or so staff of the Secretariat are drawn from the fifteen EU member states. The salaries of the staff and the work of the Secretariat are financed from the budget of the PES Group, which is part of the general operating budget of the EP, which in turn is part of the 'institutions' line in the total EU budget. Ultimately, therefore, EU taxpayers pay for the PES Group Secretariat.

In sum, the PES is the largest and most institutionalized political party at the European level, and with a dominant position in each of the three EU institutions: the EP, the Commission and the Council. However, because the main goal for the members of the PES (the national parties) is the capture and maintenance of governmental office at the domestic level, a coherent socialist strategy within and between the EU institutions is practically impossible to implement.

ACHIEVEMENTS AND CURRENT POLICIES

In the domestic arena, the strategy and policies of political parties are central determinants of the legislative agenda and governmental decisions. At the European level, in contrast, the political agenda and decision-making is primarily controlled by the national governments and the European Commission. As a result, the policies of the PES are essentially 'reactive' rather than 'proactive'. Nevertheless, the PES has begun to influence the EU policy agenda in two ways: through the organization of Party Leaders' Conferences around the European Council; and through the influence of the PES Group in the EP in those policy areas where the EP has gained significant legislative power. However, the success of both these strategies depends on two conditions: the lack of a pre-existing consensus between the national governments (or the PES policies would be overturned by a unanimity of national governments) and Commission support for the policy of the PES (to help negotiate the policy through the Council).

Strategies and Payoffs

PES Party Federation   Towards the end of the 1990s, the PES party leaders decided to hold their meetings immediately before (and, if possible, in the same venue as) the six-monthly European Councils. This allowed the Party Leaders' Conferences to focus on the agenda of the forthcoming meeting of the EU Heads of Government, issue a statement outlining a common socialist position and, in so doing, increase the profile of the meetings in the media. This strategy became particularly relevant during the Intergovernmental Conferences that negotiated the Maastricht Treaty. The PES leaders set up a working group of national spokespersons, adopted two key Leaders' Declarations (in Madrid, December 1990, and Luxembourg, June 1991), and encouraged the national parties to adopt these statements as their official 'European policies'. As a result of this process, parties that were officially opposed to EMU at the beginning of the negotiations (such as the British and Danish socialists), were in favour by the end. Also, much of the PES agenda was implemented in the Maastricht Treaty.

PES Group in the EP   In the EP, the main strategy of the PES Group is to form an alliance on technical issues and in some policy areas with the second largest Group: the EPP (Christian Democrats). The PES–EPP alliance involves over 60 per cent of MEPs. This strategy is essential since the EU rules require an absolute majority of all EP members for legislation to be passed, not a simple majority of those MEPs turning up to vote. The PES–EPP alliance enables the two groups to control the selection of the important EP offices and committee chairs and dominate the EP agenda (on issues where they agree). For example, the PES and EPP agree to rotate the EP Presidency between them, which frustrates the smaller EP Groups. When the two groups do not co-operate, as in the July 1994 vote on Jacques Santer for Commission President, it is difficult for the EP to construct a majority, and counteract the power of the Council.

Current Policies

Officially, all the policies of the PES stem from the PES Programme, the last European Election Manifesto and the latest Congress resolutions. In practice, however, detailed policies are worked out on a more ad hoc basis, independently by the EP Group and the Party Federation. In the PES Group, policies are primarily developed by the *rapporteur* from the relevant EP Committee. In the PES Party Federation, policies are drafted in working groups of national spokespersons and MEPs. Nevertheless, some co-ordination between the policies of the EP Group and the Party Federation is undertaken by the Party Federation Bureau and Party Leaders' Conference.

On EU institutional reform, the PES supports increased powers for the EP *vis-à-vis* the Council, increased majority voting in the Council in most areas of economic and social policy, strengthening the CFSP, and a greater role for the Union in internal security matters, such as open borders and a common immigration policy.

On EMU, the PES supports a single currency and an independent European Central Bank (ECB). In the negotiation of the Maastricht Treaty, the PES argued that the bank should be made 'democratically accountable' (to national Finance Ministers and the EP), and that 'convergence criteria' should include unemployment as well as inflation, interest rates and public finances. The first of these arguments was instituted in the Treaty, but the second was rejected. The PES accepted this situation, but as EU unemployment has risen there is growing pressure by many member parties for 'real convergence' before EMU is launched.

On the EU Single Market, the catch-phrase for the PES is 'Social Europe', which should be pursued in parallel to the deregulatory aspects of the single market. This has three elements. First, on social policy, the PES advocated ending the British opt-out of the Social Chapter, more majority voting, the involvement of the 'two sides of industry' in EU policy-making, and tougher health and safety rules. Second, on employment policy (the subject of the Larsson Report), the PES proposes that job creation become a main goal of the Union, to counteract the 'currency stability' goal of a ECB, and more EU investment in job training programmes. Third, on economic and social cohesion, the PES supports 'solidarity between the regions', with an increasingly large proportion of the EU budget spent on regions in industrial decline and with high levels of unemployment.

The PES is also a strong supporter of EU environmental policy, and advocates 'sustainable development' in all EU policies (especially the Common Agricultural Policy (CAP)), better enforcement of EU environment legislation and higher environmental and consumer standards. This is an area where the EP has significant influence, and the PES controls the chair of the EP Environment Committee (Ken Collins, LP–GB).

Finally, the PES advocates more action on EU citizenship. EU citizenship was proposed by Felipe González (PSOE) in the Maastricht Inter-Governmental Conference. The PES now supports greater protection of civil rights – e.g. through an EU Bill of Rights, implementation of 'freedom of movement', through abolition of internal borders and common rights for third-country nationals, increasing access to EU documents, and a common policy to combat racism and xenophobia.

Select Bibliography

Main PES Programmes
Appeal to the Electorate, 10th Congress of the CSP, Brussels, January 1979.
Manifesto of the Confederation of the Socialist Parties of the European Community, 13th Congress of the CSP, Luxembourg, March 1984.
For European Unity, Prosperity and Solidarity: Manifesto of the Socialist Parties of the European Community, 16th Congress of the CSP, Brussels, February 1989.
Europe, Our Common Future (Den Haag Declaration), 1st Congress of the PES, The Hague, November 1992.
Party of European Socialists' Manifesto for the Elections to the European Parliament of June 1994, 2nd Congress of the PES, Brussels, November 1993.
The European Employment Initative: Put Europe Back to Work (Larsson Report), PES Leaders' Summit, Brussels, December 1993, and revised, Corfu, June 1994.

Articles and Books

Bardi, L. (1992) 'Transnational Party Federations in the European Community', in Katz, R.S. and Mair, P. (eds) *Party Organizations: A Data Handbook on Party Organizations in Western Democracies, 1960–90*, London: Sage.
Hix, S. (1995) *A History of the Party of European Socialists*, PES Research Series, 1, Brussels: Party of European Socialists.
Hix, S. and Lord, C. (1997) *Political Parties in the European Union*, London: Macmillan.
Ladrech, R. (1993) 'Social Democratic Parties and EC Integration: Transnational Responses to Europe 1992', *European Journal of Political Research*, 24(1).
May, J. (1977) 'Cooperation Between Socialist Parties', in Paterson, W.E. and Thomas, A.H. (eds), *Social Democratic Parties in Western Europe*, London: Croom Helm.
Pridham, G. and Pridham, P. (1981) *Transnational Party Cooperation and European Integration: The Process Towards the Direct Elections*, London: Allen & Unwin.

Contact Information

The Party of European Socialists
The European Parliament
Rue Belliard 89–97
Brussels
B-1000   Tel: 32 2 284 2111
Belgium   Fax: 32 2 230 6933

Web page on the Internet: http://www.pes.org

Postscript: Social Democratic Parties and the European Union

Robert Ladrech

INTRODUCTION

To what extent has the development of the European Union impinged on the organization and policies of social-democratic parties? A reader of the previous sixteen chapters will note that the European Union appeared as an issue for many parties regarding the question of their country's membership. Beyond this issue, some parties, particularly those in government at the end of the 1990s, struggle to fulfil the conditions for monetary union while at the same time maintaining some distinct social democratic influence in their country's welfare and economic policies. Space does not allow a full treatment of this 'new' social democratic predicament, but the development of the Party of European Socialists (PES) does raise some questions as to the role of social democratic parties in an expanded political environment which is not, *prima facie*, conducive to traditional methods of nationally-based political-party activity. These final thoughts to a volume devoted to social democratic parties in the European Union therefore seek to raise questions and possible avenues for further reflection and research regarding the adaptation of social democratic parties to an increasingly 'Europeanized' political arena.

IMPACT OF EUROPEAN INTEGRATION

The impact of European integration on social democratic party policies and identities since the launch of the Single Market programme and EMU, it may be argued, has been more profound than for either liberal or christian democratic parties. Of course, there are exceptions to this assertion – for example, instances where explicit issues of national identity and sovereignty have been invoked, as has been the case with the British Conservative Party or the French Gaullist RPR. Apart from these cases, though, the generally regarded neo-liberal thrust of the Single Market programme and the drive to meet the convergence criteria for monetary union represent more of a challenge to traditional social democratic agendas than to parties for whom

218

these European policy agendas actually complement national policy positions.

There are several elements of the social democratic party predicament. First, social democratic parties, whether the party originally responsible for its implementation or not, have over the course of this century aligned themselves in terms of their programmatic identity with the welfare state and other public sector services. The EU's competition policy and efforts associated with the achievement of monetary union convergence criteria have in many cases come to represent a threat to the continued maintenance of these regimes in their traditional forms, as privatization of public services and budgetary constraints reduce the role of the state in social welfare.

Second, and this applies to all parties in government, yet is nevertheless magnified for social democratic parties, is the basic fact that policy competences are increasingly shared with Brussels or else eliminated altogether. The creation of a single currency and ECB further attenuates national economic tools – e.g. in the setting of interest rates. The granting of national central bank independence in this area as a run-up to monetary union is a good example of this 'paring back' of the options and thus maneouvrability for national governments. Given the relatively more interventionist economic policy orientation of social democratic parties, this reduction of influence is more of a problem, especially in terms of defending and/or proposing alternative policies.

Finally, in terms of electoral politics, the limitations placed on national government manoeuvrability means that parties are less able to (1) defend past achievements and (2) realistically promise new initiatives, at least to the extent that they relate to policy areas shared with Brussels. Social democratic parties, while certainly not the sole victims of this narrowed scope for action, are nevertheless directly challenged in terms of partisan positioning *vis-à-vis* their competitors in precisely those policy areas publically perceived as traditionally defended by social democratic parties and thus linked to their programmatic identity.

Social democratic parties, to a certain extent, have only themselves to blame for this predicament. Over the past forty years, whether in government or opposition, they voted for the construction of the European Community. During most of this period, the notion of a social democratic majority or bloc co ordinating attempts by national leaders to inject a European-level social democratic orientation both to the original Treaties or to subsequent initiatives, was virtually non-existent. There are several reasons for the absence of a truly European social democratic project, but as the previous sixteen chapters have demonstrated, a primary reason is to be found in the historical development and ideological accommodation of social democratic parties to the liberal capitalist state, which prioritized the *national state* exclusively as the motor for progressive change. Thus, to the extent that social democratic leaders later envisioned the European Community as a vehicle for promoting a particular good, the process was essentially inter-governmental (rather than transnationally partisan), and more precisely, a product of wider national foreign policy strategies. By the 1990s, social democrats, complicit in the construction of 'Europe', but more attuned to solving national problems by recourse to national means, had for the most part presided over the making of their present predicament.

SOCIAL DEMOCRATIC PARTY ADAPTATION

Political parties have a history of adapting to changes in their competitive environments, as the chapters in this book very well convey. Certainly there are examples of failures to adapt to profound changes in a political system, but parties-as-organization have a tendency, for survival reasons, to accommodate themselves to new institutional dynamics as well as secular changes in society. Social democratic parties are no exception: whether it is changes in the relations with other organizations such as trade unions in terms of internal organizational power, or the concentration of power in party leaders' hands as parliaments have declined in relation to national bureaucracies, social democratic parties have adapted to their environment. If parties adapt to their environment, do we see any evidence of social democratic party adaptation to the EU – here meaning the development of new practices or organizational features with an intent to attain some relevance in a European-level policy-making environment?

The European Union is not a parliamentary state. Regardless of the evidence attesting to the *sui generis* nature of the Union, or its state-like features, it is not a system in which the EP plays a similar function to national parliaments. Historically, and though its timing varied from party to party as the chapters in this book demonstrate, one of the key changes in social democratic parties' development was acceptance of the liberal parliamentary state. From this point onwards, electoral mobilization played a key role in the attempt to gain governmental power and implement progressive policies. The present lack of meaningful input from EP elections in regards to EU policy-making means that this defining feature of party activity is neutralized. The added fact that elections to the EP are, in most cases, national referenda on incumbents rather than campaigns devoted to truly European issues, serves only to undermine EP elections as a legitimate exercise in holding policy-makers accountable to European citizens.

If traditional party-political means to influence EU policy-making are not possible, what options then exist for parties? As Hix (Chapter 16) has demonstrated, the development of the socialist transnational party federation was to provide, at some future date, the potential organizational structure for a European political party. But in the meantime, with present economic conditions making the problem of unemployment seem intractable, social democratic parties cannot, in a word, afford to wait for EU institutional change which may or may not enhance the role of transnational party federations in EU decision-making. This being said, there is evidence of movement on the part of social democratic party leaders.

In 1990, at the Madrid EU summit, social democratic party leaders released the following declaration, seemingly attesting to a recognition of the problem and direction for possible resolution:

> The ever increasing internationalization of the economy and interdependence of our societies at every level means that it is increasingly difficult to respond on a national level to the new challenges which arise. Democratic control of the future remains possible, provided that those elements of sovereignty which can no longer be exercised in a purely national framework are pooled. (CSPEC, 1990)

This was followed up in 1992 with an organizational enhancement of the socialist transnational Party Federation, the PES. Although the 1994 EP elections continued to follow a 'national-ist' orientation (in which voter turnout declined), other activities on the part of social democratic parties, using the PES as a means of co-ordination, did produce the first evidence of social democratic input at the European level. Through the efforts of social democratic representatives from governing parties and the influence of the Socialist Group in the EP at the preparatory stage of the 1996–7 EU Inter Governmental conference (IGC), which produced the Treaty of Amsterdam, employment issues were given high profile and a subsequent EU commitment in the Treaty. The 1997 Luxembourg Employment Summit also featured among the results of these activities.

The efforts to prioritize employment for the EU's policy orientation, and indeed define this issue complementary to the construction of monetary union, does have the potential to introduce countervailing dynamics to the logic of ECB deliberations. In terms of what was possible to achieve in a process that is dominated by inter-governmental initiatives and motivations at the European level, such a development should rightly be viewed as a successful first step to introducing issues and possible solutions which complement national attempts. In short, this episode may signal the development of a social democratic transnational agenda-setting role.

CONCLUSION

The programmatic future of social democracy in its national settings seems unavoidably bound up with the European-level of policy-making, both in terms of the content of those policies and the impact of constraints on national governments. Adjusting to this reality necessitates a degree of institutionalized interaction between national parties as well as with European-level actors. In order to have some relevance in an environment beyond any single national political system, parties will have to find the will to collectively insert their combined weight in the variety of policy openings within the Union. Interest groups, free from competitive national electoral pressures, have long been engaged in this process. Perhaps the present bleak unemployment situation will, in the end, serve as the catalyst for rethinking the role of EU institutions for social democratic parties by introducing an explicit left–right dimension to EU politics. For the moment, the European Union is still in many respects regarded as the 'other', in competition to national interests, as opposed to simply another field of action to exploit for social democratic interests. The growing realization and first steps toward conceiving and executing a truly *European* social democratic agenda may signal a new chapter in the history, organization and policies of social democratic parties in the European Union.

Select Bibliography

Confederation of Socialist Parties of the European Community (CSPEC) (1990). *Declaration on the Inter-governmental Conferences* (Madrid, 10 December).

Featherstone, K. (1988) *Socialist Parties and European Integration: A Comparative History*, Manchester: Manchester University Press.

Gaffney, J. (1996) *Political Parties and the European Union*, London: Routledge.

Hix, S. and Lord, C. (1997) *Political Parties in the European Union*, London: Macmillan.

Ladrech, R. (1997) 'Partisanship and Party Formation in European Union Politics', *Comparative Politics*, 29(2).

Telo, M. (1993) *De la nation à l'Europe: Paradoxes et dilemmes de la social-démocratie*, Brussels: Bruylant.

Index

Abortion Act (Spain)   186
Adler, V.   16, 17
Agrarian Centre Party (Finland)   57, 58, 60
Agrarian League (Sweden)   189, 196
Agreement on Strategic Concertation (1996–9) (Portugal)   171
Agusta case   40
Almunia, J.   180, 187–8
Andreotti government   136
Attlee, C.   97
Aubry, M.   77
austerity policies   13
Austria   5, 212
Austrian Communist Party (KPÖ)   18, 19
Austrian Freedom Party (FPÖ)   20, 24, 26, 28
Austrian Labour Federation (ÖGB)   21
Austrian People's Party (ÖVP)   19, 20, 22, 24, 28
Austrian People's Party-Austrian Social Democratic Party (ÖVP-SPÖ)   26, 27
  government achievements and current policies   26–8
  history   16–20
    First Republic, Austrofacism and Nazi rule (1918–45)   18–19
    Second Republic: sub-cultural defence to Establishment Party   19–20
    unification and struggle for political rights (1860s–1918)   16–17
  organization and party profile   20–6
    auxiliary associations and interest-group links   21–2
    electoral performance and sociology   24–6
    party membership   22–4

party structure and organization   20–1
Austrian Social Democratic Party-Freedom Party (SPÖ-FPÖ) coalition   27
Austrian Social Democratic Workers' Party   16, 17, 18, 19
Austrian Socialists' Foreign Bureau (Alös)   19
Austrian State Treaty   20
Austrian Workers' Choir   21
Austro-Keynesianism   26
Austro-Marxism   17, 18
Autonomous Political Socialist Group (GAPS) (Portugal)   167
Aylott, N.   189–202

Baccetti, C.   137, 138, 140, 141
Bad Godesberg Programme (1959)   4, 82, 86, 130, 179
Bakunin, M.   2
Balladur, E.   75
Barros Moura, J.   172
Bataille Socialiste, La   64
Bauer, O. 17, 19
Bebel, A.   2, 79, 80
Becker, F.   157
Belgian Communist Party (PCB)   32
Belgian General Confederation of Labour (CGTB)   32, 34
Belgian Socialist Party   30–41
  government achievements and current policies   40–1
  history   30–3
    Belgian Workers Party   30–1
    inter-war period   31–2
    new party (1945)   32–3
  organization and party profile   33–40
    electoral performance   36–40
    party membership   34
    party structure   35–6
    socialist pillar   33–4

Belgian Socialist Party (*contd*)
  see also Socialist Party (Flemish-
    speaking Belgium); Socialist
    Party (French-speaking
    Belgium);
Belgian Workers Party *see* Belgian
  Socialist Party
Belgium 5, 6, 80, 212
Bérégovoy, P. 75
Bergounioux, A. 70, 72
Berlin Programme 93
Berlinguer, E. 135, 140
Berlusconi, S. 145
Bernstein, E. 79–80
Bertinotti, F. 144
Bevin, E. 95
Bildt, C. 200
Bille, L. 43–54
Blair, T. 100, 101, 105, 107
Blum, L. 64, 65
Böckler, H. 88
Borrell, J. 188
Brandt, W. 90, 91, 92, 178, 205
Braunthal, G. 86, 88
Britain 5, 204, 205, 212, 214
British Conservative Party 96, 97, 99,
    100, 101, 104, 105, 106, 107, 108,
    218
British Labour Party 7, 8, 9–10, 11,
    13, 14, 95–108, 204, 206
  government achievements and
    current policies 105–8
  history 95–101
  background 95–6
  in office 97–9
  in opposition 99–101
  organization and party
    profile 101–5
  membership and support 103–5
Brix, H. 43
Brown, G. 107
Brünn Programme (1899) 17
Brussels Federation 35
BSP *see* Belgian Socialist Party
Buffet, M.-G. 77

Callaghan, J. 98, 99, 205
Canavarro, J. 172
Cardoso, L. 168

Carlsson, I. 198, 199, 202
catch-all parties 8, 12, 117
Cavaco Silva, A. 168, 171, 173
Centeno, T. 178
Central Bloc (Portugal) 173
Centre Party (Finland) 62
Centre Party (Sweden) 199, 200, 202
Centre for Socialist Studies, Research
    and Education (CERES)
    (France) 69, 70
Centre Union (Greece) 110, 116
Chamber of Labour (Austria) 22
Chambers of Business and Agriculture
    (Austria) 22
Charte de Quaregnon (Belgium) 30
Chevènement, J.-P. 76
Chirac, J. 67, 74, 76
Christian Democratic Party (PCS)
    (Luxembourg) 150, 151, 153
Christian Democratic Union/Christian
    Socialist Union (CDU/CSU)
    (Germany) 87, 88, 93, 135
Christian Democrats 211
  France 65, 66
  Germany 81, 86, 89, 90, 93
  Italy (DC) 134, 135, 136, 139, 140,
    141, 144, 145, 146
  Netherlands 157, 160, 161–2
  Sweden 200
Christian Socialist Union
    (Germany) 135
Christian Workers' Movement
    (Belgium) 40
Churchill, W. 97
Ciampi, C. A. 145
Citizens' Movement (MDC)
    (France) 76
Claes, W. 209
Clause IV 97
Clogg, R. 110, 111, 116, 120
Coakley, J. 124, 125, 129
Co-determination Act of 1976
    (Germany) 92
co-operative movements 18, 44, 46,
    53
'Cold-War' period 3, 4, 5, 49, 65
Collard, L. 37
Collins, K. 216
Comintern 134

Common Agricultural Policy   107,
   216
Common Foreign and Security
   Policy   215
Common Programme (France)   66–7
Communal Socialist Union (USC)
   (Belgium)   35
Communist Coalition (CDU)
   (Portugal)   172
Communist International   64
Communist parties   2, 3, 5, 8, 10
Communist Party
   Finland   56, 57, 59, 60, 61
   France   65, 66, 67, 68, 73
   Greece   117
   Luxembourg (PCL)   149–50, 151
Company Statute Act (Germany)   92
Confederation of Autonomous Right-
   Wing Groups (CEDA)
   (Spain)   177
Confederation of the Socialist
   Parties   204, 205
Conservative People's Party
   (Denmark)   43, 45
constituency Labour parties
   (Britain)   101, 102
Convention of Republican Institutions
   (CIR) (France)   70
Convergence and Union (CiU)
   (Spain)   179
Corish, B.   124
Cornet Prat, J.   213
Cossuta, A.   142
Cravatte, H.   150
Craxi, B.   139, 140, 141
Cresson, E.   75
Crosland, A.   98

da Foz, F.   173
d'Alema, M.   146
Danish Communist Party (DKP)   44,
   49, 50, 51
Danish Social Democratic Party
   (SD)   8, 11, 43–54
   government achievements and
      current policies   51–4
   history   43–5
   organization and party profile
      46–51

Danish Social Democratic Party-
   Socialist People's Party (SD-
   SF)   51
Danish Socialist People's Party
   (SF)   51, 60
Dassault case   40
De Deken, J.J.   79–93
de Gasperi, A.   134
de Gaulle, C.   66
de los Rios, F.   177
De Man, H.   31
De Martino, F.   140
de Quental, A.   166
de Rivera, P.   176, 177, 181
De Waele, J.-M.   30, 40
de-proletarization   11
Defferre, G.   66, 69, 73
definition of social democracy   1–6
Delors, J.   75, 106
Delwit, P.   30–41
Democratic Alternative (Finland)   61
Democratic Centre Union (UCD)
   (Spain)   178, 179
Democratic Defence (Greece)   112
Democratic Front for French-speakers
   (FDF)   37
Democratic Left (Ireland)   127, 128,
   130
Democratic Party of the Left (PDS)
   (Italy)   136–41, 143, 144, 145,
   146
   Youth Organization   144
Democratic Renewal Party (PRD)
   (Portugal)   170, 172, 173
Democratic and Social Centre (CDS)
   (Portugal)   167, 168, 173, 174
Democratic Social Movement
   (Greece)   118
Democratic Socialist Party
   (Ireland)   128
Democrats of the Left (Italy)   146
Den Uyl, J.   157, 161, 162
Denmark   5, 6, 57, 204, 205, 212, 214
Depreux, E.   66
Dini, L.   145
Dolfu, E.   19
Drees, W.   157
Dunleavy, P.   103
Dutch Communist Party (CPN)   155

Dutch Labour Party (PvDA) 13, 14, 155–64
  government achievements and current policies 161–4
  history 155–7
  organization and party profile 158–60
Dutch People's Movement (NVB) 156
Dutch Social Democratic Workers' Party (SDAP) 155, 156

Eanes, R. 167, 168, 173
East German Social Democratic Party (SDP) 106
Ebert, F. 171
Ecologists (France) 67, 72, 76
Economic and Monetary Union 214, 215, 218
  Britain 101, 107
  Finland 57, 62
  France 75, 76
  Italy 145
  Luxembourg 148
  Portugal 173
Economic and Social Committee (CES) (Portugal) 171
Edinburgh Agreement 54
Eisfeld, R. 167, 171
electoral sociology, elements of 8–9
Engholm, B. 206
Erfurt Convention (1891) 56
Erfurt programme 155
Erhard, L. 91
Esping-Andersen, G. 196
Eurocommunist party 140
European Central Bank 215, 219, 221
European Coal and Steel Community 204
European Community Organization of Socialist Youth (ECOSY) 211
European Convention on Human Rights 108
European Economic Community
  Britain 99, 100, 106
  Denmark 53–4
  France 73
  Greece 111, 115, 120

Ireland 131
Italy 135
Netherlands 164
Portugal 173
Spain 179, 181, 185–6
Sweden 197, 201, 202
European Free Trade Association 205
European Monetary System 75, 101
European Parliament 204, 205, 206, 207, 210, 212, 214, 215, 220, 221
European People's Party 205, 211, 215–15
European People's Party-Christian Democrats 204
European Trade Union Confederation 211
European Union Bill of Rights 216
Eurosceptics 106, 201

Fabian Society 101
Fabius, L. 67, 74
Faure, P. 64
Fayot, B. 152, 206
Featherstone, K. 110
Federation of European Liberal, Democratic and Reform Parties 204, 205
Federation of German Workers' Associations (VDA) 79
Federation of Young Communists (Italy) 137
Feldt, K.-O. 198, 199
Fianna Fáil (Ireland) 123, 126–7, 128, 130, 131
Fine Gael (Ireland) 123, 124, 126–7, 128, 129–30
Finland 5, 6, 212
Finnish Labour Party 56
Finnish People's Democratic League 57
Finnish People's Democratic Union (SKDL) 60
Finnish People's Democratic Union/ Left-Wing Alliance (SKDL/ VAS) 61
Finnish Social Democratic Party (SDP) 56–62

government achievements and
current policies 60–2
history 56–8
organization and party profile
58–60
Finnish Workers' Central Union
(SAK) 56, 59
First International (1864–76) 2, 3,
43–4, 204
Fitzmaurice, J. 148–53
Flemish Green Party 40
Fontana, J. 166
Foot, M. 99
France 5, 6, 7, 205, 212
Franco, General 11, 177, 178, 181
Free Democratic Party (FDP)
(Germany) 87, 88, 89–90, 171
French Communist Party (PCF) 64,
65, 66, 68, 72, 76
French Democratic Confederation of
Labour (CFDT) 66, 69, 70
French Section of the Workers'
International (SFIO) 64, 65, 66,
68, 69, 70, 71–2, 73, 142
French Socialist Party (PS) 8, 15,
64–77, 142
government achievements and
current policies 73–7
history 64–7
reconstruction and collapse
(1920–45) 64–5
renewal and heyday of French
socialism (1971–97) 66–7
stagnation and regression
(1945–71) 65–6
unification of French Socialist
Movement (1905–20) 64
organization and party profile
67–72
electorate and electoral
performance 71–2
membership 70–1
political tradition 67–8
trade unions, relations with 68–9
FSM-PSOE (Madrid) 181

Gaitskell, H. 97, 98
Gallagher, M. 124, 125, 129
Geleff, P. 43

General Confederation of Labour
(CGT) (France) 68
General Confederation of Portuguese
Workers (CGTP-In) 171, 174
general typology of social democracy
4–6
General Workers' Association
(ADAV) (Germany) 79
General Workers' Union (UGT)
(Spain) 171, 180–1, 182
German Communist Party (KPD) 80,
81
German Federation of Trade Unions
(DGB) 88
German Social Democratic Party
(SPD) 3–4, 7, 8, 10, 11, 12, 13,
14, 79–93, 135, 155, 166, 171, 178
Gotha Programme 44
government achievements and
current policies 89–93
Grand Coalition (1966–9) 90–1
in opposition 92–3
Schmidt Governments (1974–
82) 92
history 79–83
East German Social Democratic
Party 82–3
origins to Second World War
79–81
reconstitution post-Second World
War 81–2
organization and party profile 83–9
Control and Arbitration
Commissions 84
Convention 84
Districts and Sub-district
Associations 83
Executive 84
Greens and Party of Democratic
Socialism, relations with 88–9
Länder Associations 83–4
membership developments since
1945 85–7
Party Council 84–5
Presidium 84
trade unions, relations with 88
German Workers' Social Democratic
Party *see* German Social
Democratic Party

Germany 5, 31, 99, 145, 205, 212
Gidlund, G. 190
Gilbert, M. 145
Gimle Manifesto 44
Giscard d'Estaing, V. 66
Goncalves, V. 167
González, F. 178, 179, 180, 181, 186–7, 216
Gramsci, A. 134
Greece 5, 6, 7, 12, 212
Green, P. 212
Green Party
 Austria 24
 Denmark 11
 Germany 11, 85, 86, 87, 88–9
 Luxembourg 151
 Sweden 196, 200, 201
Grotewohl, O. 81
Group of Seven 136
Grunberg, G. 70, 72
Guerra, A. 178
Guesde, J. 64
Guigou, E. 77, 213
Guterres, A. 169, 171, 174
Guzzini, S. 133–46

Haider, J. 20, 24
Hainburg issue 27
Hainfeld conference (1888) 16–17
Hansson, P.A. 192
Happart, J. 40
Healey, D. 98
Heidelberg programme (1925) 81
Hillebrand, R. 158
Hix, S. 204–16, 220
Holmberg, S. 201
Holmes, M. 123–31
Hyndman, H. M. 96

Iglesias, P. 176, 180
implementation of social democratic programme post-1945 6–10
 electoral sociology, elements of 8–9
 party organization, specific type of 6–8
 trade-off and conciliatory mode 9–10
Independent Labour Party (Britain) 95

Independent Socialist Party (USDP) (Germany) 80
Ingrao, P. 142
Institute for Industrial Reconstruction (Italy) 145
International Monetary Fund 98, 173
Internationalism 5, 17
Ireland 5, 6, 204, 212
Irish Labour Party 123–31
 government achievements and current policies 128–31
 history 123–5
 organization and party profile 125–8
Irish Trade Union Congress 123
Irish Workers' League 128
Italian Association for Recreational Culture 144
Italian Communist Party (PCI) 133, 134, 135, 136–41, 142, 143, 144, 145, 146
Italian Democratic Party of the Left (PDS) 14, 133–46
 government achievements and current policies 144–6
 history 133–6
 organization and party profile 136–44
  Communist Party, Democratic Party of the Left and Party of the Communist Refoundation 141–2
  continuity and change 142–4
  crisis of Communist Party and origins of Democratic Party of the left 136–41
Italian General Confederation of Labour (CGIL) 144
Italian Liberal Party (PLI) 140
Italian Popular Party 144
Italian Republican Party (PRI) 140
Italian Social Democratic Party (PSDI) 133, 134, 135, 140
Italian Socialist Party (PSI) 8, 133, 134, 135, 139–41, 146
Italy 5, 12, 205, 212

Jansson, J.-M. 57, 61
Jaurès, J. 3, 64, 67
Johnson, T. 123

Jospin, L. 67, 76

Karamanlis, K. 121
Karvonen, L. 57
Katsoudas, D. 110
Kautsky, K. 3, 16, 31, 79, 80
Kekkonen, U.K. 61
Kennedy, P. 176–88
Keynes, J.M. 9, 91
Keynesianism 9, 13
  Denmark 45
  France 67
  Germany 90, 91
  Greece 120
Khrushchev, N.S. 135
Kiesinger, K. 90
Kinnock, N. 99
Klima, V. 20
Knudsen, P. 43
Kogan, D. 99
Kogan, M. 99
Kohl, H. 88, 92
Koivisto, M. 57
Kok, W. 162, 163, 164, 205
Koole, R.A. 158
Kreisky, B. 20, 24, 26–7

Labour Representation Committee
  (Britain) 95
Ladrech, R. 64–77, 218–22
Lafontaine, O. 93
Landworkers' Association (FNTT)
  (Spain) 177
Largo Caballero, F. 177, 180
Larsson Report 206, 215
Lassalle, F. 16, 79
Law on the Rights and Liberties for
  Communes, Departments and
  Regions (France) 73
Leach, R. 96
Left Party (Sweden) 196, 199, 200,
  201
Left Socialists (VS) (Denmark) 50,
  51
Left Union of Socialist Democracy
  (UEDS) (Portugal) 168
Left-Wing Alliance (VAS)
  (Finland) 61
Lenin, V.I. 3, 64, 89, 111, 176

Leopold III, King 37
Levi-Sandri, L. 204
Liberal Forum (Austria) 24
Liberal Party
  Britain 95, 96, 97
  Denmark 43, 45
  Finland 57
  Luxembourg (PD/DP) 149, 150,
    151
  Sweden 200
liberal-capitalist societies 1, 2, 3, 8,
  13
Liddle, R. 100
Liebknecht, K. 2, 80
Liebknecht, W. 79
Liebman, M. 30
Lijphart, A. 156
Lindbeck, A. 199
Linz Programme (1926) 18
Longo, L. 135
Lorwin, V. 31
Luther, K.R. 16–28
Luxembourg 5, 212
Luxembourg Employment
  Summit 221
Luxembourg Social Democratic Party
  149
Luxembourg Socialist Workers' Party
  (LSAP/POSL) 148–53
  government achievements and
    current policies 153
  history 148–51
    Grand Duchy 148
    Party 149–50
    Party system 150–1
    political system 148–9
    organization and party profile
      151–3
Luxembourg Trade Union Federation
  (OGBL) 152
Luxemburg, R. 3, 80

Maastricht Treaty 205, 206, 213, 214,
  215, 216
  Austria 28
  Belgium 40–1
  Britain 107
  Denmark 54
  France 75, 76

Maastricht Treaty (*contd*)
  Greece   121
  Ireland   131
  Italy   145
  Portugal   173
  Spain   187
Mabille, X.   31
MacDonald, J. Ramsay   97
Magone, J.   166–74
Mair, P.   127
Maire, E.   68
Major, J.   101, 107
Majority Social Democratic Party
  (MSDP) (Germany)   80
Mandelson, P.   100
Mannheim Agreement (1906)   80–1
Mannheimer, R.   140
Mansholt, S.   204
Maoist People's Democratic Union
  (UDP) (Portugal)   172
Marlière, P.   1–15, 64–77
Marqués-Pereira, B.   30
Marshall Aid   134, 145
Marx, K.   2, 80, 180
Marxism   2, 4, 17, 18
  Austria   17
  Belgium   31
  Britain   96
  Denmark   44, 45, 51
  France   65, 66, 68, 73
  Germany   79–80, 82, 89
  Greece   111
  Netherlands   155
  Spain   178, 180
Marxist Radicals   16
Mauroy, P.   66, 67, 69, 70, 74, 75
Mavirs, G.   116
Mavrogordatos, G.   116
Mayer, D.   65
Meidner, R.   191
Metal Workers Union (Germany)   88
Metal Workers' Union (Sweden)   196
Miners' Federation (Britain)   95
Mitterrand, F.   66, 67, 69, 70, 72, 73,
  75, 141, 142, 178, 205
Moderates   16
  Sweden   200, 202
Mollet, G.   65, 66, 73
Moro, A.   136

Moschonas, G.   110–21
Moscow Agreement (1970)   90
Mota Pinto, C.   173
Movement of Armed Forces
  (Portugal)   167, 172
Movement for the Reorganization of
  the Party of the Proletariat
  (MRPP) (Portugal)   172
Mozer, A.   204
Municipal Workers' Union
  (Sweden)   196

National Alliance (Italy)   145
National Coalition (Finland)   57
National Federation of Education
  (France)   69
National Health Service   9, 108
National Labour Party (Ireland)   123,
  127, 128
National Progressive Democrats
  (Ireland)   128
Natta, A.   140–1
Naumann, F.   171
Negrín, J.   177
Nenni, P.   135
neo-liberal policies   13
néo-socialistes (France)   65
Netherlands   5, 6, 205, 212
Neudörfler Programme (Austria)   16
Neutrality and State Treaty Act 1955
  (Austria)   26
New Democracy Party (Greece)   112,
  117
New Democracy (Sweden)   200
New Labour   100, 101, 105
New Left (Netherlands)   157, 160
Nieuwenhuis, F.D.   155
North Atlantic Treaty
  Organization   4, 73
  Austria   28
  Denmark   45
  Finland   62
  Germany   82, 92
  Greece   111, 115
  Italy   135, 136
  Luxembourg   148, 150, 153
  Spain   179, 181
Northern League (Italy)   145
Norton, W.   124

Norway 57
Oberwinder, H. 16
Occhetto, A. 141–2, 144, 145
Occupational Qualification Promotion
Act (Germany) 91
O'Leary, M. 124
Ollenhauer, E. 81, 82
Opie, R. 98
Optenhogel, U. 171
Organization for Economic
Cooperation and Development
199
origins of social democracy 2–4

Palme, O. 197–8
Panhellenic Liberation Movement
(PAK) 110, 112
Panhellenic Militant Trade Union
Movement (PASKE) 112, 117
Panhellenic Socialist Movement
(PASOK) 9, 10, 11, 110–21
government achievements and
current policies 119–21
history 110–13
organization and party profile
113–19
electorate and electoral
performance 116–19
institutionalization of
organization 114–16
membership and party structure
113–14
Panitch, L. 99
Papandreou, A. 110, 112, 113, 115,
118, 121
Papandreou, G. 110
Parliamentary Labour Party
(Britain) 99, 102, 106
Parti Ouvrier (Luxembourg) 149
Party of the Communist Refoundation
(PRC) (Italy) 133, 143, 144
Party of Democratic Socialism (PDS)
(Germany) 87, 88–9
party electorate, changes in 11–12
Party of European Socialists 15, 153,
204–16, 218
achievements and current
policies 214–16
strategies and pay-offs 214–16

Group 207, 211, 214–15
history 204–7
organization and party
profile 207–13
in European Parliament 211–13
Party Federation 207–11, 214, 215,
221
Party of the Forcibly Conscripted
(Luxembourg) 151
party organization, specific type of 6–8
party sociology, changes in 12
Pensions Action Committee
(Luxembourg) 151
People's Democratic Party (PPD)
(Portugal) 167
People's Socialist Front (FSP)
(Portugal) 167
People's Union (*Volksunie*)
(Belguim) 40
Permanent Council of Social
Concertation (CPCS)
(Portugal) 171
Perry, J. 155
persistent features and recent changes
10–15
new trends 13–15
party electorate, changes in 11–12
party sociology, changes in 12
post-war-style policies, end of 13
social democratic paradigm, end of?
10–11
Persson, G. 198, 202
Philip, A. 66
Phillips, M. 96
Picqué, C. 40
Pierre, J. 194, 197
Pinochet, A. 135
Pio, L. 43
Pivert, M. 64
Poland 81, 141
Poos, J. 152
Popular Front Alliance (Spain) 177
Popular Front (France) 68
Popular Party (Spain) 179, 184, 187
Popular Republican Movement
(MRP) (France) 65, 66
Portugal 5, 212
Portuguese Communist Party
(PCP) 166, 167, 170, 171–2

Portuguese Republican Party 166
Portuguese Socialist Party (PSP) 8–9,
    10, 11, 166–74
  government achievements and
      current policies 172–4
    party programme 174
  history 166–9
    democratic period since 1975
        168–9
    pre-1974 period: factionalism and
        personalism 166
    revolutionary period: 1974–5
        166–7
  organization and party profile
      169–72
    centralized party structure 169
    electorate: increase in volatility
        170
    membership 169–70
    nature of the party: cartel party
        169
    other parties of the Left, relations
        with 171–2
    trade unions, relations with 170–1
  post-war-style policies, end of 13
Prieto, I. 177, 180
Prodi, R. 145
Proporz 19, 20
PS (France) 10, 11, 14
PSB-BSP (Belgium) 38–9
PSB-RW (Belgium) 39
PSC-PSOE (Catalan) 181
Public Service, Transport and
    Communication Workers Union
    (ÖTV) (Germany) 88

Quinn, R. 125

Radical Party (France) 65, 66, 67,
    72
Radicals 16
Radoux, L. 204
Rally for the Republic (RPR)
    (France) 76, 218
Ramadier, P. 66
Reagan, R. 73, 140
'Red Vienna' 18
Redondo, N. 181
Reformism 44
Rehn, G. 191, 198

Renner, K. 17, 19
Representation of the People Act 1918
    (Britain) 96
Republican Defence League (RS)
    (Austria) 18–19
Republican Party (Italy) 146
Revolutionary Socialists (RS)
    (Austria) 19
Robinson, M. 124
Rocard, M. 66, 67, 69, 70
Rother, B. 173
Rottenberg, F. 158
Russia 3, 5, 50, 56, 61, 65, 135,
    141

Sahlin, M. 198
Sampaio, J. 171
Sanders, D. 100
Santer, J. 148, 215
Santos, A. 169
SAP (Sweden) 8, 10, 11, 13
Scandinavia 99
Scharping, R. 209
Scheu, A. 16
Schiller, K. 90–1
Schmid, C. 82
Schmidt, H. 88, 92, 136
Schroeder, G. 93
Schulze-Delitsch, H. 16
Schumacher, K. 81, 90
Second International (Socialist
    International) (1889) 2–3, 4, 5
Serra, M. 167
Seyd, P. 105
Shaw, E. 100
Signorile, C. 140
Simitis, K. 115, 118, 121
Single European Act 187
Single Market 54, 215, 218
Sinnott, R. 128
Sinowatz, F. 20
Smith, J. 100, 105
Soares, M. 166–7, 168, 171, 173,
    174
Social Capitalism paradigm 13
Social Christians (PSC-CVP)
    (Belgium) 37
Social Democratic Federation
    (Britain) 96

Social Democratic League of Workers and Smallholders (TPSL) (Finland) 61
social democratic paradigm 10–11
Social Democratic Party (Britain) 99
Social Democratic Party of Austria (SPÖ) 7, 8, 10, 12, 13, 16–28
Social Democratic Party of East Germany (SDP) 16, 82–3
Social Democratic Party of the Netherlands (PvdA) 155
Social Democratic Party (PSD) (Luxembourg) 150, 151
Social Democratic Party (PSD) (Portugal) 168, 170, 171, 173, 174
Social Democratic Workers' Party (SAP) (Germany) 79
Social Democratic Working Group (SA) (Germany) 80
Social Democrats (Finland) 61
Social-Liberal Party (Denmark) 44, 45
Socialist Group 221
Socialist International 124, 133, 153, 166, 167, 178, 187, 204, 211
Socialist Labour Party (Ireland) 128
Socialist Parties of the European Community 204
Socialist Party of Austria (SPÖ) 19
Socialist Party (Ireland) 128
Socialist Party of the Italian Workers (PSLI) 134
Socialist Party (PS) (France) 32–3, 66, 67, 68, 69, 70, 71, 72, 73, 74, 75, 76, 106
Socialist Party (PS) (French-speaking Belgium) 34, 35, 36, 37, 40
Socialist Party (SP) (Flemish-speaking Belgium) 33, 34, 36, 37, 40
Socialist People's Party (MSP) (Portugal) 167
Socialist Union (Spain) 181
Socialist Unity Party of Germany (SED) 81, 82, 89
Socialist Worker Peasant Party (PSOP) (France) 65
Socialist Workers' Party (Finland) 57

Socialist Workers' Party of Germany (SAD) 79
socio-economic policies 10
Sotiropoulos, D. 114
Spain 5, 12, 212
Spanish Communist Party (PCE) 176, 177, 178, 180
Spanish Socialist Workers' Party (PSOE) 8, 10, 11, 176–88
Basque (PSE-PSOE) 181
Catalan (PSC-PSOE) 181
Galician (PSG-PSOE) 181
government achievements and current policies 185–8
history 176–80
early development (1879–1921) 176
from clandestinity to power (1975–82) 178–9
growth and political prominence (1921–39) 176–7
in office (1982–96) 179–80
wilderness years (1939–74) 177–8
organization and party profile 180–5
electorate and electoral performance 184–5
membership 182–4
party structure 181–2
political tradition 180
trade unions, relations with 180–1
Spinelli, A. 135
Spitaels, G. 33, 40, 41, 205
Spourdalakis, M. 113
Spring, D. 124, 125
Stability Act of 1967 (Germany) 91
Ständestaat (Austria) 19
Stauning, T. 43
Stoleroff, A. 171
Suárez, A. 178
Sundberg, J. 56–62
supremacy of the left wing 8–9
Sweden 5, 57, 80, 212
Swedish Communist Party 192, 199
Swedish Confederation of Workers in Finland (FSA) 58
Swedish Left Party 192
Swedish People's Party 57

Swedish Social Democratic Party 5, 7, 189–202
  government achievements and current policies 197–202
    1970s and 1980s 197–200
    1990s 200–2
  history 189–92
    background 190–1
    'Swedish Model' 191–2
  organization and party profile 192–7
    membership 195–7
    structure 192–4
Swedish Trade Union Confederation (LO) 190, 191, 193, 197, 199, 200

Tanner, V. 56
TDs (*Teachtaí Dála*) (Ireland) 123, 124, 126, 127
Tenants Protection Act (Germany) 92
Tezanos, J.F. 182, 183, 185
Thatcher, M. 73
Third International 3, 80, 134, 176
Thorn, G. 148, 150
Tilton, T. 192
Tito 135
Togliatti, P. 134, 135
trade union organizations 4, 6, 7, 9, 10, 13
  Austria 17, 18
  Belgium 32, 34
  Britain 101
  Denmark 44, 46, 53
  France 64, 68
  Germany 80
  Italy 144
  Portugal 167, 170
Trades Union Congress 7, 12, 95
Trautmann, C. 77
Treaty of Amsterdam 54, 164, 221
Trentin, B. 144
Troelstra, P.J. 155, 156
Trotskyist Revolutionary Socialist Party (PSR) (Portugal) 172
Tsovolas, D. 118

Ulburghs, J. 33, 37
Ulivo, l' (olive tree) (Italy) 145, 146
Unified General Confederation of Labour (France) 68
Unified Socialist Party (PSU) (France) 66, 70
Union for French Democracy-Rally for the Republic (UDF-RPR) coalition 74
United Communist Party of Germany (VKPD) 80
United States 3, 31, 32
Unity List (EL) (Denmark) 51
University Directive of 1976 (Germany) 91

Vallin, J.-F. 210
Vals, F. 204
van Kersbergen, K. 155–64
Van Miert, K. 33
Vienna Programme (1901) 17
Vitorino, A. 169
Voynet, D. 76–7
Vranitzky, F. 20, 28
Vredeling, H. 204

Walloon Federation 35
Walloon Rally 37
Walloon Regional Executive 40
Webb, P. 95–108
Webb, S. and B. 96
Weber, M. 7
Whiteley, P. 105
Widfeldt, A. 194, 195, 196, 197
Willey, R.J. 88
Wilson, H. 98
Woltgens, T. 206
Workers' Commissions (CC.OO) (Spain) 181
Workers' International 166
workers' organizations 16
Workers' Party (Ireland) 127, 128
Workers' Strength (FO) (France) 68
working-class atavism 7, 9

Zenha, S. 168
Zinoviev, G. 3, 64